DAY BY DAY

300

CALENDAR-RELATED ACTIVITIES, CRAFTS, AND BULLETIN BOARD IDEAS FOR THE ELEMENTARY GRADES

EDITED BY

BONNIE BERNSTEIN

David S. Lake Publishers

CREDITS

Editorial director: Roberta Suid
Editor: Bonnie Bernstein
Production editor: Patricia Clappison
Production artist: Rosemarie Singer
Contributing editors: Bonnie Bernstein, Carolyn Paine, Bruce Raskin
Illustrators:
Linda Allison, Allen Say, Jaclyne Scardova,
Mary Ann Schildknecht, Dennis Ziemienski
Also:
Frank Ansley, Martie Bracewell, Martha Hairston,
Eric Moe, Gretchen Shields
Cover designer: Dennis Ziemienski

Designed by: Hedy McAdams

ISBN–0–8224–4252–3
Printed in the United States of America

1 . 9 8 7 6 5

FOREWORD

DAY BY DAY is an anthology of 300 seasonal and calendar-related ideas and activities for the school year. Unlike other calendar activity books, *Day by Day* successfully integrates basic curricular topics with many significant calendar events and occasions. The activities in this book are either entirely new or creative innovations on old favorites. Many are based on ideas contributed by readers of *Learning Magazine*. Together they span the areas of reading, language arts, social studies, science, math, physical education, and art.

Day by Day has eleven chapters, one for each month of the school year and one for year-long learning ideas. Chapters Two through Eleven (September through June) open with calendars that include historical anniversaries, civic holidays, famous birthdays, commemorative days, and some religious festivals — an entry for almost every day of the month. The first chapter, Ideas for the Year, features a calendar of school months. Entries in this calendar are "floating" holidays, such as Easter, which derive from other lunar or lunisolar calendars; week- and month-long observances, such as Afro-American History Month; and holidays which are legally proclaimed for a day in a particular week, such as Labor Day.

The calendars are always followed by 20 or more activities, two or three large craft projects, at least two bulletin board ideas, and a list of resources for the teacher and students. *Day by Day* also features a section of MAKEMASTER duplicatable worksheets — one each for the primary and intermediate levels for every month. Together the MAKEMASTER worksheets comprise a souvenir scrapbook, complete with cover, that kids can assemble and take home at the end of the year. And we haven't forgotten you! Teachers' Planners and a subject-area Index have been included for your convenience and quick reference.

Teachers of the primary and intermediate grades will get the most benefit of the material, although middle school teachers may find ideas for their students that are appropriate and easy to adapt. All teachers will find *Day by Day* to have a format that is flexible rather than prescriptive, allowing them to select activities that suit their particular needs. Above all, teachers will find *Day by Day* enjoyable to read as well as comprehensive, informative, and easy to use.

CONTENTS

Chapters One through Eleven, pp. 2–199

Index, pp. 200 and 201

Appendix: Introduction, p. 202
MAKEMASTER Worksheets, pp. 203–224
Teachers' Planners, pp. 225–234

ACTIVITIES: *(1) School-Year Calendar Projects, (2) The Learning Booth, (3) Cafeteria Menu Graph, (4) A Darkroom in the Classroom, (5) Personal Time Capsules, (6) Kids Peddle Nutrition, (7) Photographic Seating Charts, (8) Reporter of the Week, (9) Create a Center Center, (10) TV Box Presentations, (11) The Month Train, (12) Make Your Own Magnifiers, (13) Classroom Yellow Pages, (14) Remember Us, (15) Birthday Book, (16) Roll Call Query, (17) On-the-Road Assignments, (18) That Was the Week That . . ., (19) Read All About Us, (20) A Birthday in Space*

CRAFTS: *(21) Squeeze-Bottle Printing, (22) Five-Gallon Lockers, (23) Sorter Fan*

BULLETIN BOARDS: *(24) Check-In on the Moon, (25) What's Next? (26) Pegboard Possibilities*

ACTIVITIES: *(27) Welcome Aboard, (28) Advertise, (29) Don't Just Say "Hello," (30) Meet Your Animal Double, (31) First Day Gazette, (32) Endless Summer, (33) Grand Opening Activity Center, (34) Trash Can Archaeology, (35) There's a New Kid in Town, (36) Take One Watermelon, (37) Get Acquainted With "Me" Dolls, (38) Predictions, (39) Animal Bill Of Rights, (40) Interior Design: A Mapping First, (41) Dial Neighbor, (42) Citizen's Oath, (43) Apply Here, (44) Before-School Options, (45) C-3PO's Summer Trip, (46) Tagalong Nature Trail, (47) Family Tree Greeting Cards*

CRAFTS: *(48) Twig Print Designs, (49) Recycled Soap, (50) Kachina Containers*

BULLETIN BOARDS: *(51) Baby Face, (52) Graffiti Walls, (53) A Sharing Center*

ACTIVITIES: *(135) Happy Birthday Everybody! (136) Continuous Calendar, (137) Calendar Cover, (138) Positive-Thinking Calendar, (139) Plant Plant, (140) Alien Calendars, (141) Candy Box Count, (142) Shape Ornaments, (143) Excuses, Excuses, (144) Communication Write-In, (145) Recipes by Mail, (146) Seeds of Spring, (147) Handwriting Fruit Basket, (148) Curses! (149) Color Strokes for Little Folks, (150) Stories-in-the-Round, (151) Dream or Reality, (152) Banking Center, (153) Let's Have a Game-In, (154) Read-a-thon Fundraising, (155) Save Those Hockey Cards, (156) Checking Twice*

CRAFTS: *(157) Snowball Mobiles, (158) Snow Scenes in a Jar, (159) Reading Center Projects*

BULLETIN BOARDS: *(160) While You Were Gone, (161) Clippings for Literary Terms*

ACTIVITIES: *(162) Weather Predictions, (163) A Shadow of One's Self, (164) Classy Valentine Cut-Ups, (165) Shadow-Mates on the Move, (166) Broken Heart Menders, (167) Be My First Lady, (168) Good Fortune, (169) Heart Breakers, (170) Pulse Takers and Watchers, (171) Make Your Own Stethoscope, (172) My Punny Valentine, (173) Forced Flowers in Winter, (174) Money-Wise Math, (175) Turning on Inventiveness, (176) A Change in Indoor Climate, (177) Comprehension Through Comics, (178) Alias Big Dipper, (179) Solar Walk, (180) Soft Bat Ball, (181) A Classroom-Size Time Line, (182) Fun Fridays, (183) Positive Identity*

CRAFTS: *(184) Cartoon Collaboration Kits, (185) String Painting, (186) Wear Your Heart on Your Shirt*

BULLETIN BOARDS: *(187) Wall One-Liners, (188) Valentine Post Office*

ACTIVITIES: *(189) Wayward Wind Correspondence, (190) All Steamed Up, (191) Which Way Does the Wind Blow? (192) Barometer From a Bottle, (193) Wind Erosion Recorder, (194) Send-Aways, (195) Personalized Letterhead, (196) Classroom Addresses, (197) Saving Energy Makes Cents, (198) Return to Recycling, (199) No-Paper Day Observances, (200) Garbage Ball, (201) Warm Weather Window Watchers, (202) Lookout Bingo, (203) A Pond in the Classroom, (204) Potato Day, (205) Making Research a Taste Treat, (206) Archaeology Dig, (207) Food Folk, (208) Math Facts Hot Line, (209) Edible Alphabet, (210) Compliments of the Chef*

CRAFTS: *(211) Creative Junk, (212) Migration Mobiles, (213) Bottle Cap Doormat*

BULLETIN BOARDS: *(214) Spring Weather Watch, (215) Weekly Beasties*

CHAPTER

IDEAS FOR

September

Labor Day — first Monday
National Grandparents' Day — first Sunday after Labor Day
Autumnal Equinox — the first day of autumn (astronomical)
National Good Neighbor Day — fourth Sunday
Native American Day — fourth Friday

October

Fire Prevention Week — the week including October 8
(the anniversary of the Chicago Fire in 1871)
Columbus Day — second Monday (legal observance)
National Jogging Day — second Saturday
Standard Time — last Sunday

November

Election Day — first Tuesday after the first Monday
American Education Week — second full week
National Children's Book Week — second full week
Thanksgiving — usually the fourth Thursday

December

Hanukkah — derived from the Hebrew calendar
Winter Solstice — first day of winter (astronomical)

January

Read a New Book Month
Presidential Inauguration Day — on January 20 every 4 years
Super Bowl Sunday — third Sunday

ONE

THE YEAR

February

Afro-American History Month
National Children's Dental Health Week — first full week
Chinese New Year — derived from the lunar calendar
Presidents' Day — third Monday
Leap Year Day — on February 29, once every 4 years

March

Youth Art Month
National Nutrition Month
Earth Day, the Vernal Equinox — the first day of spring (astronomical)
National Wildlife Week — the third full week

April

Passover — derived from the Hebrew calendar
Easter — derived from the lunar calendar
Patriot's Day — third Monday
National Arbor Day — third Friday
Daylight Savings Time — last Sunday

May

American Bike Month
Senior Citizens Month
Be Kind to Animals Week — first full week
Mother's Day — second Sunday
Teacher's Day — Thursday before Memorial Day
Memorial Day — last Monday (legal observance)

June

Children's Day — second Sunday
Father's Day — third Sunday
Flag Week — week including Flag Day, June 14
End of School — usually the third week
Summer Solstice — the first day of summer (astronomical)

No. 1

SCHOOL-YEAR CALENDAR PROJECTS

Every day is historically noteworthy. If tomorrow isn't a national or religious holiday or the beginning of a week of events, then it may be somebody's birthday or the day a record was set for a special accomplishment.

The *Day by Day* monthly calendars supply you with a happening for just about every day of the school year. You might like to use the calendar entries as part of an ongoing learning program or simply for their anecdotal value. The calendar will inspire many uses, but here are some learning ideas to help you get started:

● Have the class decide upon a date to celebrate. It can be a made-up event or a not-too-important date on the calendar — perhaps a week during which everyone plans to get homework completed on time or a celebration of the school's founding. Create posters to promote the day; hold an assembly with the day as the theme; travel from class to class with an interest-generating presentation; draw up a full plan for the celebration.

● Many holidays have traditions surrounding them. Ask students to pick an unfamiliar national or religious holiday and learn about the symbols and traditions that go with it. Often libraries have a section of books that describe the various holidays.

● Relate the calendar to a study of careers. What kind of work is represented by an entry (an invention, for example)? What kinds of training or background must have been necessary for the individual(s) involved?

● Students can make up a trivia calendar by finding the least significant events for each day and inserting them on a homemade calendar. For a selection of such dates, the *Guinness Book of World Records* (see resource list) will be a good place to start. Another worthwhile source is the daily newspaper, especially the short filler articles.

● Many of the important events in history relate to improvements in transportation. Have students find entries about transportation on the calendar. Ask them to use books to learn about other inventions or breakthroughs in transportation. Which of the improvements are out of date today? Which were im-

THE LEARNING BOOTH

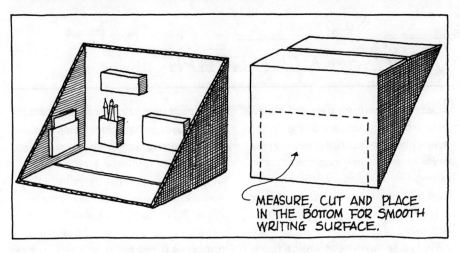

MEASURE, CUT AND PLACE IN THE BOTTOM FOR SMOOTH WRITING SURFACE.

proved further? Which never worked?
● The acronym "TGIF" stands for "Thank God It's Friday." Other days of the week have earned special sayings too: "Blue Monday," "Over the Hump Day" (Wednesday), and so on. Have kids make up expressions or create drawings for each day of the week, giving meaning according to how the day usually makes them feel.
● Cycles are part of every year. The amount of daylight varies by season; the moon goes through phases each month; the year itself is a cycle. Have kids research these and other natural cycles and explain them with models and illustrations to their classmates.
● Today the Gregorian calendar is the most familiar dating format. But this hasn't always been the case. Understanding the bases and history of other calendars will make an interesting student research project.
● The signs of the zodiac, named for constellations, are another way of organizing the year. Assign students the task of finding out the signs and their names, the date each one begins and ends and, for older groups, the historical basis of the calendar.
● In this time of conversion to metrics, some are arguing for a calendar structured on units of ten. Have students design their own version of such a calendar and then consider how the routine of their lives might change. Do they favor a calendar conversion?

If you suspect that your students would enjoy (and work better in) a place where they could have a little privacy and concentrate on an individual project, the learning booth might be an excellent addition to your classroom.

Select a cardboard box with a base about the size of a student's desk top. The base will be the "floor," and one long side becomes the back wall of the learning booth. Slice diagonally down the two short sides of the box from the top of the back wall to the front edge of the floor. Then cut along the front edge and remove this portion from the box. From this cutaway portion — or from another box — cut a rectangle that will fit into the floor of the booth to provide an even writing surface.

The booth is now ready for interior and exterior decoration. Cover the booth's wall with paint, wallpaper, self-adhesive paper or even wrapping paper.

Although paper and other work materials can be pinned or taped inside the booth, the easiest way to accommodate varying assignments and users is to glue pockets of various sizes on the booth walls. Papers, pencils, manipulatives,

flash cards, etc., can then be placed and replaced easily.

Learning booths are so simple to make that your students can help you construct extras if you should suddenly need more. If you want the booth to retain a special quality as well as serve real needs within your room, however, you may want to limit the number and to permit use by assignment only.
Idea by: David R. Adamson, Granite School District, Murray, Utah.

No. 3

CAFETERIA MENU GRAPH

Before your students start groaning about what they are or aren't getting in their school lunches this year, suggest that it may only *seem* as if the cafeteria features fish sticks every other day. Then add that the only way to objectify such objections is to gather some hard data.

First, start saving the weekly lunch menus. Then, every week or every month (or — if you relish mammoth mounds of data — near the end of the school year) have groups of students chart the food statistics. Divide the items into categories, such as main dishes, vegetables and fruits, desserts.

With each category on a separate chart, students can group menu items and keep a running tally as dishes reappear.

The charts might be filed for a few months before the first graphing takes place. The graphs could take several forms. A bar graph for each of the main categories could indicate the actual number of times each specific item was served over a stated period of time. Or challenge upper-grade students to determine percentages for each item — 27 fish stick meals out of 87 meals means fish sticks were served what percent of the time? The percentages could be graphed on a pie graph or on a 100-

percent bar graph, which is somewhat easier to construct.

The graphs could be displayed in the classroom and become the focus for graph reading activities, nutrition discussions and perhaps some speculation about seasonal food purchasing, economics, etc.

At the end of the year or at midterm, you might share your students' statistics with the rest of the school by posting the graphs in the cafeteria. See what reactions — and perhaps menu modifications — the menu graphs bring. **Idea by:** Leonard Goldberg, Fields Memorial School, Bozrah, Conn.

No. 4

A DARKROOM IN THE CLASSROOM

Sometimes being in the dark is a condition that needs to be arranged for, not avoided—especially in science teaching. Even if you have a lightproof area such as a closet, most likely there isn't much room left in it by this time of the year. So perhaps you have reason to see about constructing a classroom darkroom.

All you need is a large packing box (should be stove- or refrigerator-size, large enough for one or two children to get into comfortably), black paint and some tightly woven fabric or opaque plastic.

Cut off the top and bottom of the box. (Save the better-looking piece for a lid.) Paint the inside of the box black. Then set the box upright and cut out a small door (cut on two sides only so the door can be opened out and up). On the inside of the box hang a piece of dark fabric over the doorway, taping the fabric across the top edge only. The fabric will serve as a light lock. The top of the box can now be covered with a firmly woven piece of fabric, a blanket or a piece of opaque plastic (a fabric-lined plastic tablecloth works well). You can also set the lid on top to help seal out light leaks.

The darkroom is now ready for use. Try it out for observation of static electricity sparks; examination of things that glow in the dark; investigations of the effect of darkness on green plants, mold, mushrooms. With the top off, the darkroom can be converted into a planetarium. Plot a constellation or two on sheets of heavy wrapping paper large enough to cover the top of the darkroom. Poke holes where the stars are and put the paper over the top of the darkroom. The outside light showing through the star-holes will give children a picture of the night sky.

Fringe benefits: with the top off (and the box appropriately decorated) the darkroom can become a stage for hand- or stick-puppet productions. And the use of the darkroom may be of help to individuals who've been experiencing some apprehension about "the dark."

All this and it's portable and folds flat for storage!

Idea by: Helen Gow, Community College of Vermont, Montpelier, Vt.

No. 5

PERSONAL TIME CAPSULES

Everyone knows that things are constantly changing. Seasons recycle, bald baby birds grow feathers and fly away, skylines become crowded with new highrises, third graders become fourth graders. However, kids have a hard time noticing changes unless something sneaks up on them, like trying on last year's swimsuit and finding it's way too tight. Change is a hard thing to pin down.

A time capsule is one way a child has of keeping track of who he or she was a while back. A time capsule is like a scrapbook in a bottle. Not only is it fun to put together, but it's even more exciting to re-examine the contents on the last day of school.

Have each kid bring in a capsule that is weatherproof. A quart mayonnaise or peanut butter jar will be perfect. As a class, make a list of ideas for the contents. Your class might suggest collectibles such as these:
● An account of what you did today.
● A favorite rock.
● Movie listings for the week, or today's sports page.
● Some pictures you took at a booth.
● Tapes of your voice.
● A cassette recording of your favorite music.
● Gum wrappers, gum cards.
● A specimen from your insect collection.
● A cutting of your dog's hair.
● Bus tickets.
● Cracker Jack prizes, small toys.
● Snapshots of your best friends.
● A favorite poem.
● A brand new coin.
● A tooth that just fell out.
● Your pants size.
● Your height.

● A sample of your handwriting, perhaps on a list of your expectations for the year.
● A tracing of your foot and your shoe size.

Time capsules can have anything in them, although what seems nifty to your students now might seem silly later on. After all, they will be changed people in June.

After the kids have collected their various mementoes, have them put all the stuff in the bottles. They might want to seal the contents first in a plastic bag for a little extra insurance against water. Tell them to screw the lids on tight. Now "bury" the time capsules in some safe place—if the schoolyard doesn't seem practical, how about a dark corner of the classroom closet? Just remember they're there! At the end of the school year, have an opening ceremony. Notice any changes?

Idea by: Linda Allison, author of *The Wild Inside*, Sierra Club.

No. 6

KIDS PEDDLE NUTRITION

As fund raisers for class trips and other adventures, you can't beat bake sales and candy sales. But the extra calories and cavity-causing potential of sweet treats are not so welcome. How about a completely new approach to edible enterprise — fruit boosting!

Since fruit can add to the nutritiousness of a meal instead of spoiling it, you might be able to arrange for your students to make their fruit sales on a before-lunch tour of the school. (And imagine the colorful and appetizing advertising that fruits could inspire in your artists — all of whom can render an orange with ease.)

Managing a fruit sale means contacting a local produce supplier for fruit by the case and then preparing students for two kinds of jobs: vendors and cashiers. The head vendor becomes responsible for ordering the fruit, scheduling the classroom vendors (who goes to which room) and for checking in unsold fruit. The classroom vendors pack their boxes (they might start with 20 apples, 20 oranges and 10 bananas) and count up the fruit that's left after the sale. (Here's where you and the school budget may have to come to the aid. Be prepared to subsidize a few small, curriculum-related cook-ins.)

A cashier accompanies each vendor. Cashiers collect the correct amount for each purchase, make change and balance their accounts. The head cashier, besides scheduling the classroom cashiers, tallies the fruit sold, computes the money collected and makes the deposit.

A one-time sale could develop into a regular service. You also might consider adding peanuts, raisins and dried fruit to the line. What started out as a small project to raise money for a class trip may turn out to be a diverse learning experience. Students are introduced to supply and demand, profit and loss, cost analysis, overhead, advertising and promotion, quality control, health standards, staffing and scheduling. Nutrition consciousness is raised and math skills get a workout too.

Idea by: Penelope Zielinski, Detroit Public Schools, Detroit, Mich.

No. 7

PHOTOGRAPHIC SEATING CHARTS

Who needs seating charts? Certainly not the teacher who knows his or her kids and sees them daily. But what about classroom visitors — observers, administrators and especially substitute teachers? You can provide them with an up-to-date seating chart by obtaining a photograph of each of your students (have the kids bring pictures from home or order extra copies of class pictures) and arranging the pictures in proper order, identified below, on a piece of white paper. No chart making or secretarial work will be necessary — just a lot of smiling faces.

Idea by: C.C. Dunmore, St. Rose School, Wilmington, Ill.

REPORTER OF THE WEEK

Here is an idea for capturing and keeping the year's events and ideas—with a sound dimension. Designate a "reporter of the week"—just as you appoint students for other rotating classroom jobs—whose responsibility it is to make a tape recording summarizing classroom happenings for the week. The reporter must be attentive to the week's happenings in the ongoing program as well as to special events—humorous moments, times of excitement, shared sadness. Other students can assist the reporter by submitting story ideas throughout the week. In introducing the reporter-of-the-week idea, you might discuss the sorts of items that seem to be weekly report material. But assure the students that each reporter will have considerable freedom in choosing what to report on.

Using notes or perhaps an outline, the reporter organizes collected material by categories or in chronological order. Writing a report could be an option—a challenge for some, an unreasonable chore for others. (This news-gathering activity may lead to research about newspaper and broadcast reporters and reporting, discussion of news stories, human interest stories, commentary, sports and weather, etc.)

Reporting to the class is an every-Friday event, and students may want to devise a TV or radio "studio" setting where the action can take place. The reporter begins the tape by giving his or her name and identifying the week being reviewed. Some students may want to create individual "signature" phrases for signing off their reports in a personal way.

Tapes are preserved as a weekly log of the year's events. They can be played back on an individual basis or as a group activity, both for enjoyment and for historical research.

Idea by: Lori Goldman, Brooklyn, N.Y.

CREATE A CENTER CENTER

Suppose you discovered 25 or more teacher aides who could be called upon to prepare learning centers for use in your room. The students in your class could be just the eager-eyed and able helpers for the job. If you sense an interest in center creation among your students, you might set up a "Center Center" devoted to the propagation of new centers.

At the Center Center, post suggestions to start students thinking. Perhaps they'd like to prepare a math game, a language activity master, an art and crafts project. Students prepare rough drafts of their center plans to be worked over, improved upon and later proofread. Students also determine what materials they'll need to put their centers into operation, taking into consideration what's readily available. Then the center assembling takes place.

Schedule each student-made center for a week's use and post the schedule so that a student can check to see when his or her center will be "on."

In view of all the planning, organizing, creating and improving, as well as the drive to see a project through, you may find the Center Center to be the most valuable center of the year.

Idea by: Dorothy Hirschman, Edison, N.J.

No. 10

TV BOX PRESENTATIONS

The TV box is a great confidence builder for kids. It starts its career as a refrigerator packing box. Then a door large enough for a child is cut in the back. A window cut in the front acts as a TV screen. Children can paint on control knobs and decorations.

You might initiate the use of the TV box by trying takeoffs on TV game shows. The box will accommodate just one "contestant" at a time, so panel shows are out. And the emcee (you or a child) will also have to operate from outside the box. Gather a small group for an audience—and prospective contestant pool—and it's on with the show.

The emcee does a little warm-up interviewing at first, finding out the contestant's name, where he or she is from, special interests, family, etc. Some children will stick to the facts, but others may enjoy making up imaginary identities and life situations.

The game part of the show should be carried off in an authentic show-biz manner, but the content can consist of whatever drill material the class is working on—math facts, spelling, geography. Students should be asked to perform reasonable tasks with non-threatening time limits, or the fun will soon dissolve.

Six correct answers might win a prize—cruises, cars, homework passes, special activities, whatever your creativity conjures up.

The TV box can also be used for interviews: figures from history, workers in various occupations, visitors from countries you're studying (or from other planets). The box provides an ideal vehicle for reviewing or presenting material.

And of course the TV box has many recreational uses. You may find that children who will "do anything" for attention will be eager contenders for TV box time—to the extent of monitoring their own behavior outside the box so that they will be allowed time inside.

The charm of the TV box is in its specialness. It should never be overused. As potential uses come to mind or are suggested by the children, note them for the future, and reserve the TV box for classroom prime time usage only.
Idea by: Joyce S. Reagin, Greenwood, S.C.

No. 11

THE MONTH TRAIN

One way for early primary grade children to learn the months of the year is for them to associate each month with a symbol—something that tells what happens during that time of the year. Create a symbol for each month: a leaf for September, a witch for October, a turkey or fruit basket for November and so on. Then, on a duplicating master, draw an engine pulling 12 train cars and print the name of one month inside each car. Run off copies of the train and give one to each child. Each month have the children draw the appropriate symbol over the month's train car. At the end of the year the names of the months should be well in hand, and each child will have an artistic memento of the class.
Idea by: Delores Hines, Washington School, Chicago, Ill.

No. 12

MAKE YOUR OWN MAGNIFIERS

On those occasions when a closer look is called for, it might be nice to have a classroom supply of magnifying lenses handy. Why not make some? They can be constructed quite simply and inexpensively.

Optometrists often discard unneeded eyeglass lenses, and you might ask to be placed on their list of "charitable-cause" recipients. Being a choosey beggar, you'll select only the plastic lenses. You'll also need to pick up some Styrofoam packing material — the kind that protects "factory-fresh in the carton" TVs and radios and such. Appliance stores, hardware stores and hospitals are sources of this material.

To make the magnifiers, cut a piece of Styrofoam into a lollipop shape — with a handle narrow enough for a child's grasp and a top large enough to accommodate the lens. In the top end pierce a lens-shaped hole. The size of the opening should taper as you dig down. At the top side, the lens should just fit; on the bottom side, the opening should be slightly smaller than the size of the lens. The lens can then be pushed into place within the hole. (You may want to inscribe a groove in the wall of the opening for the lens to rest on; experiment a little.)

These lenses are fine for many projects not requiring an exact degree of magnification. And they're shatterproof.
Idea by: Davien Littlefield, New York City, N.Y.

No. 13

CLASSROOM YELLOW PAGES

Compile a classroom version of the Yellow Pages listing people resources in the class. You may be harboring a closet frog-o-phile, expert in assorted amphibian activities. You may have a clandestine genius in the gentle art of juggling. Just what kinds of talents are available? Suggest possible areas of accomplishment and discuss a few specific examples with the class to get the self-exploratory thought processes going:
● *School subjects*. Are there things you know about in science, math or reading, or subjects you do well that could help others in school? For instance, Kirk can bisect angles with compasses; Sara can demonstrate the uses of a lever.
● *Sports, games*. Dana can show how to serve in volleyball. Could you help someone improve in a sport? Do you know some new games for the playground?
● *Crafts*. Gerry knows how to make macramé knots. Are there other crafts activities that you could help with?
● *Other special interests or hobbies*. Are you a drag-racing fan? Do you like to make up plays or are you a performer? Do you speak a language other than English? Do you collect something? Could you show us your collection?

Allow students some time to mull over the possibilities and assess their potential contributions. Devise a questionnaire form through which students can communicate their capabilities — with the understanding that additions can be made and that information will be updated throughout the year. (In a few more weeks, Wendy will feel confident enough in jacks to qualify as an expert under the "Games" heading.)

The yellow pages should be categorized — various areas of the curriculum, crafts, games, research, etc. — according to what your questionnaire yields. Each category might be put into a separate booklet. (Some cross-referencing may be necessary.)

With experts available for many specific skills, students will have an alternative route for getting help when they need it. Instead of always coming to you, they can browse through the yellow pages to find a specialist suited to the task at hand. And it's no small thing to be the one that's giving the help — a real self-image booster.
Idea by: Mark Thomashow, Eastside Alternative School, Eugene, Ore.

No. 14

REMEMBER US

When a student moves away, a keepsake book filled with classmates' memorabilia can be a personal remembrance of happy times. To make the album, you'll need scissors, cardboard, colored paper, a paper punch, cord, photographs, and crayons or markers. (From *The Kids' Make-It-Yourself, Do-It-Yourself Party Book,* Workman.)

Cut two pieces of cardboard and as many same-size rectangular sheets of

colored paper as there are students. Punch two holes near the edge of one short side of one piece of cardboard and use the punched board as a pattern to mark where the holes should be on the colored paper and the other piece of cardboard. Punch the holes.

Then give a sheet of paper to each child in the room. Have the children fill the papers with their names, pictures and any words, jokes, poems or photographs that have special meaning for the departing friend. When the pages are ready, sandwich them between the two pieces of cardboard and tie the sheets and covers together.

No. 15

BIRTHDAY BOOK

What *else* happened on the day you were born? What sources could help answer that question?

Make each student's birthday an important historical occasion, or rather, give the student the opportunity to make his or her historical mark. Excuse the birthday person from regular assignments on his or her birthday (or a specially arranged alternative day) to gather data for *The Birthday Book*. In this book each class member's birthday will be observed in historical perspective with other happenings that occurred on that day.

Starting with the encyclopedia entry for the month, a student collects data about historical events that took place

on his or her birthday: birthdays of famous people in history (or current notables), battles of various wars, dates of inventions, dates when states were admitted to the Union, etc. Almanacs can be consulted, and the librarian may have other resources to recommend.

After completing a list of events, the student selects several historical occurrences to research in more depth. (All researching and reporting is to be completed in one day, which precludes "exhaustive" study.)

Current events can be collected too. Perhaps you could donate the birthday newspaper; absconding with the family's morning paper, even on a student's own birthday, might be an unwise move for a member of your class.

Have students look through the newspaper for important news items to clip for *The Birthday Book*. Selected headlines and pictures might be arranged in a collage. Some newspapers

have a "This Day in History" column that may provide more data — perhaps items of local or state history not available in other sources.

After collecting data — perhaps while others do math — the birthday student organizes the materials for the pages in *The Birthday Book* and plans a short presentation for a sharing time at the end of the day. This oral report could be chronological, carrying the audience forward or backward through history, or it might be organized by places (dateline, Pearl Harbor, December 7, 1941) or by subjects (people, sports, world news, etc.).

When the class has finished the day's work and the birthday student is ready, have a gathering time to learn the birthday discoveries. As *The Birthday Book* grows, it becomes a historical record in itself.

Idea by: Nancy Mastroianni, Placentia, Calif.

ROLL CALL QUERY

ON-THE-ROAD ASSIGNMENTS

Attendance taking is usually a matter of determining who's absent; ironically, the people singled out at attendance time are the people who aren't there. What about the people who are there? Attendance time could be a chance for giving a little special attention to those present.

The old-fashioned roll call with names and responses establishes at least a bit of recognition. You might surprise everyone some morning by saying, "Today when I call your name, let's hear the name of your favorite ice cream." Or try some of these:

● What is your favorite food?
● What is your favorite pet? . . . favorite color? . . . favorite TV show?
● Describe the best present you have ever received.
● Where were you born?
● How many are in your family?
● What do you like best at school?
● What would you do with $5,000?

You'll probably think of many more possibilities. Of course, you'll want to choose questions children will feel comfortable answering; it wouldn't make much sense to set up a situation that might keep the child from responding, since the idea of roll call is to find out — by one response or another — who's in attendance and who isn't. On the other hand, you can't invite lengthy dissertations at this particular time.

With all the diversity in answers, kids will appreciate their individuality while they sense their togetherness as a class. Next time attendance time rolls around, why not concentrate on *present* company!

Idea by: Adelle Beck, Alcott Elementary School, Riverside, Calif.

When kids are away from the classroom on extended trips or holidays, you can keep them from missing too much material by integrating class assignments with their travels. Ask the vacationers to complete some of the following or other pertinent activities while they're away:

● Write in your journal every day.
● Keep a graph of the high temperature each day.
● List the states you flew over (or drove through). Which of those states has the most vowels in its name? Which was the largest state? Which was the smallest?
● How many different types of jobs did people that you came in contact with have? What did they do?
● List all the ways a city you visited is like your own and all the ways it is different.

● Send the class a letter while you are gone.
● Collect shells (or rocks or leaves) along the way or at the final destination. Name as many of them as you can.
● Find out what food is grown in the place you visit.
● Find out about some of the animals that live in the region you visit but do not live near your home.
● Draw a picture of a bird you see and write about it in your journal.
● About how many miles is it from your home to your destination?
● Keep track of the days you are gone on a calendar.
● Bring back a menu from a restaurant where you ate.

Idea by: Patty Barrons, Pentwater Elementary School, Pentwater, Mich.

No. 18

THIS WAS THE WEEK THAT...

In the hubbub of doing activities and meeting schedules, both you and your students need a chance to stop and to reflect. What did we accomplish this week? What were the special events? What did we do for fun? What new things did we learn?

Try gathering the class at the end of the week to talk about what has been happening. In the process, you will be gathering material for a class book. Children contribute their recollections for you to record by beginning, "This was the week . . ." (With older students, recording responsibilities can be shared.) No rules dictate what constitutes a "significant" entry, though individuals' feelings should always be considered.

Children may cite the accomplishments of others. "This was the week that Mayra wrote a story." "This was the week that Stuart made a puppet." It can be a good time to reinforce cooperative or positive actions and interactions—a good time to encourage being sensitive to what will be pleasing and what might be embarrassing to individuals.

After the entries are written out, the reflection session becomes a chapter in the class "This Was the Week That . . ." book. The book can be placed on the library table for "anytime" reading. It may very well become the most popular book in your classroom collection.

Reflection can serve many purposes. It can be revealing: You may find children remembering things you scarcely recall, while, to your chagrin, that science project you thought was going to be so memorable . . .

Adding to the book can be a good way to wind up the week. You all may have had your ups and downs on various days, but looking at the week as a whole usually means highlighting the good rather than dwelling on the bad. It helps everyone to leave on the upbeat.

Idea by: Irene L. Hannigan, Fletcher School, Cambridge, Mass.

READ ALL ABOUT US

Candid classroom photos can become excellent story generators. Collect photos of both everyday activities (Wanda puzzling over a puzzle; Darryl attacking a peanut butter sandwich) and special events (the day Mrs. Webb brought the raccoon to school; Make Mine Metric Day). Be conscious too of including everyone in the class at one time or another.

Each Monday select one photo to tape on the chalkboard. (Wrapping the photo in plastic will help to protect it.) Invite each child to look at the picture and tell something about it by writing a sentence on the chalkboard. Collect a few early-bird volunteer sentences to set the "random thoughts" feeling. Others can be contributed throughout the week. Some children may be inspired to contribute more than one idea for their favorite photos.

On Friday gather the group to read over the accumulated commentary and to discuss and decide how to put the various thoughts into a kind of story about the photo. There may be a need for additional sentences. And of course the tale needs a title.

Prepare a large book in which completed stories can be copied and saved, along with the photos that inspired them. This "Read All About Us" volume can be available for the children to read at any time.

Next June you can transfer the stories and photos to a smaller scrapbook (one of those "magnetic" photo albums is ideal) for the class library shelf. Then this year's class can share with next year's class some true stories starring some familiar characters in a well-known setting. And you'll have a special record of events — a memory book of this school year.

Idea by: Margaret K. Payne, Cahokia, Ill.

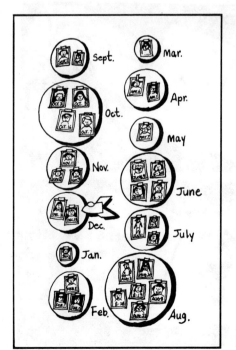

A BIRTHDAY IN SPACE

An effective way to keep track of birthdays and to help your students learn the names of the months is to make a Birthday Planet Calendar. Ask each student to bring in a recent snapshot of himself or herself. Sort the photos by birthday month and construct 12 "planets" to which you will tape the pictures. The planets, which can be made of paper or cardboard, will vary in size according to the number of snapshots they will need to hold. Also make a small rocket ship. Tape the pictures to the appropriate planets and print the children's birthdays under their pictures. Then tape the planets to the wall in order from September to August.

As the months pass, move the rocket ship (pin or tack it) from one planet to the next. You might want the children whose birthdays fall in the same month to plan an activity pertinent to their month — a special game, perhaps — or to talk about what the month might be like on another planet.

Be sure to include the children whose birthdays fall during summer vacation. Plan a special time to celebrate their birthdays and to let them plan an activity or talk about their special month.

Idea by: Diana Schrader, Bronx, N.Y.

No. 21

SQUEEZE-BOTTLE PRINTING

As a year-round art project, squeeze-bottle printing can't be beat. All your kids need is a few plastic squeeze bottles (the catsup or mustard kind), construction paper and paint.

The first time around, let the children experiment with color and design. Give each child a piece of construction paper (12 by 18 inches is a good size) folded in half. Ask the kids to unfold their papers. Then give them a number of squeeze bottles filled with different colors of paint. Have the kids squeeze small amounts of paint on one side of the fold in the paper, place the two sides together and then press (a rolling pin or heavy cardboard can be used if

hands don't press hard enough). When the kids unfold their papers, they'll discover they've created colorful prints. Put the artwork in a safe place to dry.

Once they've gotten the hang of squeeze-bottle printing, the sky's the limit. Finished prints can be used as book covers or folders. A bold, especially colorful print can be used as wrapping paper. Templates can be used to define recognizable shapes on the colorful, but abstract, prints. The fall, for instance, is a good time for the children to squeeze yellow, red and brown paint onto their papers, press the sides together and let the artwork dry. Then a leaf template can be placed over

the prints, and colorful leaves can be cut out.

Templates and appropriate paint colors can be used to make designs for a variety of seasons and occasions: a heart template (placed on the fold) with red and white paint for Valentine's Day; a tulip template (placed on the fold) with red, white and yellow paints for spring; a simply shaped turkey template with brown and gold paint for Thanksgiving. Once the designs have been cut out, they can be used as cards, gifts, mobiles or window borders.

Idea by: Beverly Lindsey, Wilcox Primary School, Portland, Ore.

No. 22

5-GALLON LOCKERS

Some schools haven't space enough to provide individual lockers for their primary and intermediate students. Others provide such narrow lockers that kids can't squeeze in more than a coat, mittens, boots and a bag lunch. What about those baseball cards for trade during recess, or a transistor radio, or an autograph book, or a jump rope, or an extra comb? If you don't want your students to stash their personal treasures in their already crowded desks, introduce them to the five-gallon locker.

The five-gallon locker is a custom-decorated ice cream container. Solicit your local ice cream shop or dairy for at least as many five-gallon ice cream containers as you have students. You might want to keep a few extra on hand for new students who come midyear — and you might even like one for yourself.

First have your kids recover the outside and lids of their containers. Construction paper, wallpaper roll ends, material bolt ends, funny pages, Con-Tact paper and leftover wrapping paper cut to size make colorful surfaces that are easy to glue to the containers. Kids may want to further decorate their personal storage containers with paint, photos, magazine pictures, decals, bric-a-brac, cut-out designs and shapes, pressed leaves and flowers or fancy lettering. The finished lockers should be as original and flamboyant as their owners.

Arrange the lockers in low stacks in the classroom. Assure your kids that the lockers are their private property, and that neither you nor anyone else will fool with the contents. Permit students to "go to their lockers" before and after school, and during recess. You may need to remind them that the five-gallon lockers are not the place to hang out during school time.
Idea by: Betsy Franklin, Columbia School, Redding, Calif.

No. 23

SORTER FAN

Classifying is a skill that pops up in most subject areas, but science is particularly rich in grouping possibilities:
- fall, winter, spring and summer happenings
- herbivores, carnivores, omnivores
- elements, compounds, mixtures

The sorter fan, composed of a stack of tagboard strips joined at one end with a paper fastener, can accommodate many classifying tasks. The fan might consist of item strips alone (a selection of things or events that kids group according to their own criteria), or it can include category strips (labels under which you wish the items to be grouped) as well as item strips.

If you provide the categories as well as the items, use contrasting colors for the two groups and cut the category strips slightly longer than the item strips. Write the name of a category across the upper end — the unfastened end — of each category strip.

On the item strips — there can be as many of these as the students can comfortably handle — put pictures or labels, one item per strip. If you wish to make the fan self-correcting, number each item and provide an answer key strip. You may also want to provide a directions strip.

Assemble the sorter fan strips with the category strips together at the bottom and item strips stacked on top. The paper fastener securing the strips should have prongs long enough to extend down through the stack and also to allow for free manipulation of the individual strips.

To use the fan, a student locates the category strips and fans them out. The item strips are then spread, one by one, in position over the appropriate category strips. (Paper clips or rubber bands may be used to keep groups grouped.)
Idea by: Janice Freeman and Joyce Freeman, Corpus Christi State University, Corpus Christi, Tex.

No. 24

CHECK-IN ON THE MOON

It sometimes seems as if a teacher's three R's are *registers*, *roll* call and "*rhino*-tallying" (nose counting). There certainly is a lot of keeping track involved when you have a class to look after. Here is an idea for handling that sort of accountability:

A large moon map can serve as an attendance-taking device. (If you can't get one, you might try mapping some mythical mystery planet instead.) Mount the moon (or planet) on a large piece of tagboard. Attach a class-sized number of brass brads to the map — at various scenic locations — bending up each brad on the front side of the map so that it becomes a hook. These hooks

will be used for skewering cards with punched-out holes. Attach an equal number of brads (also bent into hooks) to the area around the moon — to be known henceforth as "outer space."

Each student gets a 3-by-5 card with a hole punched in the top. The cards will be transformed into personalized space capsules, each clearly identified with the student's name marked in bold letters.

Every morning as students come in, each selects a moon landing site for his

or her capsule and hangs it on a "moon hook." Those capsules that remain in "outer space" provide the names of the absentees. At the end of the day, students return their capsules to outer space.

Checking in on the moon may also be of some help to messengers, special teachers and others who need to know if a student is in. The map may even stimulate some interest in astronomy.
Idea by: Donna Danowski, Newton School, Torrance, Calif.

No. 25

WHAT'S NEXT?

Kids are frequently concerned about what will happen after they finish a certain segment of the school day. Constantly informing and reassuring them about "what's next" can be a real hindrance to classwork. To relieve them of anxiety and you from continuous disruption, turn your bulletin board into a What's Next? clock.

Make a large clock face with movable hands and print the words *What's Next?* above it. (Put your clock near a real clock if possible.) On the chalkboard near the clock, print your daily schedule, showing the times of each period. On either side of the clock, put up a pocket — one for cards with the

periods' starting times on them and one for cards with subject names. Below the clock, place a frame that will display the time and subject of the next period.

At the beginning of each lesson, ask the class, "What's next?" Then have a student examine the class schedule and choose the appropriate time and subject cards. Have him pin the cards in the frame and move the clock hands to show the proper time. Now a quick glance at the clock will show everyone what's coming up and when.
Idea by: Phil Juska, Montgomery County Intermediate Unit, Norristown, Pa.

No. 26

PEGBOARD POSSIBILITIES

Pegboards — they're inexpensive, easy to store and versatile. You can use these hand learning tools in numerous teaching and display situations.

● Pegboards can be used for assigning classroom jobs. Write job names on pieces of tape positioned above several hooks and hang the name of the child responsible for each job from the appropriate hook. Name tags can be designed to fit themes or job descriptions.

● Each time a child reads a book, she can hang a construction paper book from a hook next to her name.

● A large pegboard can be divided into sections that are assigned to individual children for their personal use. On their own area, children may hang any work or items of interest that they like.

● Pegboards can be used as learning stations or centers: for practicing alphabetical order; for practicing sequential order; for practicing matching numbers, vocabulary words, contractions.

● You can wire the back of a pegboard and make an electrical answer board with a small battery-powered light bulb.

With a pegboard in hand, you'll no doubt think of many other uses on your own.

Idea by: Margaret McIntosh, West School, Jefferson City, Mo.

RESOURCES

CALENDAR BOOKS —
● "Chase's Calendar of Annual Events" by William D. Chase (Apple Tree Press [Box 1012, Flint, MI 48501]). Lists special days, weeks and months for each year. Always up to date and accurate.
● "Science Fun Every Day Calendar" by Amy Benham and Doris Ensminger (Acropolis Books [Colortone Bldg., 2400 17 St., N.W., Washington, DC 20009]). Provides one or several items of historical interest for every day of the year. Includes specific activities for many dates.
● "UNICEF Wall Calendar" (United States Committee for UNICEF [Dept. GC, 331 E. 38 St., New York, NY 10016]). Gives dates of national, religious and family holidays from around the world.

THE EVERYDAY SCIENCE SOURCEBOOK — Here is an exceptional resource book for primary through junior high science teachers. It contains more than 1,000 activities that complement just about any science curriculum imaginable.

In an introductory section, "What This Book Is Not," author Lawrence F. Lowery explains that the book is neither a text nor an exhaustive source of scientific information, and it is not to be used as a science program in itself. It is, however, a superb gathering of science activities that can serve as demonstrations of various principles and facts or as vehicles for scientific discovery.

Each activity is direct, to the point and unencumbered with superfluous content. Accompanying illustrations and descriptions of the activities are clear and easy to understand in this excellent, highly practical tool. *The Everyday Science Sourcebook* is also available in an abridged version.
Order from: Allyn and Bacon, 470 Atlantic Ave., Boston, MA 02210.
Grade level: Teachers of primary-junior high.

RECIPES FOR ART AND CRAFT MATERIALS — If, over the years, you've forgotten how many cups of water to mix with the torn newspaper and paste to get the right papier-mâché compound, then rest easy; author Helen Roney Sattler gives recipes for several different types of papier-mâché alone.

In all, *Recipes for Art and Craft Materials* supplies nearly 80 recipes for arts and crafts concoctions. The recipes are organized into eight categories of materials — pastes, modeling compounds, papier-mâché, casting compounds, paints and paint mediums, inks, dried-flower preservatives and miscellaneous. In addition to telling how to mix the recipes, the book describes how to use them and what kinds of results to expect. It also gives convenient directions for storing the prepared materials.

This is undoubtedly one of those books that a teacher or parent will refer to year after year when those standard recipes slip from mind or when new ones are in order. The book has the dual advantage of being written for intermediate level kids so they can use it on their own.
Order from: William Morrow & Co., 105 Madison Ave., New York, NY.

1

World's last passenger pigeon died, Cincinnati Zoo, 1914.

2

3

Treaty of Paris signed by the U.S. and Britain in 1783, ending the Revolutionary War.

7

Queen Elizabeth I, after whom was named the Elizabethan Era, born 1533.

8

City of St. Augustine, nation's first permanent settlement, founded 1565.

9

13

14

Francis Scott Key wrote the *Star Spangled Banner*, 1814.

15

Old Peoples's Day in Japan, a national holiday.

19

20

"Old Ironsides" (USS *Constitution*) was launched at Boston Harbor, 1797.

21

First daily newspaper, the *Pennsylvania Packet and Daily Advertiser*, published in 1784.

25

Balboa discovers the Pacific Ocean, 1513.

26

George Gershwin, American composer, born 1898.

27

First locomotive to pull a passenger train operated today, 1825.

TWO
DAY BY DAY

4
Los Angeles is founded as "El Pueblo de Nuestra Señora La Reina de Los Angeles Porcincula" in 1781.

5

Be Late for Something Day.

6
President William McKinley, 25th U.S. President, fatally shot in 1901.

10

Elias Howe patented the sewing machine, 1846.

11
The first policewoman with full powers to arrest was appointed in Los Angeles in 1910.

12
The U.S.S.R.'s *Lunik II* becomes the first satellite to land on the moon, 1959.

16

Mayflower Day, anniversary of the departure of the *Mayflower* from Plymouth, England, 1620.

17
Citizenship Day, anniversary of the signing of the U.S. Constitution, 1787.

18

22

Hobbit Day, the birthday of Tolkien's characters Bilbo and Frodo Baggins.

23

24
The U.S. Supreme Court created, 1889.

28
Cabrillo Day, anniversary of the discovery of California by Juan Rodriguez Cabrillo, 1542.

29

30
San Geronimo's Day, celebrated by Native Americans with ceremonial dancing and festivities in Taos, New Mexico.

No. 27

WELCOME ABOARD!

The first day of school, with all its newnesses, can be scary — for kids too. Instituting a "welcome aboard" letter might make a difference to both of you.

If you've gotten the facts on your new class early enough, you can get off a short personal note to each child by way of welcome — providing some pertinent opening-day data and perhaps building a little preseason rapport. Some of the items you might like to include: the name of the school, the date and time that school opens, your room number and basic supplies needed. (Though for many kids this will be known territory, reminders at the child's personal responsibility level probably won't hurt.) The rest of the content is up to your ingenuity and the kind of classroom feeling you'd like to set.

Though these letters are going out on a mission of professional importance, you might squelch the urge to turn them out on a dependable, dutiful ditto (which may be the least welcoming of the media). A hand-lettered or written message on personal note paper — as you might do when writing to a personal friend — would be more to the point.

Circumstances may favor an after-the-first-day letter instead. This sort of welcome can have the same personal-letter appeal, and there's more opportunity to individualize.

"I'm looking forward to hearing more about that train trip you went on this summer" or "It's certainly good to have a fellow caramel lover around this year." These letters won't carry the same orientation data as the "before" letters, of course, but they may refer to upcoming events:

"Next week we're going to start a special art project that uses egg cartons. Could you bring one?"

The "welcome aboard" note could help everyone get a more comfortable start on the year.
Idea by: Mamie E. Wiley, Bloomington, Ind.

Beginning of School

No. 28

ADVERTISE

The day before the start of school, greet your students with a classified ad placed in the personal section of your local newspaper. Although your students may not read the ad, many of their parents will see it and read it to the children.

Attention Third Grade Students

To my third grade students at Walter Hays Elementary School: I'm looking forward to seeing you tomorrow. Your teacher, Ann Martin

Clip the advertisement and post it where students can see it when they arrive the first day.

If you would rather not advertise, send a letter with a similar message to all of your students.
Idea by: Murray Suid, coauthor of *Made in America*, Addison-Wesley.

Beginning of School

DON'T JUST SAY "HELLO"

Greeting your class for the first time can be a special moment. You can magnify it by welcoming the children in several different languages. Here are nine greetings used by teachers around the world. You might teach some or all of these expressions to your students, who can share the greetings with their families.

Spanish:

¡BIENVENIDOS A LA ESCUELA!

(bee en benidoes ah la eskwāla)
Welcome to the school.

French:

BIENVENUS À L'ÉCOLE

(byen vneu ah laycull)
Welcome to the school.

Hebrew:

ברוכים הבאים לבית הספר

(brū heem hoc hōzreem lvayt hasayfar)
Blessed be the returners to the house of the book.

Japanese:

進学おめでとう

(shin gakoone ō may day toe)
Congratulations on the new school year.

German:

SEID HERZLICH WILLKOMMEN IN DER SCHULE

(zide helschik vilkōmen in dare shulle)
A hearty welcome to the school.

Swahili:

KARIBUNI TENA SHULENI

(ca[r] eeboony tayna shūlayni)
Welcome all of you to school.

Mandarin Chinese:

歡迎入學

(hwan nying ru sywē)
Welcome to enter your studies.

Russian:

ПРИВЕТСТВУЕМ ВАС В ШКОЛЕ

(privetstrūyem vas f schkoyeh)
We welcome you in school.

Vietnamese:

CHAÒ MǓNG BAN TRỎ LAI TRƯỜNG

(nchow meung bong tchar lie tcherung)
Welcome, friends, back to school.

Idea by: Murray Suid, coauthor of *Made in America*, Addison-Wesley.

Beginning of School

MEET YOUR ANIMAL DOUBLE

Looking for an icebreaker to help kids meet each other in September? This one, which requires some thoughtfulness, is adapted from the *Manual for Multi-Cultural and Ethnic Studies* (Inter-Culture Associates).

Ask each person, working entirely alone and without talking with others, to choose the animal that best characterizes his or her personality. Students should respond with one word: fox, turtle, bear, etc. Allow no more than two or three minutes for this.

Each person then introduces himself or herself to the person to the right, to the left, in front and behind, using both real name and animal double.

When they introduce themselves, students should explain what personal characteristics made them choose their particular animal names.

Afterwards, each participant might try to find in the group another person with the same animal double or the same characteristics. If interest in the activity holds, students might also try to meet their animal opposites.

Beginning of School

No. 31

FIRST DAY GAZETTE

Get your program off to a good start with a limited-edition newspaper, delivered on the first day of school. Getting out a paper takes some pre-opening-day preparation, but it's time well spent.

A front-page identification of the newspaper's editor eliminates the first-day ritual of "My name is . . ." on the chalkboard. A bold "published at . . ." — with the name of the school and its full address — is another important item of information for new students.

Then the articles begin. You might start out with a wrap-up of summer sports, reviewing the performances of some local teams. You could prepare a summary of summer weather with some predictions for the season ahead in *Old Farmer's Almanac* style. The vacation adventures of the editor could be dramatically presented — even if it was a fairly tame time.

After a recap of summer events, the gazette could move into plans for the upcoming year: highlights of a few study areas and topics, plans for a field trip, projects, etc. Then perhaps a section offering a few hints for a smoother year: an outline of broad expectations, standards, evaluation procedures — whatever seems appropriate for your

classroom style. (Older students particularly, notes Lovering, appreciate a sense of "where they stand" at the outset.) The final article could be an introduction to and description of a specific activity, e.g., "Tomorrow — Seaweed Candy!"

In your role as newspaper editor, you may feel inclined to round out your paper with a few jokes, puzzles, want ads (need some recyclables for a project or maybe someone to handle hamster duty?), a faculty profile or two, facts about the school (traditions, trivia). And how about a short provocative item — a school problem, local issue, sports prediction, "can you top this?" challenge — that may prompt some letters to the editor for bulletin board publication. (Communications that are intended to be private should, of course, remain so.) Time and paper rather than your imagination will be the limiting factors.

Keep in mind that the "First Day Gazette" may also be doing some communicating with parents, since many students will be taking newspapers home. This could be a good way of melting the first-day frost all the way around.

The new school year will likely bring mixed reviews as it moves along. But unlike the current crop of TV shows contending with cancellations, you and your class are probably in for the duration. Making the most of your new beginnings could help put the whole production well on its way toward a successful run.

Idea by: John Lovering, Triton Regional School, Byfield, Mass.

Beginning of School

ENDLESS SUMMER   GRAND OPENING ACTIVITY CENTER

When summer vacation ends, many kids protest strongly against returning to school. But what if summer vacation were a permanent one—and school never opened again? Here's a good way to help your students discover their true feelings about school.

Pick an upcoming date (if you save this activity for the end of the school year, use the last day of school). Then, on a large sign with very big letters, write something like this: "School closing forever on September 30, by order of the dictator. D. Stroyo." (Make sure the dictator's name is a fictitious one.) After the whoops die down, ask the students to pretend that their school really will close. Then have them write a few paragraphs about how they felt when they first read the sign and realized its meaning, how they'd feel a few days later and what they'd do in the new situation.

The results could be surprising. You may find that the kids who always talk about how much they hate school now tell you how bored and miserable they would feel (after the initial celebration). Some may talk of moving to other countries to continue their education. A few stalwarts may decide that even dictators can be dealt with. One fourth grader who was asked to consider a future with no school said, "I'd lie down and relax, watch TV and eat and stay in bed till ten o'clock, and then in a couple of years or two, I might fight with the dictator."

Idea by: Martha Snyder, Rose Hill School, Reynoldsburg, Ohio.

Beginning of School

The spirit of a new beginning can be captured in a special grand opening activity center.

Sporting such grand opening paraphernalia as pennants and posters, the center provides activity cards for ideas such as the following:

1. Create a new school holiday you'd like to have observed this year and explain the background of the celebration.

2. Draw a picture of a classmate you'd like to get to know better this year. (Socializing follow-ups could be planned for this one.)

3. Invent a new school subject you'd like to take this year. (Older students might even dream up "scope and sequence" data for their new subjects.)

4. Choose someone on the school staff to interview on the subject of _____(insert topic)_____. (The mechanics of arranging for and conducting an interview will require some outside-the-center time and discussion.)

5. Take a tour of the school with a new classmate and together make a map of the school. (Suggest a map size, the degree of detail to which the map should be drawn, and whether the map should show the interior or exterior of the school.)

6. Make an imaginary trip to a school of the 21st century on its opening day. (Where is the school? How do students get to school if they have to leave home at all? What's the homework situation? Sports program? What are the school's biggest problems?)

You might offer "let's get organized" activities, such as designing daily schedules or setting goals.

You might also include some observe, list, count and calculate activities designed to help kids get better acquainted with their room and with their classmates.

Some completed activities may lend themselves to a show-and-share time—a finale that could be the highlight of your grand opening starting-a-school-year celebration.

Idea by: Dianne Daugherty and Sharon Webb, Los Alamitos, Calif.

Beginning of School

No. 34

TRASH-CAN ARCHAEOLOGY

While we're looking at all those new faces, wondering how long it will take to really know those kids, those new faces are looking back at us and wondering what *they've* drawn this year. Trash can be a fine get-acquainted medium. (Archaeologists have sworn by it for ages.)

Prepare a box of your own personal brand of trash for the scrutiny of your student archaeologists: an appointment calendar page with a cryptic note, an advertising brochure for power tools, old family photos, an empty match folder from an intriguing place, a golf ball (tennis ball, fishing lure), a parakeet feather, a dog collar, cash-register tape from the supermarket, notes from former students (some with complimentary messages, some not so complimentary — to prove you're human), tickets torn in half, the TV page from the newspaper with a program marked, a Melba toast box, a candy wrapper, a torn calorie counter — you know your garbage best.

Allow some time for students to examine the trash and then plan for a follow-up session that will offer the archaeologists an opportunity to expand upon the raw data. Try having them frame their questions in such a way that your answers will be only yes or no. You may call attention to a few items yourself and find out what inferences were drawn — both to check on investigative prowess and to clear up any unfortunate misunderstandings. (Note: Be sure to label your box of trash "Educational Materials"; otherwise, you might discover — as Grace Welton did — that before your archaeologists have had a chance to get down to cases, an overzealous custodian has disposed of the entire project.)

Students may want to collect some get-acquainted garbage of their own, and you might arrange some student-to-student archaeology sessions.

Idea by: Grace Welton, Mills Junior High, Rancho Cordova, Calif.

Beginning of School

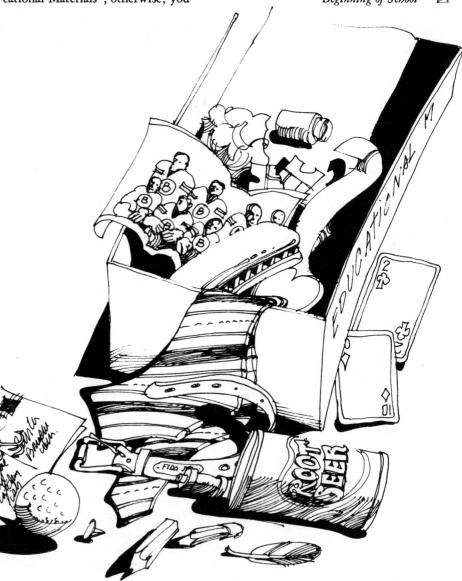

TAKE ONE WATERMELON

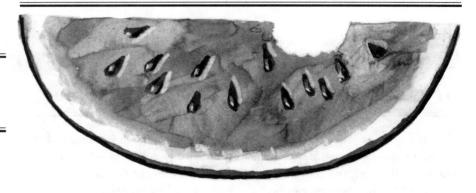

No. 35

THERE'S A NEW KID IN TOWN

Chances are you have a kid in your class who is as new a face to your other students as you are. One way of encouraging your class to get to know the "new kid" and to make his or her assimilation a little easier is to engage students in writing and compiling a local directory—a kid's guide for what there is to do and see in your town.

Since you may not be familiar with the popular hot spots, hang-outs and eating places that your kids haunt on their own time, you'd best leave the directory assignments to a class committee. Of course, you can be in on a map of the town and the guide to historical landmarks—but do you really know the flattest bike trails or the best pizza? Students might like to review local children's theater groups and book and toy stores. What goes on in the summer? They may recommend the arts-and-crafts program at one park, but the sports counselors at another. Are there any special rules, such as no skateboarding on the sidewalks downtown, or walking your bike on the school playground? Maybe the town is lucky enough to have a movie theater or a roller skating rink. And there are so many school clubs and after-school activities to consider!

Not only will one child find out that new places and new faces aren't so bad after all, but the rest of the students may rediscover that their town really offers a lot in the way of fun and interest.

Beginning of School

Even in these frenzied first days when attention fixes and flits with amazing speed, it's hard to walk away from something as large and impressive as a watermelon. And there's a lot your class can do with watermelons—besides the first thing on everyone's mind.

1. Have students estimate the weight of a watermelon. Weigh it. (Could you find a scale calibrated in metric weight for a change?) How close did the guessers come to the correct weight? Who came closest (and gets the first piece)?

2. Estimate and weigh each slice. Are the weights of various slices nearly the same? Should they be? What about variations in shape, thickness of rind, etc.?

3. Young children can draw pictures of their slices, showing the number of seeds they see.

4. Have the children save the seeds as they eat their slices, putting the seeds on paper towels for easy, non-slip counting. What is the average number of seeds? (For children who drew pictures showing seeds, how did the actual number of seeds compare with the drawings?)

5. Weigh the seeds, weigh the rind, and compare this combined weight with the original weight of the slice. How much of the slice was good for eating? What percentage of the slice do you throw away?

6. How much do all the seeds weigh together? Can you make a 5-gram mass piece with seeds? (Try balancing a nickel against it as a test.)

7. Estimate the number of seeds in the whole watermelon; then find the exact number of seeds.

8. Make a double bar graph to show the weight of each slice and the number of seeds in each slice.

9. Can you graph other data?

10. Use the rind for making stamps—potato print style—and use an ink pad to make designs.

11. Have kids make up watermelon worksheets with pictures and problems they've come up with.

12. How about planting the seeds? See what, if anything, happens.

And what else? With a slight stretch of the imagination there may be possibilities for language arts (fantasy especially), social studies (Where do watermelons grow? How do they get to us?) and even art—to say nothing of consumer ed.

Idea by: Ruth A. Manieri, Sayreville, N.J.

<u>No. 37</u>

GET ACQUAINTED WITH "ME" DOLLS

Reading, getting acquainted and building self-concepts—"Me" dolls can help with all three. And they might provide a little handwriting practice too. Me dolls serve both as alter egos and as information booklets.

Use tagboard to make a cutout doll figure about 12 inches (30 cm) tall for each member of the class. The shapes can be individualized a bit to show a dress or slacks, varying hair styles, etc. Each child may color in hair, skin, shoes—unless you'd like to spring the finished products on the class as a surprise.

For the face area, apply a disk of Mylar or foil to create a mirror effect. (A scientific supply store should have Mylar; it's also available in 48-by-42-inch sheets—enough for three or four classrooms of doll faces—from Edmund Scientific, Edscorp Building, Barrington, NJ 08007.)

Prepare clothing patterns (e.g., slacks, dress) to match the doll configurations and cut five copies for each doll from plain white paper. A sixth tracing of the clothing pattern for each doll can be on vinyl wallpaper—if you're lucky enough to have a wallpaper sample book—or on other colorful paper. This will be the doll's "outfit" and also the cover of the booklet.

On the cover goes the title: "Read about Tanya" or Tony or whomever. The rest of the book might go as follows:

Page 1. My name is _____.

Page 2. I live at _____.

Page 3. My telephone number is _____. (Skip this if unlisted numbers may cause a difficult situation.)

Page 4. My birthday is _____. I am _____ years old.

Page 5. I like _____. (You may leave the sentences open for each child to finish, or you may write in information as the child tells it to you. To make the doll more personal, allow space for the child to copy what you've written.)

Then assemble the booklet and staple it in place on the doll's shoulders, leaving the lower edge free for turning pages. Or attach the pages with a single paper fastener to make it easier for children to add pages. (The clothing patterns will need to be made available for the children's use in adding pages.)

Completed Me dolls play many roles in the classroom. Children will enjoy reading about themselves and exchanging dolls to read about others. The dolls might also be used as personalized puppets for impromptu skits.

You may even decide to add more pages of background information or to finish the backs of the dolls—for a coming-and-going Me doll.

Idea by: Mary Ellen Killelea, Belmont St. Community School, Worcester, Mass.

Beginning of School

ANIMAL BILL OF RIGHTS

PREDICTIONS

Invite your class to recall some of the big events of last year. These could be things that happened in their class or in town, or national happenings—*Star Wars*, the coal strike, the Yankees winning the World Series.

Now ask your students to join you in making predictions for the coming year. You might prime their imaginations with the following predictions made by two California futurists:

• Scientists will learn how to control a person's moods from a distance by beaming mood messages directly to the brain.

• The number of smokers will decline.

• The U.S. government will greatly expand its support of research into ESP.

• Monster toys will be the rage.

You, the teacher, can make safe predictions about what the kids will learn: "By March, you children will know how to solve a hard math problem like this! And by May, you will all know how to spell every word on this list."

Write the predictions on a "Futures Poster" that you can display in the room, or appoint an editorial committee to put out a "future issue" of a newspaper. Or you can simply write out the predictions on scraps of paper, store them in a box, and reopen them in June to check the class's accuracy.

Idea by: Murray Suid, coauthor of *Made in America,* Addison-Wesley.

Beginning of School

On September 1, 1914, the world's last passenger pigeon died. Since then many species have qualified for the endangered list and continue to face extinction. Children often have an affinity for animals and will eagerly respond to the opportunity to espouse the inalienable right-to-life of these creatures. But rather than have a group of budding ecologists and preservationists convene for discussion of a one-sided issue, why not have the animals themselves attend an Endangered Species Convention and draft their own Bill of Rights?

Have each child research and assume the role of an animal whose survival is endangered. An almanac will provide an endangered species list, or you can write to the U.S. Fish and Wildlife Service at the Department of the Interior in Washington, D.C. Recent issues of natural history periodicals and other topical publications should provide information and statistics.

With information in paw or under wing, have the various creatures—the blue whale, the auk, the grey wolf, the bald eagle, the crocodile, the gorilla and the rhinoceros—describe their plights and speculate on their chances for survival.

After each animal has had an opportunity to speak, have the convention appoint a chaircreature and a scribe (preferably an animal with a good supply of plumes!). The chaircreature will call upon the various participants for items to include in the Animal Bill of Rights. Sample clauses might be (1) The right not to be hunted for sport, (2) The right not to be killed for clothing or (3) The right to have natural habitats left undisturbed. The scribe will write a draft on a scroll of newsprint or brown wrapping paper. After the convention is over, students may make their own souvenir copies, and the class as a group might submit the original to their school or local newspaper.

September 1

No. 40

INTERIOR DESIGN: A MAPPING FIRST

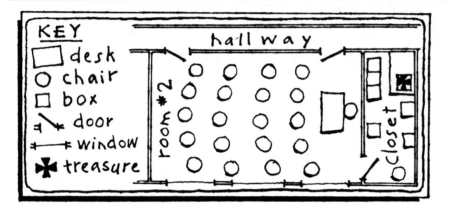

If you're about to introduce mapping to your class, you're probably starting out "where the children are"—in their own classroom. Here's one way to go about mapping the classroom.

Provide each child with a sheet of construction paper, along with an assortment of cut-out squares and rectangles to represent furniture. Have children try placing the furniture pieces on the construction paper "floor" according to the present room arrangement. After this, the children may enjoy rearranging the furniture pieces on their own maps; then you might try recreating some of these new interior designs, moving the real furniture to match the maps.

A further step might be converting shapes to symbols—such as an X for a chair, a box for a table and an X inside a box for a chair-table combination. Children can come up with their own symbols, providing a map key to explain what each stands for.

A treasure hunt using these maps can put children's map-reading skills to work. A child hides an object in the room, marking its location on his or her map with an agreed-upon symbol. It's up to a friend then to find the hidden object by using this treasure map. Even children who've become quite proficient using their own personally designed maps may find that reading someone else's map can be a challenge. And the map key takes on special importance.

When the class seems ready for bigger things, help them sketch the layout of the school—in much less detail, of course—and try a treasure hunt within these broader boundaries. As before, the hider maps the treasure spot and the hunter follows the hider's map in tracking down the treasure. And in this large-scale map activity the hunting may be more determined if the treasure is known to be worth finding—in lieu of jewels, try brownies!

Idea by: Clara Greisman, Richmond U.S.D., Richmond, Calif.

Beginning of School

No. 41

DIAL NEIGHBOR

Students can help their families and their neighbors' families by researching all the local telephone numbers for direct assistance in emergencies. The compilation of a list of neighborhood numbers can be a homework assignment, or a classroom project if you are able to obtain several phone books from your local telephone company headquarters.

Have each child find the numbers of the emergency and repair services nearest his or her home. Such a list might include:
- Police station
- Fire station
- Ambulance service
- Hospital
- ASPCA or animal control center
- School
- Emergency or Civil Defense shelter
- Baby-sitter service
- City sewerage service
- City garbage service
- Local bus service
- Train station
- All-night garage
- All-night pharmacy
- Local electric or gas utility
- Reliable neighbors (ask permission to list their numbers)

When the children have completed their directories, have them make additional copies for each of their neighbors, or take a class trip to a local copy shop where each child can order and pay for the necessary number of copies.

National Good Neighbor Day

No. 42

CITIZEN'S OATH

What better way to have your students observe Citizenship Day than to have them take the oath of allegiance that immigrants must take in order to become naturalized citizens?

I hereby declare, on oath, that I absolutely and entirely renounce and abjure all allegiance and fidelity to any foreign prince, potentate, state or sovereignty, to whom or which I have heretofore been a subject or citizen; that I will support and defend the Constitution and laws of the United States of America against all enemies, foreign and domestic; that I will bear true faith and allegiance to the same; that I will bear arms on behalf of the United States when required by the law; that I will perform noncombatant service in the armed forces of the United States when required by the law; that I will perform work of national importance under civilian direction when required by the law; and that I take this obligation freely without any mental reservation or purpose of evasion; so help me God.

As a group writing assignment, you might have the class rewrite the oath in "plain English." Be sure to follow up with a discussion. Are there any students in your class who will someday have to take the oath of allegiance? (An applicant must be at least 18 years old.) Are those students who are citizens by birthright willing to undertake all the obligations of the oath? An applicant for naturalization must be able to read, write, and speak the English language. Do all Americans demonstrate such abilities? Does citizenship mean more to the person who must undergo naturalization than the citizen who is born with it?

You may also want to assign research projects for the children to learn about immigration and naturalization laws, or about immigration trends and statistics. Perhaps each child can research the immigration history of his or her ethnic or national group.

Citizenship Day

No. 43

APPLY HERE

Classroom jobs may not be in the same league with electrical engineering, interior decorating and law, but they certainly count with the kids. You can imbue these tasks with additional status — and skill-building value — by introducing a system of recruiting and hiring that includes job applications, interviews and remuneration.

You might give your class operation a name (such as Brain Power Plant) and then prepare staff recruitment materials: a newsletter with descriptions of the jobs available and a supply of job application forms.

Some of the jobs might be described as follows:

President. This person has leadership qualities. The president chairs opening activities as well as takes charge of class meetings, voting, etc.

Executive Secretary. This person carries messages to rooms within the building. The executive secretary must know how to get to the main office, the library, the counselor's office, etc.

Ecological Engineer. This person is concerned about the environment of the Brain Power Plant. The ecological engineer passes the wastebasket around the room, issues violation tickets to litterbugs and presents commendations (worth five bonus points) to classmates (coworkers) who take good care of the environment.

Other employees (with appropriate job descriptions) might be: chalkboard engineer, superintendent of pencils, physical fitness counselor, teacher assistant.

The job application forms — besides requesting name, address and telephone number — ask for the position being applied for, the applicant's experience, acceptable alternative positions and references (classmates, teachers, principals). Applicants are asked to sign and to date their applications.

Interviews are conducted, and newly hired workers are assigned to two weeks' work with individual salaries of 20 bonus points, which are credited to their bank accounts.

Periodically, a bonus activity is offered to employees who have earned a required number of points. The points may be used to purchase a reserved seat at the showing of a special filmstrip or may secure a game period during which popular board games are played. Crafts projects could be other bonus activity options.

Reading and following directions, writing checks, balancing check registers and handling an interview with poise are skills that students practice at the Brain Power Plant.

Idea by: Rosalind Wiley, Cooper Elementary School, Detroit, Mich.

Labor Day

No. 44

BEFORE-SCHOOL OPTIONS

Has your collection of before-school ideas petered down to a choice between having students copy the week's spelling words or drill with math facts? Injecting more diversity into the early-morning activities isn't as much of a chore as you might think, and it could make a big difference in the morning mood of everyone concerned.

The relatively uncrowded before-school period is a good time for using the typewriter, the microscope or other popular equipment. Ongoing projects can be taken a few steps further — building the maze for the gerbil, constructing a model, creating a mural or a map. The special housekeeping tasks can be rotated among early arrivals: watering plants, feeding animals, setting up the listening center.

But for students not involved in these activities, you might provide a daily offbeat alternative or two:
• Have a dictionary scavenger hunt. Post a few dictionary-dependent queries on chart paper. Ask, for example: On what continent does an *aardvark* live? Are you a *native* of Boston? What would you do with a *busby*?
• On the chalkboard, write a coded message for students to decipher.
• Provide hand lenses and have students sketch their thumbprints or make detailed drawings of leaves.
• Draw two lines on the chalkboard. Students can copy the lines on paper and build a design or picture around them.
• Provide copies of a map — a mysterious island or an exotic alien planet. Students "bury" a treasure and write directions for finding it. Then they test their directions on a friend.
• Provide string and ask students to measure their ankles, knees, wrists and necks in centimeters.
• Provide one or several mystery boxes (sealed) that students can explore by sight, sound, smell. Ask students to record their observations and inferences. At the bell, reveal the contents — and perhaps pass around a treat.
• Provide puzzle sheets, hidden pictures, mazes, word-search matrices.
• Play recordings of popular songs and have students transcribe lyrics for a sing-along book.

Concoct a few more ideas, and before-school time becomes something special.
Idea by: Doanne Marks Dunn, Brockton, Mass.

Beginning of School

No. 45

C-3PO'S SUMMER

Back to school and "What I Did on My Summer Vacation" — this is a traditional combination in many parts of the country, but it is a routine that often produces deep sighs from prospective Hemingways. Why not try a variation on this timeworn theme? Ask your returning students (you can do this after any vacation) to write as though they were famous people (or animals, space beings, etc.) just back from a holiday. "John Travolta on Vacation," "Jaws' Happy Holiday" or "C-3PO's Summer Trip" may provide better clues to individual interests and writing abilities than does a description of the proverbial trip to Uncle John's.
Idea by: Kathleen Richko, Paradise Knoll School, Oak Ridge, N.J.

Beginning of School

No. 46

TAGALONG NATURE TRAIL

A supply of blank baggage tags (the large heavy-stock kind with stout strings) can be the start of some travels that have nothing to do with baggage whatsoever. You'll also need one of the following: ample school grounds, or access to a vacant lot, or an outdoor education site.

Trail-tagging is an activity that will require several on-site sessions, so it's a good idea to begin early in the fall season. The first visit to the nature site is one of true exploration. Depending upon background and experience, your explorers may discover habitats, a variety of plants, signs of animal life, evidences of the action of sun and water, evidences of interactions between living things and their environment. Take notes.

Back in the classroom, discuss what you found. You may want to enlist the aid of a recorder—human or tape. Take down at least enough trail "features" for one per student.

Now to the baggage tags. Describe one trail feature from the list on each tag, e.g., "This is a plant that cannot make its own food"; "This is a home for a social insect." Before the second visit to the trail, each student gets a trail-feature tag to study and speculate about. (Descriptions may fit more than one situation.)

The group should probably stick together on the second visit to the site in order to consult and share information.

When the group comes across a feature fitting a tag description, the tag is read aloud, the feature specifically identified on the back of the tag (if you wish) and the tag tied in place at that location (bring some sticks or stakes). Tags left over after the walk can be discussed and placed by consensus.

Tags can remain at their locations as very temporary markers, or they may be collected, laminated and replaced for a more permanent nature trail. (On the final placement trip try to see that students get different tags from the earlier trip.)

Other classes may now be invited to retrace your steps and study the markers on the Tagalong Trail.

Idea by: Lib Roller, Nashville Metropolitan Schools, Nashville, Tenn.

No. 47

FAMILY TREE GREETING CARDS

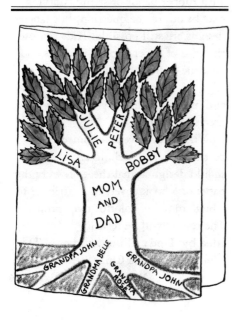

Don't let your kids forget to celebrate National Grandparents' Day! It's the Sunday following Labor Day, so you'll have to introduce this project within the very first few days of the school year.

A very appropriate way for students to show their appreciation for Grandma and Granddad is to put them in a place of honor—at the roots of the family tree. Have the kids first list all their immediate first, second and third generation family members. Make sure the kids include themselves in the third generation. Then, on the front face of a folded sheet of 8½" x 11" paper, have them draw a branching tree. Within the root system the kids write in the names of their two sets of grandparents. Mom and Dad's names come together in the trunk of the tree, and the various branches bear the names of the child and the child's siblings.

The kids can adorn the trees with very small leaves that have fallen from deciduous bushes, or color their own leaves with paints or felt markers. Each child should include a personal greeting on the inside of the card and sign it. Remember to provide ample time for students to make a second card for the second set of grandparents.

Grandparents' Day

No. 48

TWIG PRINT DESIGNS

Making designs with sticks is an ancient method of decorating objects. Native American Indians are among the many peoples around the world who have used sticks for decorative printing. The method is very easy and therefore ideal for kids in the classroom. But they should be challenged to use a simple design to derive more complicated patterns.

Make twig-printing a two-day crafts project. On the first day, take your kids for a hike in a wooded area or a tree-lined park. Bring along a sharp knife. Have the kids find several green branches of varying diameters. As they make their selections, harvest the branches from the trees. If you're worried about permission on public grounds, let the park official or groundskeeper know beforehand that you only intend to cut about 15 slender branches and twigs for a school project. Probably no one will object.

Before the next class, cut the branches into three-inch lengths with sharp pruners. You want a flat, clean edge for printing. Throw the branches together in a big box. In class, allow each kid to select 3 or 4 twigs from the box. Provide them with lots of jars of thick paints or ink pads, and sheets of absorbent paper such as newsprint.

To print, a child must dip the end of the stick into ink and press it onto a sheet of paper so that it leaves an impression. If paint is used, have the child paint the color onto the end of the stick with a paintbrush, making sure that the entire printing surface is coated with paint.

Encourage your kids to be innovative. Have them experiment by printing with more than one twig at a time. Suggest that they bind twigs together with rubber bands or string. Carving may be out of the question, but fancier designs are still possible. Kids can use the ends of paper clips as punches and nick the sticks by rubbing along the edges of their desks. Nails and screws also have enough of a point to do some precise tooling.

When they have ascertained their best designs and techniques, the kids should design a final sheet of wrapping paper or a book cover, or contribute to a huge mural of colorful twig prints. The results will be terrific!
Idea by: Linda Allison, author of *The Wild Inside*, Sierra Club/Scribner's.

Native American Day

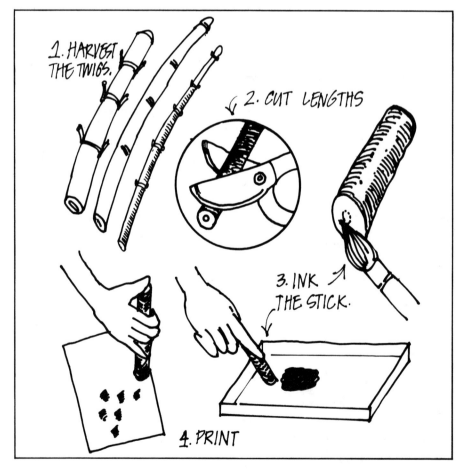

1. HARVEST THE TWIGS.
2. CUT LENGTHS
3. INK THE STICK.
4. PRINT

No. 49

RECYCLED SOAP

Another school year begins, and you're back in the business of collecting cast-offs for crafts. The following project calls for recycling soap scraps.
Materials:
• pieces of leftover soap (as soap pieces are brought in you may want to store them in a covered container, adding a little water to start the softening process);
• assorted cookie cutters (not intricate shapes; roundish are best);
• cookie sheets;
• egg turner;
• large spoon;

• double boiler;
• hot plate or stove;
• newspaper and paper towels.
Procedure:
1. Spread newspapers to cover work area.
2. Boil water in the lower part of the double boiler. Put soap pieces and a little water in the top part and set over the boiling water.
3. As the soap warms and softens, use the spoon to smooth out lumps, adding a bit more water if necessary. (Mixture should not be thin; soap will take longer to dry out if it is.)
4. When the soap has softened to the consistency of thick oatmeal, turn it out on a cookie sheet, smoothing and stretching it. It should be about three-eighths inch, or one centimeter, thick.
5. Allow to cool and harden a few

minutes. Then cut shapes with cookie cutters.
6. Remove soap "cookies" with egg turner and place on paper towels to dry.
7. Gather up scraps and resoften or mold into soap balls.
8. Allow soap to harden at least overnight.

If you're adventurous, you may want to experiment with the addition of food coloring or scents.

An early start on soap collecting will assure an adequate supply, and soon the children will be prepared for the next gift-giving occasion with some useful and attractive presents.
Idea by: Lillian Cooper, ACT-ED Headstart, New York, N.Y.

Beginning of School 🖌

No. 50

KACHINA CONTAINERS

Kachinas are the embodied religious spirits of the Hopi Indians. Hopi children play with kachina dolls and their elders perform ceremonial dances dressed in kachina costumes. In this project, kachinas are the colorful containers kids make to hold pencils, dried flowers or a variety of small things they like to collect.

Ask your kids to help you accumulate the cylindrical cardboard containers that potato chips, cornmeal and oatmeal come in. In addition, you will need lots of colorful paint, construction paper, feathers, beads, yarn, macaroni and whatever other decorative items you store in your crafts closet. You might also want to check out a number of library books that have pictures of au-

thentic Hopi kachina dolls or costumes for the kids to use as models.

Provide each child with a container. First, the container must be painted a solid color or covered in construction paper. Leave the rest to your kids' design and crafts ingenuity. Arms and legs may be painted in, or kids can roll construction paper cylinders and glue them on. Another possibility is to provide pre-cut lengths of the cardboard

tubing that comes on dry cleaner hangers. Feathers, beads, and any other adornments may be added.

When the containers are complete, exhibit them around the classroom. They make a particularly appropriate display for Native American Day. Afterward, let your kids take home their containers and fill them with whatever they like.

Native American Day 🖌

No. 51

BABY FACE

A good way to share personal histories and to help your students know one another better is to ask class members to bring in baby pictures of themselves and then guess the identity of each baby.

For easy viewing, hang the pictures on the bulletin board and place a number next to each. Have your class study the pictures. Tell the kids that at the end of a specified time, perhaps a week, they can put forth their guesses as to who's who. Encourage students not to tell others which picture is of them, but don't be surprised if some kids can't hold out.

During the week, the baby pictures can be the focus of several other activities:

A caption telling what the baby may have been saying or thinking can be attached to each picture.

The class can discuss the very first thing each student remembers. Stories about the events could also be written.

The class can vote on baby "winners" — the cutest baby, the baby most likely to be president, the baby most likely to be a movie star and so on. Students can write short campaign speeches for their favorite candidates.

Hold a class discussion about the differences in raising a baby now and then. Topics could include expenses, medical care, clothing, toys and life-styles, and would require some research.

Baby pictures of teachers, administrators, and business and maintenance staffs could be included in an all-school baby-face bulletin board, and a contest could be held to identify each picture. **Idea by:** Barbara Parry, M-F-L Community Schools, Monona, Iowa.

Beginning of School

No. 52

GRAFFITI WALLS

If you, like many teachers, have a problem with graffiti, you can channel the wayward writing to an area other than desks, walls and floors. Buy an inexpensive window shade and attach it at the top to a wall in your classroom. When one of your students feels a graffiti-writing urge coming on, the graffiti wall is there to use. (You might want to include some ground rules about language.) The shade can be rolled up when not in use and when no one wants to read it. When the shade is completely covered with messages, you can make a new graffiti wall by removing the shade from the roller and replacing it with brown wrapping paper. You might occasionally give the grafitti wall a theme, such as books or movies. **Idea by:** John Petrasun, Jefferson Junior High School, Mount Lebanon, Pa.

No. 53

A SHARING CENTER

Your classroom's bulletin board is often a place where you post and share pictures and information with your students. Why not turn it — or a section of it — into a place where students share ideas, knowledge and goodwill?

The sharing center can be designated as such with a title like "I Want To Share This With You" or a similar heading. Then kids can fill the space with favorite comic strips, original drawings, pictures of admired athletes and movie stars, birthday cards to classmates, easy-to-use recipes, ads for useful products, favorite short stories or just about anything else the children want to share. You may want to have a few simple guidelines for the center, such as requiring that photographs be mounted or that certain kinds of material be screened by you before going up on the board. Students should have the option of signing or not signing their names to their contributions.

A sharing center can be an exciting source of fun and learning, and it can also tell you a lot about your students' hobbies and interests.

Idea by: Cory D. Spears, Cypress, Calif.

RESOURCES

TRACING YOUR ROOTS — *Record and Remember: Tracing Your Roots through Oral History*, by Ellen Robinson Epstein and Rona Mendelsohn. Monarch Press/Simon & Schuster.

Thanks to Alex Haley and ABC, tracing family roots has become a national craze right up there with jogging and disco dancing. For those who are serious about discovering their family background but are not able to do a full-blown genealogical search, this book suggests the alternative of compiling an oral history. By interviewing family members who are good storytellers and who are old enough to know a lot of family lore, an individual can create a permanent, open-ended oral archive that can be enjoyed now and passed along to posterity.

The authors have determined the very best way to produce an oral history and have written a superbly detailed handbook about accomplishing all the necessary tasks. Included is information about how to be a good interviewer, whom to interview (grandchildren interviewing grandparents tends to work better than children interviewing parents), how to choose a good tape recorder and good cassettes, how to operate the recorder, transcribing interviews, editing tapes and much, much more. There's also a section written specifically for teachers, "Oral History for Classroom Use." But the fact is, the entire book is an excellent resource for teachers who want to direct students in family or community oral history projects.

BOOKS FOR KIDS —
● *Grandpa and Me*. Stephanie S. Tolan. Scribner's. Recommended reading for the intermediate grades.
● *The Art of the Southeastern Indians*. Shirley Glubok. Photographs by Alfred Tamarin. Macmillan. Recommended reading for the primary grades.
● *The Girl Who Married a Ghost and Other Tales from the North American Indian*. Edited by John Bierhorst. Photographs by Edward S. Curtis. Four Winds. Recommended reading for the intermediate grades and up.
● *In Defense of Animals*. J. J. McCoy. Illustrated with photographs. Seabury. Recommended reading for the intermediate grades and up.

THE WORLD OF ENDANGERED WILDLIFE — The National Wildlife Federation has put together a serious and absorbing filmstrip that broadly discusses the causes of the problems faced by threatened and endangered wildlife. Without being alarmist, the strip makes clear that the very real danger of extinction constantly threatens great numbers of both large and small animals.

The World of Endangered Wildlife deals with many different species; the ferret, bald eagle, whooping crane, brown pelican and grizzly bear are some of them. The animals mentioned are primarily but not exclusively from the United States.

Two copies of the special issue of *National Wildlife* magazine, a list of endangered species, a set of wildlife notes and an extensive teaching guide come with the filmstrip.

Order from: National Wildlife Federation, 1412 16th St., N.W., Washington, DC 20036. **Grade level:** Intermediate–high school.

2

Thurgood Marshall, first black Supreme Court Justice, is sworn in, 1967.

3

Abraham Lincoln declared the first Thanksgiving to be celebrated this day in 1863.

7

Anniversary of the Great Fire of Chicago, 1871.

8

9

Viking explorer Leif Ericson lands in America, 1000.

13

In 1792, the building of the White House begins.

14

Speed of sound broken in 1947.

15

World Poetry Day.

19

20

21

In 1879, Edison invents the incandescent lamp.

25

First postcard mailed in the U.S., 1870.

26

The Erie Canal opens in 1825.

27

Anniversary of the Cuban Missile Crisis, 1962.

THREE

DAY BY DAY

4

Dinosaur National Monument created, 1915.

5

First World Series broadcast over radio on this day in 1921.

6

The Jazz Singer, the first "talkie" (moving picture with sound), released, 1927.

10

11

Eleanor Roosevelt born, 1884.

12

Christopher Columbus discovers America, 1492. Traditional Columbus Day.

16

Pope John Paul II, the first non-Italian pope since 1522, elected in 1978.

17

Albert Einstein arrives in the U.S. from Nazi Germany, 1933.

18

Alaska transferred from Russia to the U.S. in 1867.

22

First parachute jump from a balloon in 1797.

23

The swallows' winter migration begins from San Juan Capistrano, Calif.

24

United Nations Day.

28

Statue of Liberty dedicated, 1886.

29

Stock Market Crash, 1929.

30

"War of the Worlds" radio panic in 1938.

Halloween.

31

No. 54

OPERATION OPEN HOUSE

Now that we're several weeks into the school year, can Parents' Night be far off? Here is an idea for an informative and enjoyable evening.

Parents' Night usually means sharing information about your daily program. The class can help by making a filmstrip-and-cassette show about a "typical" day. (Use a do-it-yourself filmstrip kit or take slides of children's art showing a day's doings.)

Divide the daily schedule among the students and add enough other events — such as a trip to the nurse and buying lunch tickets — to total one frame for each student. Each student then writes a few sentences describing his or her portion of the day and designs a filmstrip frame — simplicity is a must — to illustrate the activity. Frames for title, credits, etc., will also need to be worked out. (If you plan to photograph a slide program, have students prepare their illustrations on posters.) Sequence must be firmly set before stu-

dents actually draw their frames in place. Taping students' prepared narration is next. A bell or clicker can signal frame changes.

If the class makes posters for this project, there's a plus. Have students title their posters and add clock faces to show when certain activities usually take place. Then display the art in the hall as a sneak preview.

Sharing "A Day in the Life . . ." takes preparation, but it can be a hit.
Idea by: Connie Curtis, Ackley Elementary School, Ackley, Iowa.

Open House

No. 55

SPEED OF SOUND

The speed of sound? This concept is very difficult for most youngsters to grasp. Finding out how long it takes a sound to travel down the hallways of your school can bring this seemingly cosmic concept down to earth.

Tell your students that the approximate speed of sound is 1,125 feet per second. Divide the class into several groups, one for each major hallway in your school. Give each group a yardstick to measure the length of its assigned hallway. Then have each group

calculate how long it takes sound to travel the length of its hallway. Your students will be surprised to find that sound whizzes down the hallways in a fraction of a second. Post the traveling times in the various hallways to interest other classes.
Idea by: Karen Boetcher, Arlington Heights, Ill.

October 14

No. 56

JOB SHEETS

If parents are accompanied by their children as they come to Open House, present the adults with job sheets.

Have the children take stock of the room and their activities and then let them decide on ten things they'd like their parents to be sure to see. Items may vary widely from child to child — magnets, a special library book, even last week's spelling test. Children write descriptions of their choices and give directions to guide parents looking for items on the lists. (Even if parents can't come, job sheets can go home to provide an idea of children's school interests.)

As parents arrive for Open House, children hand them their job sheets. Children keep track of parents' progress, checking off items as they're discovered. The "finds" serve as conversation starters between parents and children as well as between parents and teachers.

A successful hunt is duly rewarded with the affixing of a star on the completed job sheet. The star sticking is, of course, the child's proud duty.

Job sheets effectively break up the traditional line-up-to-meet-the-teacher pattern, giving you a chance to circulate and to join the fun. Job sheets also provide parents with a current sample of their child's writing and a souvenir of Open House.
Idea by: Donna Anderson, Churchville-Chili Elementary School, Churchville, N.Y.

Open House

No. 57

METRIC MONSTERS

If your class has already measured the metric length, width, height and perimeter of everything in the room including themselves, it could be time to start measuring their imaginations. To this end you might set up a center for the creation of metric monsters.

Directions for metric monstering can be handled in a number of ways:
● Draw a geometric shape that has a perimeter of (state number) centimeters. Add to this shape in any way you'd like to make the most monstrous monster you can imagine.
● Create a monster with straight-line segments, measuring as you create, keeping all measurements in even centimeters (no extra millimeters). Keep a record of the measurements. Challenge others to estimate the length of the segments and/or the entire perimeter of your monster. Estimators can then check by measuring.
● Draw a metric monster with straight-line segments, and, without measuring, try to come as close as you can to (state number) centimeters for its perimeter. Check by measuring.

Whatever the method of monster manufacture, all monsters eventually can be corralled and displayed in a metric monster zoo, ready for additional creative adventures.
Idea by: Kari Yokas, Arcadia, Calif.
Halloween

No. 58

GHOSTLY VISITATIONS

You can never tell where ghosts will go, and tracing their travels around a haunted house can give your students plenty of practice with prepositional phrases.

First each student prepares the setting — a drawing, painting or other art piece portraying a haunted house. Suggest the possibility of a cutaway view showing the house's interior. This may offer more material for students to write about later on.

When the illustrations are complete, have students imagine and describe the wanderings of their own personal ghosts. Every sentence begins with "My ghost . . ." and is completed by a verb and prepositional phrase chosen by the student: "My ghost flew up the chimney." "My ghost arrived after midnight." "My ghost slithered behind the dresser." "My ghost sulked beneath the sofa." Challenge students to see how many sentences they can think of without using the same preposition twice.

After students have worked on their sentences awhile, they may decide where in their pictures they'd like to locate their ghosts (made out of tissue, perhaps).

Have a "My Ghost" sharing session with darkly dramatic reading, sound effects and some laughs.
Idea by: Bettie Weber, Houston, Tex.
Halloween

No. 59

PRIVATE EYE

The Private Eye is an easy-to-make and fun-to-use system for self-correcting. And it has built-in motivation features.

Materials: posterboard, scissors, tape, glue, clear Con-Tact paper and red acetate (or use red permanent marker to color either overhead projector film or clear acetate). You'll also need markers in red, orange, yellow, pink and a light shade of green.

Directions:

1. From posterboard cut two identical magnifying-glass shapes. Cut out a large viewing-area hole in both pieces.

2. Cut two pieces of red acetate a little larger than the center holes you've cut.

3. Tape both pieces of acetate tightly over the hole in one of the magnifying-glass shapes.

4. Glue the two shapes together with the acetate sandwiched in between.

5. To complete the Private Eye, cover all but the viewing area with clear Con-Tact paper for greater durability.

Preparing answer keys that can be checked by use of the Private Eye is not difficult. First write the correct answer in light green marker. Then, with the other markers, write random words, numbers, phrases directly over the green answer. Soon the answer space will appear to be a meaningless scribble—until the Private Eye is applied to the task. Because the red acetate masks all the red tones, the correct answer alone will be visible to your wondering eyes.

With a little color adapting for use of the Private Eye, the answer keys for worksheets, activities and games take on new excitement.

Note: Be aware that Private Eyes tend to discriminate against the color-blind.

Idea by: Candace Purdom, Christopher Elementary School, Christopher, Ill.

No. 60

READING UNDERCOVER

In a project called "Mystery Library Pals," students become intrigued with one another's reading personalities. First the class draws names. Then each student sets out, in undercover fashion, to discover the interests of his or her library pal, to determine the sort of book that person might enjoy.

Each student picks out, checks out and reads a library book for his or her pal. The next step is for the student to make up a list of six or seven questions relating to the book. Each set of questions is then put into an envelope and slid into its respective book. Then the book-and-envelope sets are presented to the library pals.

After the pals have had a chance to read the books chosen for them, pairs of students who've now read the same book get together to discuss the answers to the questions. There'll be two discussion sessions for each student, because each drew someone and was drawn by someone.

Besides heightening interest in reading, this kind of book sharing can help broaden some reading habits—moving some students out of horse stories, for the moment, and into mysteries, or out of science fiction and into black history—expanding and enriching everyone's reading menu.

Idea by: Melody Dian, Crown Point, Ind.

No. 61

FALL COLORS

You know it's fall when those gaudy leaves start showing up in class as kids scuff their way to school through the autumn mornings. Unfortunately, those bright colors have a way of fading and drying into a crumbling brown as the season wears on.

Here is a trick for preserving fall colors indefinitely. It will change the colors of some of the leaves you preserve, but that is part of the magic.

Purchase a bottle of glycerine at a drug store. You will also need several empty jars, and the leaves that your students have brought in from the cold. Here's how to do it:
1. Mix up a solution of one-third glycerine and two-thirds water in a jar. There should be enough liquid so that the solution reaches three to four inches up the stems when you immerse the leaves.
2. Pick a handful of leaves.
3. Crush the tips of the stems with a hammer to make it easier for the solution to be absorbed.
4. Set the leaves in the solution for a week or so.

The treated leaves will stay soft for a long time — in fact, they may last for years! You can store them away when your class has tired of them.

Single leaves can be fixed by laying them in a pan and pouring a mixture of half water and half glycerine over them. Pour the extra solution into a bottle and save it to preserve your next batch of leaves.

Experiment with as many different kinds of leaves as you can and see what colors result. For instance, birch leaves turn dark red, forsythia turn very dark, and magnolia turn bronze.

Idea by: Linda Allison, author of *The Wild Inside*, Sierra Club/Scribner's.

No. 62

MAKING MONSTERS

Any number of children can take part in this exercise from *Giving Form to Feeling* (Drama Book Specialists). The activity requires that kids exercise their imaginations, respond to fantasy, create a collective fantasy, project feelings and situations, and work in cooperation with one another.

"Create a monster, determining where it lives, what it eats, how it relates to other creatures. . . . Use simple props or materials such as cardboard tubing, old wire, colored paper. When each person's monster is ready, share them. Perhaps separate monsters would like to interact or combine to form a group monster. Encourage the group to work with as much detail as possible, so there is diversity and complexity.

"Pose problems . . . such as: How would this monster differ if it lived at the bottom of a lake, on top of a high

mountain, in the midst of a rain forest or in a desert? How would your monster be affected by similar monsters or different monsters? Could it live alone? Consider how cold, heat, rain, snow and ice might affect it. Does it relate to humans, can it respond to machines, is it from outer space?"

Then try more personal questions: "How would your monster react to being in school, living in your home, meeting your family, going on vaca-

tion? How was your monster born? How does it die? What pleases it? What angers or frustrates it? What might cause your monster to be sad and to cry?"

Halloween

No. 63

MEET A MONSTER MATH

Bring kids face to face with multiplication facts in a way that doesn't intimidate even the most math-shy among them. And preparing the Meet a Monster game shouldn't be an overwhelming chore for you, either.

The game requires a die or spinner, place markers and a follow-the-pathway gameboard. The number of spaces in the pathway will depend upon the size of the multiplication products you'll be working with; the larger the products, the more spaces you'll need to make.

On some spaces write short directives advancing players or sending them back (e.g., "You forgot Granny. Go back to Start"). Mark several spaces Meet a Monster. When a roll of the die lands a player on one of these spaces, the player draws a special Meet a Monster card — of which you've prepared 20 or so that are similar to the following:

The Bobo
The Bobo has 7 toes with 3 bells on each toe. How many bells does a Bobo have?
The Noonoo
The Noonoo has 3 tummies with 3 navels on each tummy. How many navels does a Noonoo have?
The Chumpchump
The Chumpchump has 4 heads with 3 chins on each head. How many chins does a Chumpchump have?

A player drawing a Meet a Monster card gets an extra move equal to the problem's answer. (Answers can be verified by an answer key.) The first player to reach the end of the pathway wins.

Meet a Monster problems can be written as division problems, too:
The Dotto
The Dotto has exactly 63 freckles. There are 9 freckles on each head. How

many heads does the Dotto have?

Art activities — writing too — are natural extensions of Meet a Monster. (See how many written or drawn interpretations of a Bobo students can come up with.)

To ensure a constant variety of new monsters for the game, invite kids to create a few — following the pattern of multiple parts used in your game cards. You might slip in a few monster cards that call for addition, just to keep your monster meeters on their collective toes.
Idea by: Pamela Pieper Johnston, Hillsdale Elementary School, Salt Lake City, Utah.

Halloween

No. 64

INVASION!

The closest our nation has come to a threat of attack in recent years was in October of 1962, during a period known as the Cuban Missile Crisis. Recall for your students how panicky Americans built or converted their basements into bomb shelters, and how schools participated in civil defense drills.

Because they lack such experience, it is hard for American children to understand what it is like to face an alien force near or in one's own homeland. One way to simulate the experience—

for older children at least—is to produce the radio drama "The War of the Worlds," Orson Welles's famous Halloween prank radio program (the script of which is found in *The Panic Broadcast* [Avon]). Older kids will have a lot of fun performing the play, which can be tape-recorded for use throughout the school. Even very young kids should gain from this story some sense of the terrible psychological impact of an invasion.

October 27 and October 30

No. 65

KBOO TO YOU TOO IN RADIOLAND

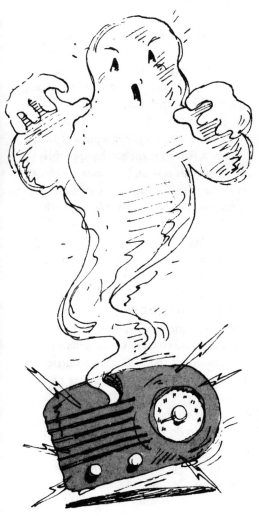

If you've ever considered starting a class radio station, now's the perfect time to try it. At Halloween time a day's broadcasting can be influenced by the spookier side of life. Discuss and divide responsibilities for planning, writing and presenting a number of radio features. Plan for either one continuous session or several "spots" to be performed throughout the day.

Broadcast features should have a Halloween content, mood and style of delivery.

News—Zeta Chapter of Zombies International meets at Dracula Hall today.

Weather—perfect forecast: typhoons followed by tidal waves. And don't forget, we're going on darkness saving time tonight.

Sports—For Frankenstein's Monsters and the Galloping Ghouls it was a sudden-death playoff.

Entertainment—Take your pick of ghastly stars and diabolical divertissements.

Fashion—what the well-dressed witch and warlock will be wearing.

Food—recipes and hints for bubbling brews and magic potions.

Add commercials, lost and found notices, gardening tips and commentaries on the whole scary scene.

Have students write their scripts and prepare to go "on the air." You may want to invite another class to tune in, or you may be able to have the show broadcast over the school PA system. **Idea** by: Melody Dian, Crown Point, Ind.

Halloween

No. 66

CREEPY CREATURE CREATIONS

Young children, who may be surprised at their monstrous creations, might easily use this composite-art activity from *150 Plus! Games and Activities for Early Childhood* (Fearon Pitman) as a springboard for a language experience.

"Have the children sit in a circle or around their tables. Give each child a crayon and a sheet of drawing paper folded in thirds across the short way. Caution them not to open the paper. Then tell them to draw a creepy creature head on the top surface. When they finish, have them turn that surface under so the next person can't see the head they have drawn. Now each child passes his or her paper to the child on the left. Everyone then draws a creepy creature body on the middle surface. (The first child draws little lines on the fold to indicate where the body attaches. The second child indicates where to attach the legs.) When the bodies are finished, fold and pass the papers along again. The third child completes the creepy creature by drawing legs on the final surface.

"After all the creepy creatures are finished, the children can take turns opening the papers up. Give each an opportunity to show a creature and tell a creepy story about it."

Halloween

No. 67

CLASS IMPORTS

If you could put a flag on every object in your classroom that would represent the country it came from, your room would look like the United Nations. You don't believe it? Check it out for yourself. Most products have the place where they were made stamped on them somewhere. A quick survey will prove that goods from all over the world are assembled in your room.

Turn your survey into a colorful classroom demonstration. First, have the kids make a complete list of countries whose exports have found their way into your room. Do a little research to find out the rules for marking foreign imports. Then have your students make a small paper replica of each country's flag to plant on the appropriate items. An easy and accurate way to do this is to trace flags from an almanac or the encyclopedia with colored markers. Toothpicks are just about the right size for flag poles. Cut the flags out and scotch tape them to the poles. Roll up balls of plasticine clay and use them as flag stands wherever they are needed.

Here are some follow-up questions:
• Is every continent represented?
• Is there one country whose products far outnumber those of other countries?
• What do we mean when we say "Buy American"?
• What is an import tax? What does this have to do with the Boston Tea Party?
Idea by: Linda Allison, author of *The Wild Inside*, Sierra Club/Scribner's.

United Nations Day

No. 68

COMPASS COURSE

Mariners of long ago feared falling off the edge of the world, but in this compass-reading, directions-reinforcing game going "over the edge" is the only way to win.

The materials consist of a gameboard, instruction cards and place markers. On 3-by-5 cards (use about 25) write instructions such as "Move NE two squares" and "Move S three squares." For the gameboard use a 13-by-13-inch piece of tagboard. Rule the board into 1-inch squares. In the center square mark START. In the bottom right-hand corner of the board make a compass rose with all cardinal and intercardinal directions labeled. If you wish to carry out a theme, you may want to decorate the gameboard accord-ingly and perhaps add appropriate hazards that warn players to change directions.

As many children can play as can fit comfortably around the board. Each child puts a place marker into the START square. Player One draws an instruction card, reads it aloud and moves in the designated direction the number of spaces indicated. Play passes to the left. The winner is the first player to move off the gameboard — out of the gloomy woods or off the edge of the ancient world, if that appeals to the adventuresome travelers in your social studies class.

Idea by: Sister Mary Robert, Holy Angels School, Appleton, Wis.

Columbus Day

No. 69

CREATE A WEST COAST LANDMARK

With the Bicentennial long behind us, perhaps your class has been somewhat less than excited about studying American landmarks and symbols. But what if the students were commissioned to take on a monumental project in symbol study — the creation of a new American landmark!

Bishop Fulton J. Sheen once quoted an author who thought that America should be bounded on the East Coast by the Statue of Liberty and on the West Coast by a Statue of Responsibility. Discuss the idea of establishing a West Coast counterpart of the New York landmark with your students. What reasons might there have been for the suggested pairing of *liberty* and *responsibility*? What other qualities might be equally appropriate for the partner landmark? What forms could such a landmark take? Where might the West Coast landmark be located? What famous individual should be asked to make the formal dedication?

After raising some of these questions to start some thinking, suggest that students — working in pairs or individually — follow through and develop plans for the creation of a West Coast landmark complementing the Statue of Liberty. They'll need to decide on its theme and form, explain its symbolism, and provide some rationale for selecting the quality symbolized.

Students may demonstrate their thinking in a number of ways, possibly using illustrations or models along with oral or written reports. There may even be those who'd like to plan for a suitable inscription — quoted or original — on the order of the Statue of Liberty's poem welcoming the "huddled masses yearning to breathe free."

Who knows — perhaps by the nation's Tricentennial we'll have that new West Coast landmark!

Idea by: Sister Mary Philip De Camara, Georgetown Visitation Preparatory School, Washington, D.C.

October 28

No. 70

CLASSIFICATION SAFARI

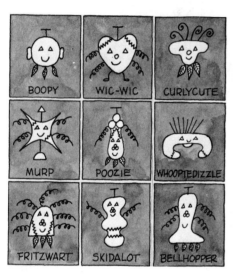

Children's first forays into classification of animals may result in their being confused by strange words.

Perhaps classification is intimidating because the Latin seems formal and austere. Lighten things up a bit with your own classification labels and some artwork. Great talent is not a prerequisite.

Prepare a collection of strange and wonderful creatures according to a system of characteristics. For instance, you might start with the kingdom Animalia, phylum Teetopsum. These animals would have T's on their heads. Within the Teetopsum phylum there might be two classes: Springzata and Spikezata. These groups would be recognized by their springs and spikes.

Depending upon the skill of your students, you might move on to more detailed classifications: order, family, genus and species. And for those who

are ready for real adventure, provide a silly safari on which students search for the animal that has the following classification:

Kingdom: Animalia
Phylum: Teetopsum
Class: Springzata
Order: Zigzagtia
Family: Noseocirculisee
Genus: *Trinoseocirculisee*
Species: *Trinoseocirculisee leafola*

Can the hunters find the *Trinoseocirculisee leafola* among the animals pictured in the illustration? To track the animal down, hunters must separate animals with T tops from those without; T-topped animals with springs from those without and so forth. The animal they seek has a T top, springs, zigzags, a circular nose — three circular noses — and leaves. Who else but the poozie?

Once students become adept at analyzing word clues to animal characteristics, they may want to invent new classes, orders, families, etc., and draw animals based on their descriptive nomenclature. And after a few successful hunts on silly safaris of this sort, students may approach the Latin jungle with more confidence.
Idea by: Bob Hauch, Our Saviour Lutheran School, Chicago, Ill.

No. 71

INVENT-A-FORM

Haikus, cinquains and other forms of structured poetry have long been popular with kids. Usually students must create a poem to fit the form, but here's a way to have them work within their very own constraints and the constraints of their classmates. *Write To Communicate: The Language Arts in Process* (Reader's Digest Services) explains how students can create their own poetry forms.

"Make up your own rules for writing a form of poetry. Write the rules on a card. Then follow the rules. Be as serious or as silly as you like.

"For example, you might set up rules like this:

Line 1. *Use a word ending in* ing.
Line 2. *Use three words that name colors.*
Line 3. *Use a word ending in* est.
Line 4. *Use five words as a direct quotation.*
Line 5. *Use a word ending in* ing.

"Following the rules you set up you might write:

Falling
Red, green, orange
Harvest
'Let's rake the dried leaves.'
Crunching.

"If you wish, pass the card to some classmates. See what they write. Post the pieces of writing on a bulletin board. Keep the cards in a file for classmates to use later."

World Poetry Day

No. 72

HAVING A WONDERFUL TIME

The next time you get a postcard from your Aunt Minnie, who is having a glorious vacation in Greece, don't just wish you were there. Save her card — and others you receive or purchase on trips of your own — and use the greetings from faraway places to stimulate social studies, geography, history and a variety of other valuable activities.

Place all the colorful postcards you can collect in an attractive box or on a learning center table and ask each child to choose one to investigate. Have the students find out as much as they can about the areas or persons the postcards depict and then present their information in oral or written reports. The activity requires use of research techniques as well as clear, descriptive language. Children will be fascinated to learn about famous and not-so-famous people and places.

Idea by: Frances Leahy, St. Bede the Venerable, Chicago, Ill.

No. 73

FINDING POETRY IN THE NEWSPAPER

The headlines in the daily newspaper seldom sound like poetry: They're concerned with facts, the events of the day. Poetry, on the other hand, often seems to be about feelings and opinions. If your students find news very real and poetry otherworldly, you might try drawing these two forms of written expression together to see if the reality of one can help students find meaning in the other.

Bring in a stack of newspaper as resource material for the class. Present a collection of headlines and have students characterize the subjects dealt with. Discuss the different purposes of a news story and a poem, the differences between a poet's point of view and a journalist's perspective. The poet and the journalist, after all, do live in the same world; they simply express their experience of the world differently. You may want to introduce the terms *objectivity* and *subjectivity* in this session.

Share a poem that tells a story and have students suggest ways it is like and unlike a news account. Whittier's "Snow-Bound," for instance, might translate into a few paragraphs about the depth of the snowfall, the wind-chill factor and the number of buses stranded in Buffalo. Have students write a news story covering an event that's described in a narrative poem. When students finish, compare the two accounts with respect to word choice, attention to detail and coverage of the familiar who, what, when, where, how and why of the news. Discuss the effect of these stylistic differences.

Now turn the assignment around. Read aloud a news item, such as the report of a fire or an update about local strike activity, and ask students to write poems based on the article. Be sensitive to students who may need help when deciding how to focus on particular aspects of the story. Follow up with discussion of the various ways students approached the same story to create their poems.

Then challenge each student to choose a newspaper article to use as the basis for a poem. Don't be surprised to see everything from the ski report to Dear Abby in poetic form.

Idea by: Julie Crawford, Scio Central School, Scio, N.Y.

World Poetry Day

No. 74

ALIEN CAPTIVITY: METRIC SURVIVAL

If your class feels less than pressed to learn metrics, present this scenario: "Alien beings are holding us captive in an airtight compartment the same size as this room. How long do we have to plan our escape before the air runs out?"

An unusual emergency of this sort might tempt your class to try some calculations with metric volume.

Data needed:

1. number of people in room

2. volume of a breath (Find out from a science text or use one cubic decimeter as a reasonable estimate.)

3. average breaths per minute (Count breaths per minute for a sample of students and take an average. Note: oxygen-carbon dioxide exchange might be mentioned, but it's best to ignore it in calculations.)

Sample data:

1. people — 30

2. breath volume — 1 cubic decimeter

3. breaths per minute — 20

4. room volume — 170 cubic meters

Computations:

1. How much air is the class using each minute?

   a. Each person uses 20 cubic decimeters per minute. Thirty people use 30 times that, or 600 cubic decimeters.

2. If the class uses 600 cubic decimeters per minute, how many of those 600 cubic decimeter minutes are in the room?

   a. To find how many 600 cubic decimeters are in your 170 cubic meter room, you'll need to change the cubic decimeters to cubic meters. One cubic decimeter equals .001 cubic meter, so 600 cubic decimeters equal 600 times .001, or .6 cubic meter.

   b. To find how many minutes of air for the class are in the room, divide 170 cubic meters by .6 cubic meters. There are 283 minutes of air in the room.

You have about 4 hours and 43 minutes to escape. While you have been calculating your survival time, you have used metric measures, averages, volume, decimals and regular arithmetic.

Idea by: Homer Clark, Oregon Episcopal School, Portland, Ore.

Halloween

No. 75

DANGER DRILLS

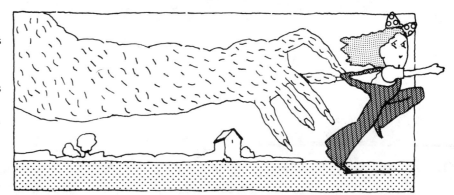

A set of self-correcting drill cards—math facts, picture-word match-ups—can be the basis for an appealing game for one person or a group. All you need to add is markers and an easily made gameboard with a "dangerous mission" theme, such as outmaneuvering a monster, avoiding an ambush, outdistancing an alligator or racing an oversize spider.

Plan the gameboard with two widely distant starting areas, each opening into a pathway of blocks or circles. One pathway is for the player (or players); the other is for the pursuer (monster, alligator or whatever). Plot the pathways on a collision course, the intersections being marked with a star. When preparing the pathways, give the pursuer the advantage of a much shorter path; the spider reaches the star in just three moves, but the player must move eight or ten spaces to arrive at the goal. Artistic touches can develop the theme: monster land, gloomy swamp, sticky spiderweb, alligator alley, vampire valley or creepy caverns.

The player simply draws a drill card, makes a response and checks it. A correct answer allows a move of one space along the player's track. If the answer is wrong, the pursuer is advanced one space.

If the player does not reach the star before the pursuer, the player is ambushed, eaten or caught in the web; success means survival.

Write the directions for the game on the gameboard and store the board and drill cards together for independent use by the children. And some afternoon, try putting a gigantic version on the chalkboard.

Idea by: René Ravanelli, St. Paul's Lutheran School, Concordia, Mo.

Halloween

No. 76

MUCH MORE THAN A MILE

Running and jogging are activities that are often done alone, with no interaction or sharing taking place among participants. An afterschool, mile-a-week jogging time, however, can encourage groups of kids to become more physically fit while they get to know one another and members of the teaching staff and administration.

Before you begin, send notes home to parents of interested children to OK their child's participation in the program (it will be after school, optional and strenuous; so you'll need their permission and a doctor's approval). Then determine the speed at which the mile should be run: A 10-minute mile is probably run at a pace appropriate for intermediate-aged children, but the target speed can be adjusted to account for initial lack of endurance (the first few runs might even be less than a mile to help joggers get into shape gradually) and later, runners' improving fitness.

On the day of the first full-mile run, caution all participants that a mile is a long distance. Remind runners that the object is to have fun, to converse and to build fitness—not to "win." Encourage everyone to walk or to slow down when necessary but to finish. Begin at a comfortable pace and ask everyone to stay with you or behind you. (But allow able runners to speed up their pace.)

You'll probably find that most kids will enjoy the run, participation will increase as the weeks go by, runners will increase their pace, and overall conditioning will improve. As an ongoing event, a mile-a-week program will also encourage closer relationships and strong feelings of self-worth.

Idea by: Raymond P. Albert, Central School, Riverside, Ill.

National Jogging Day

No. 77

ORIGAMI BATS FOR HALLOWEEN

Even if your children's earlier origami efforts ended in utter frustration and mounds of unrecognizable folded forms, you might try just one more time. Origami bats are easy to make, and they'll be quite at home hanging around your room this time of year.

For each bat you'll need a 6-inch square of black paper. Then follow these steps:

• Fold the square in half, corner to corner, to form a triangle. Press the crease firmly. (See illustration 1.)

• Open the square. Then fold it in half, this time putting the already-creased corners together to form a triangle. (See illustrations 2 and 3.)

• Open the square and see how the fold lines cross at the center (E). (See illustration 4.)

• Pinch at E, pushing the triangles AEC and BED inward as you flatten triangles CED and AEB against each other. (See illustrations 5 and 6.)

• Fold the flap with point D toward the center so that there is a vertical line from E to D. (See illustration 7.)

• Fold the flap with point C toward the center so that there is a vertical line from E to C. Lines EC and ED meet in the center of triangle AEB. (See illustration 8.)

• Fold point E down ½ inch over the flaps to make the bat's head. (See illustration 9.)

• Hang the bat from points C and D. Attach the bat to a branch or a bat perch made out of a rolled paper cylinder.

• Make lots more bats. They're easy!

Idea by: Barbara New, Pittsburgh Public Schools, Pittsburgh, Pa.

Halloween

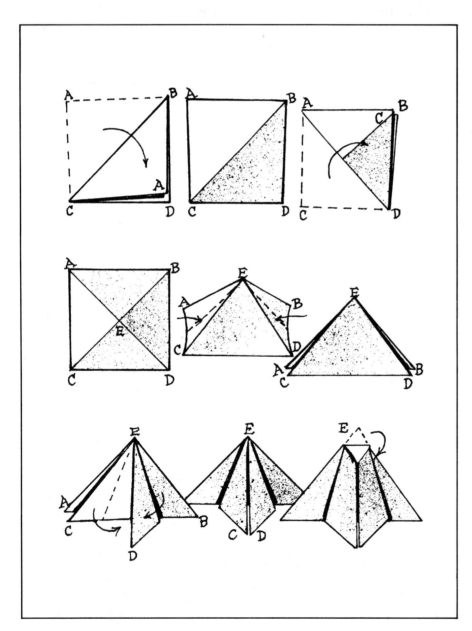

No. 78

HAUNTED HI-RISE

Save display space in your room for an architectural project designed especially for Halloween: an impressive multi-unit dwelling for ghosts, bats and the season's other creatures. The building is a construction of shoe boxes — each one a separate diorama — that become rooms in a house. If the finished building is to be an apartment house, each diorama can be an individual living unit. Or the building could be one large mansion with a variety of rooms. In any case, don't forget the attic, or the tenants — particularly the bats — may be disappointed.

Your designers might brainstorm about what should be in the rooms: furniture; dramatic doorways; dark, heavy draperies; scary portraits; massive fireplaces; jack-o'-lanterns; tissue ghosts; skeletons (in the closets or just hanging around).

The bottom of each box will become the back wall of individual rooms because the building will be formed by stacking the boxes with their open side to the front.

Staple the rooms together to build a house as wide or as tall as you wish. You may want to add a cardboard piece for a peaked roof if the dwelling is to be a mansion. A medium-sized house could be displayed by attaching it to a bulletin board.

The haunted high-rise is a likely setting for some unusual goings-on that might give students ideas for stories to share at your Halloween party.
Idea by: Linda L. Wangerin, Hope Lutheran School, Pompano Beach, Fla.

Halloween

No. 79

SPATTER PRINTS OF LEAVES

Instead of actually preserving leaves, your students may prefer to make leaf prints. The prints, which can be used while the class studies plants, also make excellent greeting cards. *A Guide to Nature Projects* (W. W. Norton) offers an easy way to make prints.

To make spatter prints of leaves, you need an old toothbrush; india ink, poster paint or some other thin coloring; a jar lid; a knife or thin strip of wood; some straight pins; a leaf collection; a flat board; a scrapbook with removable pages.

Make prints as soon as possible after collecting your leaves, while the leaves are still flexible. After they have dried out, it will be more difficult to make prints.

"Tack a sheet of paper on a flat board. Then, using common pins, pin a leaf in the center of the sheet. Be sure that all of the leaf is fastened flat on the . . . sheet. All lobes or teeth should be flat. Insert the pins at angles so that the heads point toward the center of the leaf. Another way is to weigh down the leaf with small pebbles. When the leaf is flat on the sheet, it is time for the spatter job.

"Pour some ink into a flat container, such as the top of a mason jar. Dip the toothbrush into the ink and shake off any surplus ink. . . . Then scrape the bristles of the brush with a knife or thin stick. The object is to spatter ink on the paper — not in your face. So be sure to scrape the bristles toward you. This will throw the ink in the opposite direction. Perhaps you will want to practice first, using water instead of ink.

"After you have spattered ink on the page . . . let the ink dry. Then carefully remove the pins from the leaf and remove the leaf. You will have an outline print of the leaf on the paper. You may want to define the outline with a thin line . . . and to sketch the veins of the leaf. Do this with several leaves, and you will have an attractive collection of prints. Do not forget to print only one tree's leaf to a page and to write in your notes on the opposite page."

No. 80

MENU FOR A MONSTER

Feed
Me

To feed the monster, a child takes a "Monster Menu" worksheet, fills it with things that will please the monster's palate that day, signs it and puts it in the lunch basket. (Magazines, catalogs, picture dictionaries and other helpful reference materials should be nearby.)

If the students feed the monster in the morning, later in the day they can share their menus or help compile a class composite menu.

For older students, menu mandates might include such items as, "Look through the food section of this newspaper and feed me four things whose total cost is less than $1.00." Or "Look through the restaurant menus in the folder and feed me something that has protein and carbohydrates." Or "Look through the dictionary and feed me three words you think no one in the class knows. (They'll probably give me indigestion!)"

Monster menus can be a way of introducing material and reviewing or carrying out mini-studies in special areas, as well as reinforcing skills in working with categories.

Although it does eat a lot, this monster can earn its keep.
Idea by: Penny Moldofsky, Benchmark School, Media, Pa.

Halloween

Although you may feel that your classroom already holds something of a menagerie, adding one amiable monster to the roster won't crowd anyone, and it could be just what the curriculum ordered.

Because monsters are at their best when full-grown, plan on using a large-sized piece of paper or tagboard for the construction job. This monster has a unique feature—a lunch basket, attached with drapery hooks. Herein lies the curriculum tie, for what the monster does best is eat written tasks

prepared by individual members of the class.

On the front of the monster's lunch basket, under a bold "Feed Me" label, is a place for posting a bulletin telling what the monster would like to eat that day. For young children the meal order might be, "I want to eat things that begin with the same sound as *toy*." Or "I'd like to eat *at* words today." Or "I'm hungry for foods that grow on trees." An additional note might tell whether the monster prefers words or pictures.

No. 81

WHICH WITCH

Here is an easy way to incorporate a standard language arts lesson in a colorful holiday activity bulletin board. This bulletin board idea is featured in *Language Arts Ideas for Bulletin Boards* (Fearon Pitman).

From black construction paper, cut out the silhouettes of two slightly dissimilar Halloween witches. Also cut out the letters of the words which will head up your board: "Which Witch Is Which?" From orange construction paper, cut out ten or fifteen rings about eight inches in diameter. Tack up the words, the witches (so that they face one another), and the rings. Within each ring, tack a narrow strip of paper on which you have written one word from a homonym pair. Leave several blank strips tacked to the bottom of the board. It's up to your students to fill in the strips with homonyms for the words in the rings. Limit contributions to one per kid.

Halloween

RESOURCES

EXPLORERS 1 — What was it like for explorers like Columbus or Magellan to sail out into uncharted seas and stumble across unknown lands? Books may describe it well, but simulating the experience gives an even better idea.

Explorers 1, a simulation game, recreates the process of discovery — in this case by boat — of a make-believe body of land that is as yet unmapped. Groups of students take off from starting points on a large wall graph that represents an ocean. As they move from cell to cell across the chart and sail within sight of land, the teacher draws in symbols (found in a master key) that represent land, forests, deserts, mountains and rivers, keeping just ahead of the explorers. The game is over as soon as all the land is discovered and claimed by the teams.

The game requires only a few minutes per day for about a week. Teachers and kids have the option of adding rules and making the game more complex as they play.

The game manual, a short, easy-to-understand booklet, describes additional activities and questions for relating the game to a class study of the period of exploration and discovery.
Order from: Simile II, P.O. Box 910, Del Mar, CA 92014. **Grade level:** 4–junior high.

EDISON EXPERIMENT BOOKLETS — Though we remember him primarily for the light bulb and the phonograph, Thomas Edison actually created more than 1,000 inventions. The Charles Edison Fund offers a set of ten booklets — most of them related directly or indirectly to Edison or his work — for students or teachers to use as the basis for science lessons.

Most of the booklets include experiments that can be done in school or at home. Among the booklet titles are "Energy Conservation Experiments You Can Do," "Environmental Experiments," "Electrical and Chemical Experiments," "Edison Experiments" and "Selected Experiments and Projects."
Order from: Charles Edison Fund, 101 S. Harrison St., East Orange, NJ 07018. **Grade level:** Teachers of all grades. (Requests should be made by teachers using school letterhead.)

BOOK FOR KIDS —
● *Who Found America?* Johanna Johnston. Golden Gate. Recommended reading for the primary grades.
● *America's Most Haunted Places.* Bruce and Nancy Roberts. Photographs by Bruce Roberts. Doubleday. Recommended reading for the intermediate grades.
● *An Album of the Great Depression.* William Loren Katz. Illustrated with photographs. Watts. Recommended reading for the intermediate grades and up.
● *The Mystery of Masks.* Christine Price. Illustrated by the author. Scribner's. Recommended reading for the intermediate grades and up.
● *The Pumpkin People.* David and Maggie Cavagnaro. Photographs by David Cavagnaro. Sierra Club/Scribner's. Recommended reading for the primary grades.

1

The Stamp Act imposed on American Colonies, 1765.

2

First commercial radio broadcast from Station KDKA in Pittsburgh, Pa., 1920.

3

U.S.—Alaska Highway completed, 1942.

7

Marie Curie, discoverer of radium, born in 1867.

8

Dunce Day.

9

Smokey the Bear, symbol of fire prevention, died in retirement at age 26, 1976.

13

Robert Louis Stevenson born, 1850.

14

Robert Fulton, inventor of the first steam boat, born in 1765.

15

19

Descubrimiento de Puerto Rico. Today is Columbus Day in Puerto Rico.

20

Peregrine White is the first child born in the New England colonies, 1620.

21

Edison applies for a patent for his invention of the phonograph, 1877.

25

Carrie Nation, famous hatchet-wielding saloon smasher, born in 1881.

26

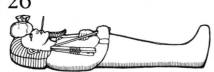

King Tutankhamun's tomb opened, 1922.

27

Nobel Prize established, Sweden, 1895.

FOUR

DAY BY DAY

4

First immigrant wagon train arrives in California, 1841.

5

6

John Philip Sousa born, 1854.

10

"Sesame Street" made its debut on this day in 1969.

11

Veterans Day.

12

16

First public display of a rock mined on the moon, 1969.

17

Suez Canal opened, 1869.

18

Mickey Mouse's birthday. He first appeared in the animated cartoon "Steamboat Willie," 1928.

22

John F. Kennedy, 35th President of the U.S., assassinated, 1963.

23

Boris Karloff, king of horror movies, born in 1887.

24

Scott Joplin, musician and composer of piano rags, born in 1868.

28

HELLO, U.S.A.

First skywriting appears, 1922.

29

Louisa May Alcott, author of *Little Women*, born 1832.

30

Winston Churchill, former British prime minister, born in 1874.

No. 82

POLITICAL DECISION-MAKING GAME

Local issues take on more meaning for students if they find themselves "in the mayor's chair." A gameboard and a set of "situation cards" can place students in this decision-making position.

The gameboard is of the basic follow-the-path kind around which students travel according to numbers rolled on a die. But there are 14 or 15 blocks in the pathway marked with X's where the path divides into an A route and a B route. Whenever a player, in the course of counting out his moves, reaches or stops on an X, he draws a situation card. These cards describe local issues on which the player must act. Each card offers two courses of action, marked A and B. The player reads the card aloud and selects either option A or option B. The player who has additional moves left from his throw of

the die continues along the selected route. The player who ends his moves on an X must wait until his next turn to proceed along his chosen path.

Of course, constructing the game — gathering the situations and providing the alternative actions — is the most challenging part of this activity. But students can assist and, in the process, learn a lot about special interests and politics.

Prepare students by generating discussions of local issues, eliciting suggestions of action alternatives, and encouraging speculation about the effects of various actions on the differing interests within the community. Then students, working individually or in teams, search the newspapers for issues and come up with two alternative actions. Example: "A lot at the corner of

Front Street and Eighth Avenue has been donated to the city. What should be done with the land?

A. Construct a park.

B. Build low-income housing."

The card collection should be added to and weeded out continually.

The winner of the game is the one who finishes the course first, reaching the "Reelection" block. But the shortest path should not be obvious — so that players will make decisions on other than the "most expedient" grounds.

Add to the complexity of the game by scattering "vote points" on various blocks. The winner in this variation is the one reaching reelection with a required number of votes.

Idea by: Sue Bianco, Norfolk, Va.

Election Day

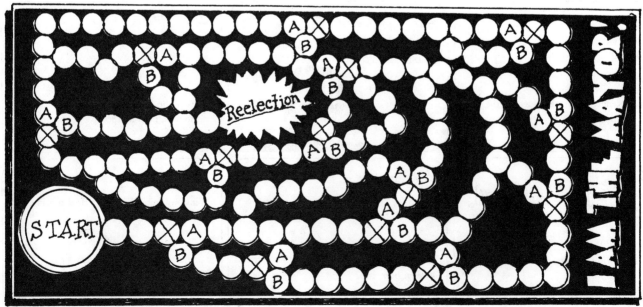

No. 83

STRAW VOTE

As Election Day rolls around this year, take the opportunity to engage your kids in politicking and participating in a straw vote ballot.

A straw vote is an unofficial vote which gives an early indication of a trend of opinion on an issue or candidate. Many states have party caucus straw votes before primaries to gauge the popularity of various candidates.

Have your kids prime themselves on a number of issues and general election candidates. On election day, give each child two drinking straws, each a different color. One color will stand for a *yes* vote, the other a *no* vote, on ballot issues. When voting for candidates, one color will stand for Conservative Craig and the other for Liberal Louise.

Set up a polling place in the front of the room. A shoe box will do admirably for a ballot box. After the children have cast their straw votes, have an official poll counter tally and announce the results of the balloting. Repeat the process as many times as you have issues and office races.

Compare the classroom trends with the actual election results the following day. Was your straw vote an accurate indicator of voter sentiments? You may also want to discuss the criteria upon which a responsible voter should base his or her decisions. For instance, how many children voted as they did because that's the way their parents voted? In order to provoke further thinking and discussion, the class could hold a real election — where the results actually matter — on some controversial issue concerning the class directly.

Election Day

No. 84

YELLOW PAGES GRAND PRIX

As part of a community resources unit, try a yellow pages board game. Besides providing some local phone books, you'll need to prepare the following materials: a gameboard, a set of "Look 'em Up" cards, and a set of "Information Please" cards.

The gameboard is a simple pathway of blocks, 50 to 100 of them, some of which will need special labels; these will be described further on.

Each "Look 'em Up" card resembles a yellow pages entry, minus the phone number:

Pharmacies

    Smith's Pharmacy
    431 Bridge St.

A player draws a card, looks up that listing in the yellow pages, notes the final digit of the phone number and moves that number of blocks. (If the digit is 0, the move is 10 blocks.)

As students become proficient at this, add an element of choice to some of the cards: If there are two branches of Smith's Pharmacy, don't give the address. In this way students can choose the phone number with the most beneficial final digit.

Label four or five blocks on the board "Information Please." A player landing on one of these blocks picks up an Information Please card. Each of these cards describes a situation requiring a special service, the kind that might send someone on a search through the yellow pages. For instance: "A buffalo bumped into your car. The buffalo is fine, but the car's back bumper is badly bent. Move to _____." The needed service (in this case "Automobile Body Repairing") is shown by a labeled block on the board — yellow pages headings such as "Caterers," "Advertising — Outdoor," "Veterinarians," "Pest Control." A player drawing an Information Please card reads the problem, surveys the services on the board, selects the appropriate one and moves forward or back to that block. (As you write each Information Please card, be sure to label a block providing the help that's needed. Consider how "creative" solutions will be handled, to avoid war later on.)

The winner of the game is the first player to land — by exact count — on the final WIN block.

Not only does the game help students use the yellow pages, improve their scanning skills and their alphabetical-order efficiency, it also gives them the opportunity to become more familiar with the kinds of services and businesses in their home-town area.

Idea by: Penny Moldofsky, Benchmark School, Media, Pa.

No. 85

MOTHER NATURE PRESERVES

One way to save those souvenirs from field and forest is to put them under glass. In anticipation of this, have students bring in some medium-sized clear glass jars with screw-on tops. A late fall nature walk could yield a wide variety of dried plants, seeds, seed pods, nuts, burrs, twigs, bits of bark, etc. After these items have served their science-exploration purposes, collect them in a box for "preserving."
Procedure:

1. Each student gets a covered jar, some clay and a self-selected "bouquet" of the field-trip goodies.

2. Apply clay to the inside of the jar cover in a layer deep enough to support the stems of the dried plants. (Be sure not to apply clay all the way to the edges; leave room for the jar to fit back inside.)

3. The plants and other items are then arranged and fixed into the clay base. Keep the dimensions of the jar in mind.

4. Place the jar carefully over the arrangement and tighten into the cover.

For extra color, invest in a bunch of tiny straw flowers. With each student using only a few, one bunch will go a long way.

Tiny animals made of modeling dough can be added to the arrangement. For each batch of dough (about 30 animals), use three cups of flour, one cup of salt and enough water to make a workable dough. Allow the models to

dry (or bake them), paint them, then let them dry and apply a coat of shellac.

And in case you're thinking ahead, Mother Nature Preserves make nice gifts.
Idea by: Sue Morrow, Old Hickory, Tenn.

No. 86

WHAT TO SEE IN OUR TOWN

Your city or town may not have a Statue of Liberty or a Space Needle, but still there are probably a number of spots worth visiting. In connection with a study of your city, students could develop tour attraction folders describing points of interest — for tourists and townspeople alike.

Post a city map and divide it into four sections, right through the city center. Each section will become the

focus of operations for a group that will research the tour potential of that area. This will require careful map reading as well as the use of a city directory and pamphlets from the chamber of commerce. On-site visits to tour-worthy locations for exploring and sketching will need to be arranged, perhaps with the help of parents. These spots might include the museum, stadium, zoo, courthouse, schools, places of worship, library, post office, fire station, parks, major stores, auditoriums, apartment complexes, hospitals, etc.

Since the folders are to accommodate student artwork, they'll need to be larger than the usual business-envelope-size format. Try butcher paper

in portions several yards long, which can be folded into panels accordion-style. Drawings can be stapled or taped to both sides of the panels.

Labels identifying the buildings or other attractions, as well as notations of street addresses, will be needed. And some students may wish to research and write up information on the history of a building or area, or the hours an establishment is open, or other pertinent data.

When all have completed their work, students in each group may use their folder to take the rest of the class on a "guided tour" of their part of the city.
Idea by: Florence Rives, Selma, Ala.

No. 87

GRANT PROPOSALS

What could you do with half a million dollars? Just suppose a $500,000 two-year grant is to be made available to improve the quality of life in your city. Your students have the task of submitting proposals for use of this grant.

The student proposals may deal with any of several areas of a social, scientific or cultural nature: senior citizens programs, transportation systems, pollution control, community centers, recycling programs, arts extravaganzas. Ideas for proposals might come from investigation of library resources, newspapers, attendance at meetings of special-interest groups or the city council. Or you might invite advocates of

various "causes" to talk to the class. Students should not consider the development of proposals which involve programs that have already received funding, but may investigate programs which are currently under study by community groups.

Set a deadline when brief outlines of proposals are to be submitted for review and suggestions. Then more detailed proposals are worked out, including goals, costs and methods of implementation. Students will need to research the present situation, justify the need for their plans and set up practical ways of carrying out the scheme. You may want to enlist the aid of appropriate community resource persons in various stages of the proposal-making process.

Written proposals are to be presented, discussed and defended before a "panel of experts" you've recruited from the community or perhaps

a local college. The panel evaluates the proposals and makes determinations about the "awarding" of the "grant." The decision of the panel and factors involved in awarding the grant should be explained and discussed.

At the end of the project, you may want to submit the proposals to the mayor, the chamber of commerce or the newspapers as evidence of the interest and involvement of some young citizens.

The $500,000 grant project can have a feeling of reality about it. Proposals must be clear and logical — not just for a grade, but because the plans must be effectively communicated to the panel. And the project takes on special appeal with a half a million dollars riding on the results.
Idea by: S. Donn Campbell, The Pittsburgh Academy, Pittsburgh, Pa.

No. 88

THANKS A MILLION

"I've chosen you as one of the persons to share my fortune. Please accept the enclosed amount." Several hundred-dollar and thousand-dollar bills are tucked inside the envelope that carried that message.

Now that should wake them up! Everyone in the class gets a letter in an envelope full of money and, not so incidentally, a reason for composing an unusual sort of thank-you note. Preparation on your part for this event involves:

1. Composing and duplicating a letter concerning the fabulous fortune of some fictitious eccentric.

2. Buying or making some play money (large denominations preferred).

3. Placing letters and play money in envelopes addressed to each member of the class.

The fortune-bearing letters may arrive at whatever point in your language arts program it seems that such motivators are needed to spark letter-writing practice.

When the right time comes, and the money's in hand, the next sounds most likely to be heard will be wild plots for spending the windfall. You might suggest that students try to keep their best ideas secret for sharing later on, and that meanwhile something ought to be done about acknowledging these most generous gifts. Perhaps the mysterious donor would be interested in reading what plans each recipient has for his or her money — the more exotic the better.

Letters should, of course, follow the form the class recently has learned, the idea being to write good letters while having fun with the content.

The finished letters can be shared aloud or posted for everyone to read. Twenty-five or 30 ways to spend a lot of money can make for enjoyable reading.

And perhaps all that money floating around could be rounded up for other activities — a little math perhaps?
Idea by: Alyse Rynowecer, Chicago, Ill.
Thanksgiving

No. 89

RADIO DRAMA SOUND EFFECTS

The unique aspect of radio drama is that speech alone characterizes the whole person. Students can experience this art form by listening to "The Shadow" or "The Lone Ranger" on recordings available in most record shops. Discuss how voice, sound effects and music combine to convey emotion and action. Note the trick of tagging dialogue lines — "Which way did they go, *Tonto?*" — in order to clarify who is talking to whom.

Radio scripts are available in playbooks. It's also possible to adapt stage plays or write original scripts. Improvisation is another possibility. In all cases, rehearsals are a must and playing back successive recordings helps.

Radio drama provides a great chance for voice play: have kids listen to, and try to imitate, the voices of old people and babies, people with accents, and people in special vocations such as telephone operator, telephone time voice or police dispatcher. For pure invention, there are always voices of talking animals, plants, objects or extraterrestrial beings. Suggest experiments such as talking with the nose held closed or speaking through cloth or paper.

Taping the dramas not only facilitates evaluation but also permits students to gain maximum impact from their own manufactured sound effects. A sound-effects "production table" might include bells, buzzers, a pan of water, gravel for walking on, a rusty door hinge for a haunted house, a clock that ticks loudly (time bomb?), and other everyday noise-makers. A few classic effects can be produced as follows:

• *Fire*: Crinkle cellophane six inches from the microphone.

• *Bird flying*: Shake a partly opened umbrella up and down.

• *Breaking down a door*: Crunch a piece of balsa wood in a fist held near the microphone.

• *Rain*: Trickle grains of rice onto a sheet of canvas or paper stretched tightly above the mike.

• *Chase through underbrush*: Beat two leafy twigs together.

• *Guillotine*: Chop a head of cabbage near the mike.

Kids can also use their voices to make sounds like sirens, wind and airplane engines. While the sounds should be subordinate to the drama, kids will have fun producing them and may even get story ideas based on an intriguing squeak or sklush.

Share polished tapes with other classes. You might also send outstanding productions to a local radio station with the helpful hint that they play it as part of the FCC-required public-service broadcasting.

November 2

No. 90

HEAR ALL ABOUT IT

They're noisy and come in all sizes, shapes and colors. Not the children — transistor radios! And they just might be the way to generate interest in world and national news — while sharpening listening skills and providing a break from the books.

Getting a transistor or two into the classroom should be easy. (And it's probably best to limit it to one or two at first.) Getting the kids to "tune in" should be easy too (even when you designate the station and set the dial for news). Activating true listening is something else.

You might consider a listening concentration aid in the form of a worksheet with categories such as states, cities, foreign countries, national leaders, world leaders, domestic problems. You might also indicate what might be a reasonable number of entries under each heading. The categories may help focus listening.

It will probably take more than one newscast to gather enough data to catch all the information put forth; newscasters tend to talk fairly fast, and of course there's no interrupting to ask that something be repeated.

The news data collected on the worksheets can provide some starting points for discussion and further study. Maps can be used to locate cities and countries in the news. Newspapers can be skimmed for photos of newsmakers. A few students may decide to follow certain continuing news stories and report developments to the class. (Transistors with individual earphones can help here.) Careful listening and efficient note taking become important with this kind of responsibility.

Another thought: Those transistors are meant to be portable. How about a small-group news-listening-activity-time taking place outdoors some warm afternoon?

Idea by: Isobel Livingstone, Rahway, N.J.

November 2

No. 91

AND NOW FOR THIS ANNOUNCEMENT

Radio disc jockeys regularly make announcements about community meetings, local happenings and miscellaneous events. They must present the messages concisely, with complete information and in understandable terms. Writing this type of announcement is at first demanding, but comes more easily with practice. Here are 15 possible topics (from *Mass Media*, activity cards published by Creative Teaching Press) from which kids can make up announcements:

1. a community arts-and-crafts show
2. the results of a track meet
3. a golf tournament
4. a new bus schedule
5. tickets for a church spaghetti dinner
6. a contest with $10,000 in prizes

7. the opening of a new shopping center
8. a canned goods collection for needy families
9. a class reunion
10. a garage sale
11. a paper drive
12. a lost child
13. a news bulletin
14. a reward for the return of a missing pet
15. your choice of topics

Have students choose three topics from the list and prepare announcements about them. Limit each announcement to 30 seconds.

An interesting variation is to have students make 30-second spot announcements about items and events that have real meaning to their class or school. School announcements can be broadcast over the school's public address system.

November 2

No. 92

PRESERVING AND CONSERVING

The concepts of conservation and preservation have much in common. *Creative Learning and Teaching* (Dodd, Mead & Co.) gives the following background information and discussion questions to stimulate thinking about preservation on both concrete and abstract levels. The discussion will help kids to explore the reasons for preserving things and to understand the idea of conservation of natural resources.

"We preserve things in many different ways. In order to keep fish fresh, we use ice. By bronzing them, many people keep the baby shoes of their children in the same condition that they were when the shoes were outgrown. When we want to preserve something nowadays, we may encase it in plastic. In this exercise, think of how a variety of things might be preserved — that is, how they might be kept, maintained, retained or sustained.

"How would you preserve:
1. raspberries?
2. the flavor of mint?
3. the fragrance of roses?
4. the excitement of a holiday?
5. dignity?
6. honesty?
7. a friendship?

"Which of the items above would you like to preserve or have preserved for you? Why? Would it really be the same if you tried to keep it just as it is? Explain. Is there anything that actually never changes? Why or why not? What is the difference between conserving something and preserving it?"

No. 93

NO MORE MEAT

Experts tell us that someday meat on the table will be a thing of the past. Ask kids to imagine that day has come — meat is gone and with it have disappeared all our short-order hamburger restaurants. Working in small groups, have children remake the fast-foods empire in the vegetable image. New names for restaurants — Carrot King, Kentucky Fried Beet — and new menus — spinach shakes, grilled zucchini sandwiches, cornburgers — are in order. Have the students write recipes and tummy-tempting menu descriptions for their new concoctions.

Continuing the meatless idea, kids can plan a full day of vegetarian meals. Ideally, this would be followed by the classroom visit of a bona-fide vegetarian. Students and guest could then discuss their scheduled meals and make plans for preparing one or more of them in the classroom. An effort should be made to have meals contain a variety of items likely to surprise kids who think the universe of vegetables begins and ends with limp spinach or soggy peas. If you don't know any vegetarians, try asking at a health-food store. Failing that, your discussion leader could be the school dietitian, a hospital dietitian, or the food editor of a local newspaper.

THE JAM JAR

CURRICULUM À LA CARTE

What would your students do if they were home alone and suddenly saw smoke coming from the kitchen? What if they were playing in the park with a friend and the friend had a bad fall? Kids can deal with such problems when they dip into the Jam Jar.

Ask the students to decide what kind of jam they'd like to make (strawberry, grape or whatever) and decorate the front of a large jar accordingly. Then have the children cut the chosen fruit shape out of several sheets of colored paper. The shapes should be large enough to write a sentence on, and there should be enough of them so that each child receives one.

Now give the children an example of a "jam," a difficult or unlikely situation, and ask each child to write an original jam on a fruit cutout. Place all the jams in the Jam Jar and then have each child take one. Have the students write short stories or solutions that explain how they got out of, or solved, their particular jams.
Idea by: T.S. White, Montclair School, Omaha, Nebr.

A menu has potential for providing a variety of teaching materials (an idea that may have been born in a busy restaurant as a teacher-patron tried to creatively occupy the seeming eternity between "This way please" and "Are you ready to order?"). Menus can, in fact, be used to generate activities representing almost every area of the curriculum.

Assembling adequate quantities of this sort of resource can be handled without resorting to furtive measures. You may find a number of local establishments willing to part with single samples of their menus, and this way you can collect a variety of kinds. Or a restaurant that's updating or replacing menus might donate the old ones in such quantities that each child could have one.

Language and math activities spring quite naturally from menus. There is bound to be intriguing vocabulary to explore: *à la carte, side order, garnish, à la mode, poached, julienne, croquette, soup du jour, cold cuts*, as well as food names that some children may not have encountered. Children can also look for ways descriptive language is used in presenting, explaining and glorifying food items.

Math problem situations abound — as any diner-out well knows. You might suggest tasks such as these:

1. Plan a complete meal for five for under $25.

2. Plan the most expensive meal that a person could order. (Would you want to eat this meal?)

3. Plan the least expensive full meal.

4. Look at the items listed under "Country Breakfast." Find each of those items listed separately (à la carte). Add up their prices. How much money would you save by ordering the Country Breakfast instead of ordering items separately?

5. What would you have for a snack for under $1.00?

Tipping is a math concern, of course, but tipping also has a social studies aspect. Children might research the custom of tipping and find out how it is handled in various places. Taxes on meals can also be a matter for both math and social studies activities and investigations.

The menu provides material for nutrition studies and explorations into kinds of food. If someone ate only items from this menu, would the diet be well balanced and healthy? Are some needed foods lacking? Are there unfamiliar foods on the menu? Dishes deriving from other countries? Familiar foods prepared in new ways? (Would the class like to prepare and try some?)

Children may enjoy dramatic play with the menus, ordering meals and serving them — which could lead to discussion of careers in the restaurant field.

And of course, simply reading through an attractive two-page listing of foods instead of dealing with a text can be a happy change of reading fare that will please many children.
Idea by: Diane S. Bailey, Majestic Elementary School, Birmingham, Ala.

No. 96

JAR DRAW

This upper grade language activity calls for three large-mouthed jars (check your cafeteria) that you label first person, second person, third person. You also prepare a large collection of colored-paper strips. On each strip write a single noun or a noun phrase. You might start with common things, places and people (both names and roles: Jesse James, sister, race car driver). You might also include names of books, movies, TV shows, songs and abstract terms — courage, procrastination, curiosity.

Randomly distribute the strips among the three jars, and then the activity can start.

Each student draws a strip, being careful to note which jar it came from. Whatever is on the strip becomes the subject for a riddle to be phrased in the first, second or third person, according to the label on the jar. For instance, if the strip is drawn from the first-person jar, the student must write about the item by taking on the personality of the item, by describing it as if talking about himself or herself:

"Good morning, I'm glad you came by. I enjoy visitors. As you can see, I'm pretty tied up here being a floating museum."

Drawing a strip from the second-person jar means describing the item as if talking to it directly:

"You're really looking good for your age. I understand you've been a national landmark for over 100 years."

Third-person jar items are described as if the student were talking to someone about the item:

"See that character over there? He's been hanging around that cornfield for years. They say he doesn't have brain in his head."

At the end of each description, students write the appropriate riddle-concluding query; e.g., "Who am I?" "Would you like everyone to try to guess your identity?" "Who is it?"

If you find more jars, you can expand your collection to include verbs (several tenses) and perhaps adjectives or prepositional phrases for building sentences with an interesting point of view.
Idea by: Jule Marine and Barbara Woll, Jordan Junior High School, Salt Lake City, Utah.

No. 97

PEAS ON THE PATIO

Without being doomsayers, let's imagine grocery stores with empty shelves, forcing us to grow our own food. What do we do? Have kids survey the neighborhood to find all usable space for growing things. Have them draw pictures and make maps and diagrams of the neighborhood turned into a community farm (corn on the baseball diamond, cabbage in the front yard).

Younger kids might simply pick out all likely spaces — parks, yards, vacant lots — or they might go further by suggesting rooftop gardens, window boxes, etc. Older kids could study such problems as: neighborhood population; how much land to support how many people; what crops in what climate; soil analysis; will available open space be enough or should buildings be razed, streets torn up?

No. 98

APPLE FRACTIONS

Introduce your students to fraction basics with worms and apples in a matching game.

Cut several apple shapes from red construction paper and divide them into equal pie-shaped parts. Then cut away several of the parts from each apple to represent various fractions. The cutout parts represent the numerator of the fraction.

Now cut out some brown construction paper worms. On each worm, print a fraction that corresponds with a cutout apple fraction. As a group or individual activity, display an apple and then ask a student to choose the corresponding worm from all the available worms. New fractions are introduced when students are asked how much of each apple is left for the worms to eat.
Idea by: Patricia Zell, Miami Elementary School, Wabash, Ind.

No. 99

DRYING FOOD

Drying is a method of preserving food without refrigeration. Here are instructions for drying fruits and vegetables in school or at home. (From *The Heritage Sampler: A Book of Colonial Arts & Crafts*, Dial.)

"Materials: clean old sheet; sharp knife; needle; several coat hangers; broomstick or long wooden pole; piece of cheesecloth; heavy-duty thread; scissors; containers with lids; saucepan.

"Ingredients: vegetables—peas, corn, green beans, or peppers; fruit—apples, blueberries, blackberries, peaches, or apricots.

"Vegetables take six to twelve hours to dry, depending on the size of the pieces and the amount of humidity in the air. Fruits take eight hours or longer to dry. Dried fruit feels dry and leathery on the outside but slightly moist inside. Vegetables should be brittle.

"*Peas*: Shell and lay ripe peas on a clean sheet in the sun to dry. Bring them inside at night. The hulls will crack. When the peas are dry, tap them with the side of a knife to remove the loose hulls. Store the peas in a closed container.

"*Corn*: Husk and clean ears of corn. Cut the corn off the cob with a sharp knife and dry the kernels in the sun on a clean sheet. Store the dried corn in a closed container.

"*Green Beans*: String green beans on a length of strong thread and hang in a warm, shaded place. Hang until the beans dry and store them in a closed container.

"*Peppers*: Wash and string hot red peppers with a needle on a length of strong thread. Try long red cayenne or chili peppers. Make several pepper strings, tie them on a coat hanger, and put it in an airy closet to dry. A dried pepper skin feels dry and wrinkled.

"*Fruit and Berries*: Peel and slice apples into slivers or core peeled apples and cut into half-inch thick rings. String the rings on a broom handle or on a pole and hang in the sun. String apple slivers on a length of strong thread and hang, or lay apple slivers and rings on a clean sheet in the sun to dry. You can peel, slice, and dry peaches and apricots in this way; whole blueberries and blackberries can be spread on a sheet to dry. Apples and other fruit will turn brown and rubbery. Cover the fruit you dry outside with cheesecloth or lightweight cloth to

protect it from dirt and insects. Store dried fruit in closed containers. You also can heat dried slices in a 225°F. oven for about five minutes to kill any germs.

"To cook dried fruit and vegetables, you must replace the water taken out during the drying process. Pour about 1½ cups of boiling water over 1 cup of dried food. Let the food absorb the water until it will hold no more. Dried vegetables usually soak up enough water in about two hours, but fruits usually take longer, from two to four hours or more. You can bake the fruit in pies and other desserts."

No. 100

GOALS FOR REVIEW GAMES

Perhaps you've forgotten how much interest can be generated by using a popular sport, such as football, as a vehicle for review. Although young children may not appreciate the details of the game, most kids catch football fever and enjoy using the sport's terms.

Collect your review questions and organize two teams with a coach for each. The coaches are responsible for keeping track of plays, recording touchdown points and selecting extra-point kickers after each touchdown.

The toss of a coin determines which team goes first. A question is then "kicked off" to the starting team.

You may want to try football review in its simplest form, which doesn't involve yardage. One team tries to keep the ball through four questions. Questions are responded to by individual team members after the team has huddled and agreed on an answer. If a question is missed, the team has another chance to answer correctly before losing the ball. If the team handles the four questions well, it earns the chance to answer a six-point touchdown question. If the touchdown question is missed, the ball goes to the other team without a second try. If it's correctly answered, there's an extra-point question — after which the ball goes to the other team for it's "first down."

You may have to call "interference" (subtracting three points) if the defensive team gets noisy. A "fumble" (minus one point) could be called if a team doesn't know who's supposed to answer next.

If the class can handle a more challenging format, you might modify the game by using a football diagram, timing the quarters, and organizing material into yardage questions — each worth a specified number of yards lost if missed — and touchdown questions — worth touchdown points. Play starts at the 50-yard line. The team with the ball has the option of either trying for a goal after traversing a specified number of yards or going for a touchdown question anytime — and risking loss of the ball.

Whether trying for extra points or making dogged progress down the field, students should enjoy the football atmosphere — even if it's related to social studies review.

Idea by: Andrea D. Windsor, Philadelphia, Pa.

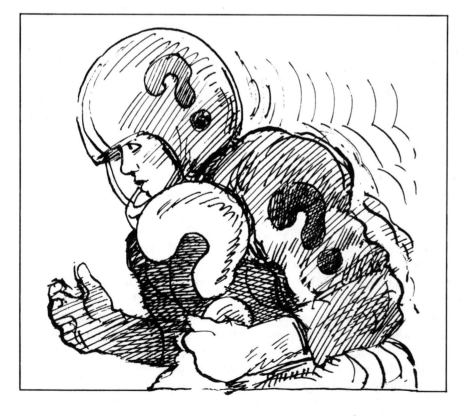

No. 101

RE-INVENT THE PHONOGRAPH

Recorded sound requires both motion and amplification to be heard. Edison figured that out when he invented the phonograph. Of course, electronics and stereophonic sound have brought the phonograph a long way since Edison had it patented in 1877. But this experiment from *Science Activities With Simple Things* (Fearon Pitman) will resimplify the system so that your kids can see how it really works.

You will need a hand drill, an old record, a pin or needle, a 12" x 18" piece of construction paper, glue or a stapler and a ⅜" x ½" stove bolt.

Make your turntable by inserting the stove bolt through the hole in the record and clamping the bolt firmly into the hand drill. Next, roll the piece of construction paper into a cone and secure the shape with glue or a stapler. At the small end of the cone, insert a pin or needle at a slight angle and push it through so that it extends down from the tip of the cone. Now you're ready to "play" the record.

Have one child hold the drill upright and turn the handle at a steady rate. Have another child hold the cone by the large end so the needle rests on the record with only the weight of the cone holding it down (see illustration). When the record is turned at the appropriate speed, the class should clearly hear the sounds on the record.

November 21

No. 102

A FLOWER A WEEK

Frost may already have finished off the flowers in your part of the world, but that doesn't have to mean an end to the welcome color and the many opportunities for science discovery that flowers can bring — not so long as there are flowering house plants or a florist's wares to be tapped. Perhaps you'd rather not promise a flower a week — once a month might be more realistic — but try scheduling in some flowers as classroom visitors on a regular basis for learning and enjoyment.

Depending on your area's climate and the season, you might be able to brighten the room with local wildflowers, chrysanthemums, African violets, carnations, poinsettias, daffodils, magnolias, camellias, lilacs, pansies and dozens of others over a year's time.

If you're dependent on the florist for your flower curriculum materials, this need not be an expensive venture; a single stem of a featured flower set up in a special spot can be quite effective. Or if garden flowers or field flowers are available in abundance, it may be possible for each child to have a sample to study.

The learning opportunities inherent in flowers are many and varied. The shape and color of flowers may inspire art projects in a variety of media. Or perhaps some more technical science drawings can be tried. New vocabulary can be generated in recording sight and scent observations. Research can be enlisted to cover all sorts of facts about a plant's origin, range, varieties, etc. Writings surrounding a flower might range from poetry to factual science records. (Cumulative spelling lists from flower study, including some of the flower names, could be a challenge too.) A notebook of the year's flowers — format to be discussed and set up at the beginning of the project — could be a shared responsibility among the class.

With some planning and planting, a later month's flower bulb could be growing while the current period's flower is in bloom. Groups of students could alternate in taking care of the developing plants, recording growth data and noting other changes.

Looking forward to flowers through the cold, dark winter months can be something quite special. And even in warm climates where flowers are part of the scene year round, singling out a flower for special treatment may help focus attention on one small miracle that can easily be taken for granted. **Idea by: Elizabeth B. Huband, Chestnut Street School, Wilmington, N.C.**

No. 103

CORN HUSK MAT

"One of the more important contributions of Indian life to the settlers was the plant called maize, or corn. The new Americans found many uses for the plant they saw growing in the villages of the first Americans. The Indians used the corn plant in many clever ways. The ear of corn was eaten fresh or dried and ground into meal. The husks, or leaves that surround the ear, were braided into ropes and mats. Children made dolls from corn husks. The settlers tied the husks into brooms and used husks as mattress stuffing." (From *A Child's American Heritage*, Troubador Press.) The following project provides kids with an opportunity to work with corn husks, the same material used by Indians and early settlers. The mat is from *A Child's American Heritage*.

You'll need carpet thread, a heavy-duty needle and the husks from at least 12 ears of corn. Prepare the husks by placing them between two sheets of paper. Allow them to dry for two weeks. The day before use, sprinkle the husks with water and flatten. Carefully place them in a large plastic bag and close it tightly until you are ready to use the husks. Then spread the husks flat on a damp towel. Keep them damp as you work.

Trim all pieces to an even length, 6 to 8 inches long. Cut three husks with an angle at one end; trim the first one, then cut the second one an inch shorter than the first. The third husk should be 1 inch shorter than the second. (See illustration A.)

Roll the three husks into long narrow strips. (Illustration B.)

Fasten the three husks at the straight end with carpet thread. (Illustration C.)

Fasten the tied husks to a steady hook to hold them while braiding. Braid the husks into a rope. (Illustration D.)

To add husks, slip a rolled husk into the short strand. (Illustration E.) Continue to braid, adding husks until your rope is as long as you'd like. Bind both ends with carpet thread. (Illustration F.)

If you make a rope 6 feet long, you can coil it into an 8-inch mat by stitching the coil together with carpet thread. It makes an excellent hot-mat for a table. (Illustration G.)

No. 104

CORN HUSK BROOM

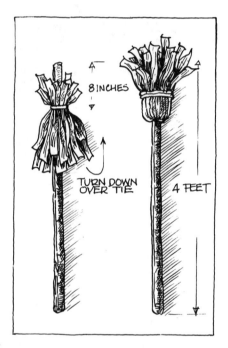

The directions for making a corn husk broom come from *Project 1776: A Manual for the Bicentennial* (Bicentennial Commission of Pennsylvania).

The following materials are needed: a stick about 4 feet long for the handle, corn husks and string.

Gather a large bunch of dried husks together and soak them. Tie them tightly around the handle about 8 inches from the end. The long ends of the husks should hang down toward the long end of the handle, as shown in the illustration.

Fold the long ends of the husks carefully over the tied part and tie them tightly near the short end of the stick, as shown. Trim the ends of the broom.

No. 105

MAKING AN APPLE-HEAD DOLL

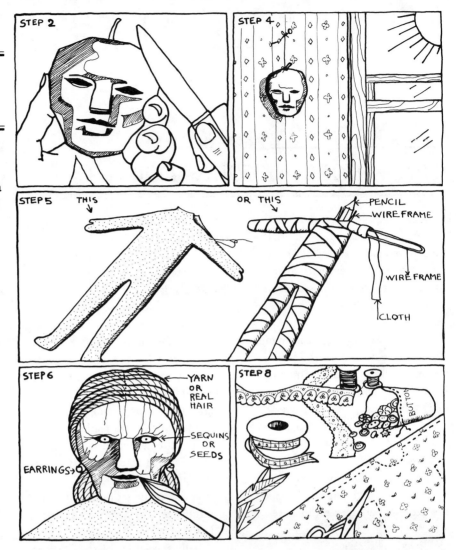

Students are thoroughly enthralled to find that a mere apple, a familiar dessert or snack, can transform itself into a human face. The technique and process of making an apple-head doll is quite basic, but as the student brings imagination and skill to the task, each doll becomes an individual and a unique work of art.

Materials for one doll:

apple (choose hard cooking type)

knife

pipe cleaner (optional)

paint or lemon juice

needle and thread

straight pins

glue

flannel fabric (or wire), cotton, fabric
    scraps (for body)

beads, seeds, sequins (for eyes)

cotton, yarn, real hair (for hair)

fabric, notions, jewelry (for clothing
    and ornament)

shellac or nail polish

Note: In the drying process the apple may shrink 50 percent or more; keep this in mind in selecting apple size.

Procedure:

1. Peel the apple. Leave the stem — and a bit of peel around it — for a "handle." Or run a pipe cleaner down through the apple, bending the wire on both ends to secure it.

2. Use a knife or sharp tool to carve the features of the face. These should be fairly exaggerated, allowing for shrinkage.

3. The apple will turn a caramel brown as it dries. A darker shade can be achieved by painting after the apple has dried. For a lighter tone, soak the apple in lemon juice for 45 minutes before the drying begins.

4. Hang up the apple in a well-ventilated place to dry. Allow two to four weeks.

5. A rag-doll-style body can be made from flannel cut to a simple outline, stitched and stuffed with cotton, old stockings or fabric scraps. The head will be attached with straight pins.

Or, a wire armature can be constructed for the body, to be padded with cotton and wrapped like a mummy with fabric strips. A doubled wire extending upward from the neck area can provide for the attachment of the head. A pencil incorporated into the body section and extending up into the base of the apple can add support.

6. In the drying process the facial features may close; you can gently pry them open. Beads, seeds or sequins can be inserted for eyes. Features may be emphasized with markers or paint. Earrings can be pinned in place. Hair can be applied with glue or pins.

7. Shellac or nail polish adds sheen and helps preserve the face.

8. The clothing can be simple or elaborate. Offering a rich variety of fabric scraps, trims, buttons, feathers, etc., can be inspiring. Clothes can be sewn without thought for intricate or workable fasteners, since the dolls are only for display. Pattern design, cutting and stitching can be organized into small group projects.

No. 106

START A HOLIDAY COUNTDOWN

As a holiday approaches, the I-can-hardly-wait excitement takes over. Because children are counting the days anyway, providing them with a set of countdown activities (things to do on your way to the holiday) can bring benefits all around.

You might start the countdown eight days before the holiday period begins. Set aside a bulletin board as the countdown site and choose an appropriate holiday symbol as the countdown device. For Thanksgiving you might have a turkey — with removable tail feathers numbered one to eight and keyed to special activities. For Christmas or Hanukkah a stack of brightly wrapped, numbered gift packages could serve.

Thanksgiving activities might include directions such as:

1. Put a list of Thanksgiving dinner foods in alphabetical order.

2. Write a thank-you note to someone who has done something you're thankful about.

3. Read a Thanksgiving story or poem.

4. Decode a Thanksgiving message.

5. Write a story about a surprising Thanksgiving visitor.

6. Make table decorations.

7. Make a picture or word collage of things you're thankful about.

(For other holidays, activities could explore seasonally appropriate topics, themes and traditions.)

Eight days before Thanksgiving, invite a child to choose a feather on the turkey and thus select that day's special activity. As the turkey loses its feathers, the holiday slips closer.

Before the poultry plucking begins, you might want to designate a particular "last feather" and cook up something really special for blast-off day at the end of the holiday countdown.
Idea by: Donna Milanovich, Bon Meade Elementary School, Coraopolis, Pa.

Thanksgiving

No. 107

CAN YOU LOCATE?

Map study takes on the lure of a puzzle when you put up a Can You Locate? bulletin board. Suppose your class is studying your own city or a nearby area. You can provide materials for a scavenger hunt by touring the area and taking snapshots of well-known buildings and attractions, businesses, parks and even street corners. Photograph a few "giveaway" locations as well as sites that take detective work to identify.

Post the city or area map and pin the photos around it. Next to each photo staple a piece of yarn. Then challenge the children by labeling the bulletin board "Can You Locate?"

Children use research skills to identify the photos and to pinpoint locations. The telephone directory will help with street addresses, and the map's street index — with its guide letters and numbers — must be mastered so that students can zero in on locations. As each photo is "found," the yarn is attached to the appropriate spot on the map.

Children may want to augment the display with photos they take themselves — to test the investigative prowess of their friends while extending everyone's knowledge of the city.

Other maps may be used in this way — but magazine pictures, rather than snapshots, might have to suffice when the map is of Brazil or Antarctica.
Idea by: Lisa Kass, Lincoln School, Pontiac, Ill.

No. 108

CONCENTRATION

Concentration, that perennial game show favorite, also can be enjoyed as a manipulative bulletin board game. Using yarn and thumbtacks, hang word cards with the words facing the bulletin board and attach a score pad or sheet, as shown in the illustration.

Concentration words can reflect the month (Thanksgiving words for November Concentration), the weather, specific subjects (dairy products, mathematical equivalents, sports equipment) or anything under class discussion. Two children play at a time (the rest of the class can observe), each trying to find a matched pair. Uncovered pairs are quickly learned by both the players and the peanut gallery.

Idea by: Patricia Smoak, Kadimah School, Buffalo, N.Y.

RESOURCES

PIONEERS — Until recently, most simulation games had been developed exclusively for high schools. Now producers are beginning to create new games and adapt old ones for use by elementary students. *Pioneers: A Simulation of Decision-Making on a Wagon Train* may be used as early as the intermediate level. Its purpose is to allow students to "vicariously participate in situations and events similar to those experienced by pioneers who headed west in early wagon trains."

Over the course of the 15 one-hour sessions, students take on the roles of pioneer family members heading west to Oregon in the mid-19th century. Along the way, simulation participants encounter many problems, including flooding rivers and unfriendly Indians. Participants also do a research paper, keep a journal, read maps, select and keep track of supplies and, in general, make short- and long-range decisions which will affect all members of the train.

The game comes in the form of two booklets. A student workbook provides information, background, assignments and space for writing. The workbook serves as a permanent record of the journey for each student. The teacher's guide tells how to carry out the simulation, explains the components of the game and gives a working schedule for the sessions.

Setting up the game requires a small but worthwhile investment of time on the part of the teacher — reading the two booklets and gathering research and other background material for students. Teachers are encouraged to adapt the game in any way they see fit.

Order from: Interact, Box 262, Lakeside, CA 92040. **Grade level:** Intermediate–junior high.

JAR AND BOTTLE CRAFT — All but a few of the knickknacks in this book of crafts projects are both decorative *and* functional. Author Helen Roney Sattler gives ideas for many practical gift items that will travel well from school to home.

There are directions for making, among other things, a spice rack (out of baby-food jars and a detergent box), a toothbrush holder and a cookie jar. Some of the purely decorative items are ornaments for Christmas trees.

The book is written for intermediate grade children, who will be able to follow the clear directions on their own. Teachers also can use the book as a resource to explain the same projects to primary graders.

The book is indexed, divided into chapters and includes an introductory section that explains many of the decorative techniques used throughout the book. These techniques can be applied to any number of original projects as well as those described in the book.

Order from: William Morrow & Co., 105 Madison Ave., New York, NY 10016. **Grade level:** Primary–intermediate.

1

First drive-in gasoline station opened in Pittsburgh, Pa., 1913.

2

Monroe Doctrine declared, 1823.

3

Anniversary of the first successful heart transplant, by Dr. Christiaan Barnard in 1967.

7

Pearl Harbor Day.

8

The American Federation of Labor organized at Columbus, Ohio, 1886.

9

Joel Chandler Harris, author of the *Uncle Remus* stories, born in 1848.

13

14

In 1799, George Washington died at Mount Vernon.

15

Bill of Rights Day.

19

Benjamin Franklin published his first *Poor Richard's* Almanac, 1732.

20

Transfer of the Lousiana Territory from France to the U.S., 1803.

21

Forefathers' Day — the landing of the pilgrims at Plymouth Rock, 1620.

25

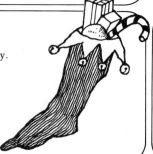

Christmas Day.

26

Mao Tse Tung born in 1893.

27

Louis Pasteur, inventor of the pasteurization process, born in 1822.

FIVE
DAY BY DAY

4

5
Walt Disney, the creator of Disneyland and the father of Mickey Mouse, born 1901.

6

"Mary had a little lamb . . ." First sound recording by Thomas Edison, 1877.

10
The French set the length of a meter to equal one ten-millionth of the distance between the equator and the North Pole, 1799.

11
UNICEF established by the United Nations in 1946.

12
Decision to move the U.S. Capital from New York City to Washington, D.C., 1800.

16

Anniversary of the Boston Tea Party, 1773.

17
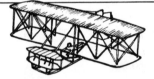
The Wright Brothers fly over Kitty Hawk, N.C., 1903.

18
Slavery abolished with the passage of the 13th Amendment to the Constitution, 1865.

22
International Arbor Day.

23

24

Kit Carson born in 1809.

28
Congress officially recognized the Pledge of Allegiance, 1945.

29
Anniversary of the Wounded Knee Massacre, 1890.

30 Author Rudyard Kipling born in 1865.

Touch a Pig for Luck Day in Australia.

31

No. 109

ADVENTURES IN ALMANACKING

You don't have to be an Old Farmer to appreciate an Old Farmer's Almanac or to compile one of these useful compendiums. Your class has the resources and creative energies to turn out an almanac quite as captivating as anything Old MacDonald could come up with.

A good start for an almanac-writing project is to expose kids to a number of different kinds of almanacs. They're fairly inexpensive and can be found at most bookstores. The kids will soon

have a good idea of the sorts of things almanacs include—just about anything. Topics easily touch on nearly everyone's special interest, and the format— everything from charts to poetry— provides fine variety in modes of expression.

Step two in almanacking might be a class brainstorming session to produce a suggested outline of content. Then implementation of various items may be worked out through small groups and individual projects. Here are some possible topics (subject matter groupings are only for convenience, not chapter headings):

Science
1. home remedies ("For toothache, hold vanilla on tooth with tongue.")
2. herbs, plant lore, kitchen cosmetics
3. tide tables, phases of the moon
4. planting tables, weather predicting, science folklore ("When cows lie down, it's going to rain.")
5. identifying flowers, trees
6. windowsill gardens
7. ecology tips—saving energy, recycling, natural pest control

Language Arts
1. poems, stories, local legends
2. proverbs and sayings
3. silly horoscopes
4. jokes, riddles, tongue twisters, jump rope rhymes, folk games

Math
1. games, puzzles, brain teasers
2. tables of metric weights and measures

Social Studies
1. famous birthdays
2. walking tours of town with maps
3. town history time line, interviews with townspeople on history of town
4. holiday customs around the world

Arts, Crafts, How-To
1. kites, folk toys (willow and grass whistles, apple dolls, corn husk dolls, cat's cradles)
2. pomanders, quilts
3. quilling, origami
4. terrariums, bird feeders
5. tying knots, uses of knots
6. recipes for homemade "clay"

Information for almanac items can be drawn from reference books, resource persons and the children's own experiences. Written work can be channeled through student editors with teacher assistance. Making illustrations, choosing a title and designing a cover are finishing touches that generate considerable interest.

Whether the completed almanac is turned out on a hand-cranked ditto machine or an offset press, the pride on the faces of the kids will be the same. Ben Franklin could hardly have asked for more.

Idea by: Laurie E. MacGuire, Branford Intermediate School, Branford, Conn.

December 19

No. 110

INNER TUBE ART

Old rubber inner tubes are an easy-to-work-with medium for making prints. And the materials needed for working with them are manageable for even young children. This activity from *Art Survival Guide for the Elementary Teacher* (Fearon Pitman) shows you how.

These are the materials you will need: a rubber inner tube, a brayer (hand-inking roller), ink, scissors, white glue and paper. The tools can be shared by the students, but be sure you have enough inner tube rubber to go around.

Give these instructions to your kids: Cut a rubber inner tube up into small pieces with interesting shapes and glue the pieces on a piece of cardboard or heavy paper (see the illustration). When the glue is dry, roll ink on the surface

of the rubber pieces with a brayer. Place a piece of paper on the inked surface and rub with your hand until most rubber areas have made an imprint on the paper. Try different colors and tex-

tures of paper. Peel off the paper and allow it to dry. Have students save their best impressions for greeting cards.

Christmas and Hanukkah

No. 111

STYROFOAM PRINTS FOR GIFTS

Even the most devoted potato printer might think about switching to a non-nutritive medium in these food-

conscious times. Consider Styrofoam packing material. It's readily available and easy to handle. Its composition — tiny round particles bonded together — gives the finished print an interesting textured look. Shapes can be easily "carved" into Styrofoam surfaces with pencils, rulers or even fingers — no knives needed. (Note: Intricate designs should be avoided since particles tend to break off if care is not taken.)

In trials against the potato, Styrofoam gained points with fifth and sixth graders because it didn't get soggy, the printing block washed easily and would accommodate two or more colors simultaneously without getting too runny.

Students may enjoy blending a variety of colors in their prints and can achieve a "ghosting" effect by printing one design overlapping another. Styrofoam prints can be used to make greeting cards, gift tags, holiday wrapping paper and a number of items with gift potential, such as stationery or wall hangings.

And think of all the delicious ways you can enjoy those liberated spuds!
Idea by: Judi Benvenuti, Feltwell American School, Feltwell, England.
Christmas and Hanukkah

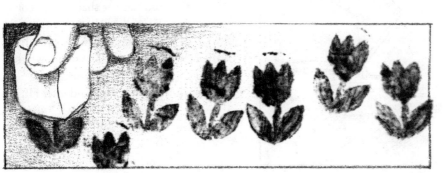

No. 112

RAINBOW-WRAP TISSUE PAPER

Science and art blend effectively in this color-mixing activity. And the final product comes in handy for the holiday season. You'll need: white tissue paper, food coloring (red, yellow, blue) and shallow containers for colors (jar lids are good for this).

Before the project begins, students might observe and discuss colors in nature — fruits, vegetables, flowers, animal coverings — and colors in the man-made world. Which colors are easier to describe and name? Why? How many different colors (crayons or jars of paint) do students think they need to make a true-to-life picture of their classmates? Suppose they had only red, yellow and blue — how many colors in their classmates' outfits do they think they could match?

The rainbow-wrap process begins with preparing the paper. Each child takes a sheet of tissue paper and folds it back and forth to make a fan. The strips should be about 2½ inches wide.

Have the children fold their strips as if folding a flag for storing. All folds should be pressed firmly. The final shape is a triangle.

Provide a number of areas for the coloring phase. It would be best if each pair of children could have a set of the three colors.

The coloring process is a matter of dipping each corner of the triangle into one or two colors. Encourage the children to try mixing. They may have particular results in mind, but they should expect things to "just happen" as well.

Children may decide they'd like to mix up containers of secondary colors before starting to dip. (They can try out these colors with small strips of tissue paper.) But many will dip-mix — put a corner into yellow then into blue. (Light colors before dark seem to work best.) A soft, fuzzy, pastel effect can be achieved by dipping triangles quickly into water first, then into the colors.

When all the dipping is done, children carefully unfold the triangles until they are back into long strips. (Don't open papers out flat yet.) Have the children look carefully at the patterns and color mixtures. Any surprises?

Each strip is then placed inside a newspaper sandwich and ironed with a warm iron. (You'll be the one doing this part of the project, of course, if you have younger children.) Now the strips can be opened out into flat sheets. What new patterns appear? More surprises?

Allow the sheets to become almost dry, then iron them again between newspaper.

While the first sheets are drying, take students on a "field trip" among the projects to observe, discuss and share dipping techniques. Your science/art students will very likely discover new ideas they'd like to investigate with a second sheet of paper — to see if they too can get that special color or design. Encourage them to rainbow-wrap as many sheets for which you have the time and supply. The rainbow-wrap tissue paper makes lovely wrapping paper for holiday gifts. And after all, 'tis the season!

Idea by: Carol Chesley, University of Vermont, Burlington, Vt.

Christmas and Hanukkah

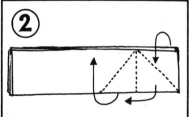

No. 114

URBAN RENEWAL GOES HISTORICAL

No. 113

SILKSCREEN CARDS

Tis the season . . . and here is an easy way of designing and printing original greeting cards for the holidays, or any occasion. (From *Shopping Cart Art*, Collier Books.)

Make a screen by stretching some thin, transparent or transluscent material — such as an old nylon stocking — over an embroidery hoop and fasten it tightly with a rubber band.

On a sheet of paper the same size as the hoop, draw the outline of the design you want to use on the greeting cards.

Place the hoop upside down over the sketch and outline the drawing on the fabric with a dark colored crayon, pressing down heavily.

Place the screen over the greeting card paper and pour thick tempera or finger paint onto the screen. Use a match folder or a piece of cardboard as a squeegee to pull the paint across the screen.

The paint will pass through the fabric everywhere except on the crayoned design. The process can be repeated to make many cards in a variety of colors.

Christmas and Hanukkah

While rote memorization of the dates of British monarchs from Egbert onwards may not be required by your curriculum, there probably are at least a few names and events you feel students should be able to recognize and locate in time — give or take a few hundred years. But keeping track of historical data is often a ponderous, confusing task.

One approach to organizing certain bits of history — one which provides a helpful focus — is urban renewal on a historical theme. Suggest that each student choose a state capital (U.S. history) or the capital of any country (world history). Then announce that the center of each of these cities needs to be completely redesigned and rebuilt. Each student gets a chance to develop and present a master plan for the renewal of the downtown area of his or her chosen city. Stress that the city's center should reflect the great achievements and noted personalities of the city's (or state's or nation's) past.

The students determine for themselves what will be memorialized and by which means — street names, parks, monuments, schools, museums. When the planning is complete, students map

out their renewed city center with labels indicating the commemorative structures. Then students prepare background materials explaining the rationale for their memorials.

Though most memorials will honor well-known people or events, an occasional off-beat, purely local commemoration would be fun.

As students share their city plans, they may be able to attach history to places for easier recall. They may also discover that some famous people pop up in a number of different cities. How many renewed capitals wind up with Franklin Squares or Lincoln Parks? If your students are enthusiastic about their individual projects, suggest a group undertaking. Have the class redesign their own city or town center. Make it a historical free-for-all. Memorials may honor revolutionary patriots, great reformers, or just local heroes and heroines of old.

Idea by: James W. McCoy, Farrer Junior High School, Provo, Utah.

December 12

No. 115

MAGNETS: THE REPULSIVE SIDE

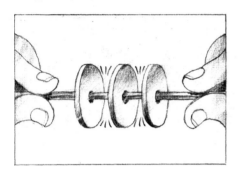

Magnet activities are nice to reserve for indoor weather when you need to "attract" short attention spans. The magic of magnets is always a crowd pleaser. But as attractive as the standard "look-what-the-magnet-picks-up" activities are, there's another side to be explored.

Get some repulsive discovery started by using the "no-visible-means-of-support" gimmick. You'll need eight doughnut-shaped magnets (three-eighths-inch-hole size; rubberized magnets are durable and not too expensive) and a couple of pencils fixed upright in wooden (or cardboard or Styrofoam) bases.

Start with four magnets in a stack in your hand. (Note: Magnets will not lie quietly in a stack unless attracting surfaces — opposite poles — are in contact.) Now slip magnet number one over the pencil and let the doughnut slide down to the base. Then, one at a time, slide the other magnets onto the pencil. Clunk. Nothing new here.

Moving along, go to pencil number two with the other stack of four magnets. Slide the first magnet on as before. But this time, *turn magnet two over* before slipping it on the pencil. No clunk this time. The magnet hangs suspended on the pencil shaft, not touching the magnet below. Slip the third magnet on as is; then, turn over the last magnet before sliding it on the pencil, and you'll have a column of "floating" magnets.

The "show" part is now officially over. Let the inquiry begin:
● What happens when you try pushing the magnets together with your fingers?
● What do you observe about the amount of space between the pairs of magnets? (Note to person coordinating the inquiry: The illustration shows that the bottom magnets are closer together than the top ones. Cumulative weight is pushing on the lower ones. Even though the magnets don't touch each other, their weight is a factor. If you remove the pencil from the base and hold it as you slide the magnets on one at a time in an alternating pattern, you can feel the weight increasing.)
● What happens to the spacing when you turn the pencil on its side? (With the factor of cumulative weight eliminated, the spacing should equalize.)
● Take off the top magnet and move it near the suspended ones — up, down and around the rims — to see if anything happens.
● What about the rim of the magnet — does it seem to have any kind of force?
● If magnets are not already marked, devise a system that will allow you to know ahead of time which surfaces are going to repel each other.

And so on.

Idea by: Philip White, Queens College, Flushing, N.Y.

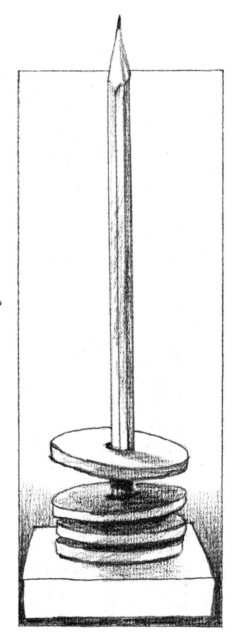

No. 116

PAINTING IS THE ATTRACTION

The concept of the magnetic field surrounding magnets can be reinforced by creating magnetic-field paintings. The materials needed are newspapers, heavy gauge construction paper, spray paint, a straightedge, iron filings and at least one magnet. A number of different-shaped magnets, though, is a plus.

After placing the magnet on a newspaper-covered tabletop, cover it with a sheet of construction paper. Sprinkle iron filings on the paper. Students can then explore the force of the magnetic attraction by tapping the paper lightly and allowing the filings to be moved by the magnet. When the filings have taken the shape of the magnetic field, you're ready to apply a bit of color.

Carefully and from a distance, spray a light coat of paint over the entire sheet of construction paper (too close may disturb the filings; too heavy will make the paper sticky and difficult to work with). Allow the paint to dry about five minutes. Then, with the straightedge, gently rake the iron filings from the paper. The results are a silhouette, spatter-painting style, of a magnetic field—and an unusual piece of art.

Students may want to try a variety of colors of both paint and paper. Contrast is important, of course, in achieving a boldly defined design. Using different-shaped magnets will also create a variety of designs.
Idea by: Bob Windham, Dunn Elementary School, Arlington, Tex. ▨

No. 117

VERY ATTRACTIVE EXPERIENCES

What will a magnet pick up? Here are two activities (from *Science Experiences for Young Children: Magnets*, Teachers College Press) to help kids find out.

For the first activity, you need a timer, and a magnet for each participant (work with groups of six to eight children). Check the room beforehand to become familiar with the objects a magnet will attract; this will enable you to give clues to children who may have difficulty finding an object.

Give each child a magnet and explain that the children have three minutes to find objects a magnet will pick up or attract. Advise them to use their magnets to touch *all parts* of the objects. Tell them to bring all movable objects to the science area.

Set the timer to go off in three minutes. At the end of three minutes, gather the objects and, as the children test them, ask questions:

Why does the magnet pick up that object?

Why won't the magnet pick up the object when you touch it here? (It may be that only a part of the object is metal, e.g., a metal spoon with a plastic handle.)

Why does this object fall off the magnet when you pick it up? (The magnet may not be strong enough to hold it.)

After the children have tested and talked about the objects, ask them if they found any magnetic objects that they could not move. Discuss these objects (pipes, refrigerator, radiator).

The second activity requires the following materials: construction paper for making fish; various magnetic and nonmagnetic materials (paper clips, nails, washers, small magnets, etc.; cloth, pieces of crayon, tape, etc.) to attach to the fish; sticks, string and magnets for making "fishing poles."

"Make several fish out of construction paper. Tape one kind of material to the head of each fish. . . . Put out about six fishing poles with magnets attached to the ends of the strings.

"Allow the children to play a 'Go Fishing' game. Observe those children who test each fish and those who only choose fish they know they can 'catch.' When all the fish have been caught, throw them back in the 'pond' and play again." ▨

No. 118

PLANE FUN—METRIC STYLE

With winter weather closing in, you may need an activity that uses pent-up energies and invites creativity—with metric practice added for good measure.

Challenge your students to build a better paper airplane—one that can travel a long distance. Each student designs his or her own—from experience, with the help of resource books or by pure aerodynamic intuition. And because there's no way to know how a plane flies without trying it out, plan to provide opportunities for test flights before staging a final contest.

On the day of the contest, have students measure a course 20 meters long in the gym. (You may want several "lanes" if your class is large.) Put markers along the course at 5-meter intervals. The markers should be readily visible from the starting line.

Now for the contest! Each student is entitled to two flights down the course. When the plane lands after the first flight, the pilot estimates the distance the plane went, using the markers as rough guides. Then the pilot measures, first determining the point on the course that is even with the plane's landing site, then measuring the distance from the nearest marker to that point. The distance is carefully recorded in meters and centimeters. Having "officials" to verify the distances and to record the data on a master chart may encourage accuracy—and also provide materials for graphing activities.

The better of each student's two tries becomes that student's bid for the title of long distance champ.
Idea by: Jim Heus and Jean Taranta, Friends' Central School, Philadelphia, Pa.

December 10

No. 119

METRIC FAIR

Why not have a little celebration and welcome in the entire metric system. Its anniversary is December 10.

Students can help set up a metric midway. Games involving a hierarchy of points—ring toss, darts and variations thereof—can be labeled with metric measures. Possible activities might be guessing the weights of various items in grams, the circumference of a cake in centimeters, the capacity of a bucket in liters, the temperature inside or outside (each within a stated range) in degrees Celsius, or drawing a line of a specified length. A guess-your-weight or guess-your-height concession might run a brisk trade if you have an estimator equal to the task. And for thrill-seekers, how about a sponge throw—a 360-gram water-loaded sponge from four meters, five meters or whatever—at the victim of your consensus?

Athletic contests could be a part of the program too, with all distances and weights in metric, of course. As a test of agility and compatibility, see how many people can stand in a one-meter square. Use your creativity for other odd events.

You'll probably even start figuring how to portion out eatables in grams, or estimating the number of servings per liter of punch, once you start (and we hesitate to say it) thinking metric.
Idea by: Paul Hampel and Bill Stein, AMY Learning Community, Philadelphia, Pa.

December 10

No. 120

BOTTLE GRAPHS

Bottle graphing provides practice in metric measuring and graphing, and also gives kids a chance to develop puzzles they can challenge their friends with.

Materials:

1. a collection of bottles in a variety of distinctive shapes. You might have one or two straight-sided containers, but the rest should have angles, curves, bulges and "wasp waists."

2. a measuring cup—calibrated in milliliters—with a pouring lip. (You may have to use one marked in fluidounces and make the conversion: 1 fluidounce equals 30 milliliters.)

3. a 30-centimeter ruler.

4. two or 3 liters of water colored with food coloring.

5. graph paper and lined paper.

Procedure: Set up a bottle-filling, bottle-graphing center with directions similar to these for the students to follow:

1. Choose a bottle to graph and make a rough sketch of it.

2. Prepare a chart with two columns: one headed "milliliter"; the other, "height in centimeters."

3. Fill measuring cup with colored water to the 30-milliliter mark and empty it into the bottle.

4. Measure the height of the water level and record the data on your chart.

5. Continue steps 3 and 4 until the bottle is filled.

Pause for discussion: When the water reaches a place where the sides of the bottle bulge out, does the water level rise more quickly or more slowly than where the sides are straight?

Where the sides curve inward to make a skinny place, does this affect the way the water rises? How?

6. On your graph paper, draw axes and plot milliliters along the horizontal axis, centimeters along the vertical axis.

7. Take the data from your chart and plot points for your graph. Connect the points.

Compare your sketch of the bottle's shape with your finished graph. What does the graph curve look like where the bottle is straight sided? Where it is

skinny? Where it bulges most?

Look around at other graphs. Can you spot one with a pattern similar to yours? Is its bottle a similar shape too? What about the size of the other bottle compared with yours?

Following up: You might use completed graphs to set up a matching game. Label each graphed bottle with a letter. Number each graph. See if students can match the graphs and bottles.
Idea by: Randall J. Souviney, University of California at San Diego, San Diego, Calif.

December 10

No. 121

FESTIVE SYMBOLS OF LIGHT

Apollo and his fiery steeds were responsible for the life-giving powers of the sun, according to the early Greeks. The ancient Egyptians, Babylonians, Incas and Aztecs worshipped the sun. The retreat of the sun each winter made ancient peoples apprehensive, and they greeted lengthening days with joyful festivities. Many believe that the

gloomy Stonehenge sun temple was oriented to the rise of the sun on the year's longest day. Even today Danish people celebrate that day in June with huge bonfires.

Some research and a lot of imagination can furnish the resources for some older students to dramatize their version of an ancient festival to welcome the sun's return. Original songs, dance, choral speaking and, of course, the use of lights can be part of the ceremonies.

Light is very much a part of the symbolism of religious writings and ceremonies today. Children may enjoy sharing experiences from their own traditions concerning the use of lights or

candles, particularly for holidays or other special occasions. You may call on community resource people to add further light to the subject.

Light is important in the observance of the midwinter holy days, Christmas and Hanukkah. Children might like to create some holiday greeting cards using the symbolism of candles and light in art and words.

Some individuals may want to research other customs involving the use of lights: Where may "eternal flames" be found? Why do we use candles in birthday celebrations? When did the tradition of the Olympic torch begin?

Christmas and Hanukkah

No. 122

HOLIDAY MATH PROBLEMS

In this problem-producing project, kids work out the mathematics of "what I want for Christmas." At the same time, they get more practice in reading and understanding what to do with a problem as well as extra practice in calculation. And you get what you want—a sizable supply of new math problems!

Start by gathering ads from newspapers and old magazines; cut out 100 to 200 pictures of products and their prices—choosing items that fall into the "most likely to be devoutly desired" department, e.g., minibikes, tape decks and the like. Have each student choose a picture or two and create several problem situations involving each product, using the price information given. (Ads with installment-buying data offer a special challenge.) Writing more than one problem for a picture allows for some selectivity; you can help each student choose the problem version he or

she feels is best, and you'll be better able to vary the types of problems represented in the total collection.

As an added incentive you might make provision for kids to use a calculator to work out the arithmetic of their own problems, recording the results for an answer key.

Students then set up their cards (5-by-7 size is good), copying off the problems they've selected and attaching the appropriate pictures to each card. You may want to devise a system of coding cards to facilitate use of the answer key.

Everyone gets a chance to try someone else's problem card(s) and some students may decide they'd like to create more. Here's one time when having lots of problems can only be a plus.

Idea by: Jim Bettendorf, North Junior High, St. Cloud, Minn.

Christmas and Hanukkah

No. 123

SANTA WORK BAGS

Heigh ho, the holidays! It's the time when spirits become so spirited that it's almost impossible for you to steer young minds toward any kind of work. Perhaps the children will have more success in steering each other.

During the last week of school before vacation, invite each child to prepare a Santa Work Bag for a secret pal— whose identity won't be known until the last morning of school. Into the bag go things to do: review questions (for which "Santa" must also prepare an answer key), puzzles, cartoons, original dot-to-dot pictures, etc.

Post guidelines so that the work bags will have similar contents—at least in number and kinds of tasks. For example, you might have each student create: five math computation problems, five math word problems, five dictionary questions, five sentences to finish and punctuate, five map questions, two health questions, etc.

Creating the materials and decorating the work bags call for considerable concentration, and the ingenuity shown can be marvelous.

On the big day, hold a name drawing and distribute the Santa Work Bags—to the delight of both givers and receivers. These collections of activities will provide enjoyable and educational diversions to launch everyone on a happy holiday vacation.

Idea by: Janet A. Lundquist, Washington School, Burlingame, Calif.

Christmas

No. 124

SECRET PAL MYSTERY GIFTS

A gift of something imaginary can be almost as exciting to young children as the real thing—especially if there's an element of magic involved.

Prepare slips of paper with the names of class members and have the children draw names for secret pals. Ask the children to think hard about what they'd give their secret pals if it were possible to give the most wonderful present in the whole world. Allow thinking time, but because the gifts are to be surprises, everyone must make plans privately.

When each child has the perfect gift in mind, the preparation can begin.

Materials:
1. 12-by-18-inch white paper
2. white crayons
3. crayons in other colors
4. large paint brushes
5. containers of watered-down tempera paints.

Procedure:
1. Have each child tape the slip telling the name of his or her pal on one corner of the paper—without letting anyone see—and turn the paper over.
2. With any color, the child draws the outline of a large gift box and adds a bright bow in a different color.
3. With the white crayon, the child writes his or her own name inside the box along the bottom edge. (Using white on white is a little tricky. Advise

the children to go slowly.)
4. The child then uses the white crayon to draw a simple outline picture of the gift he or she has decided to give.

When everyone has finished Step 4, ask a child to collect the papers. You may then read the name slips and have the children come up to receive their gifts.

5. Children use the large brushes to cover the gift boxes with thin paint. The gift and the giver's name magically appear on each paper.

A follow-up show-and-share session gives all the children a chance to tell what they got. This makes a magical gift-giving and gift-receiving time even more special.

Idea by: Patricia Mays, Ridley School District, Folsom, Pa.

Christmas and Hanukkah

No. 125

METRIC LABELS

Although most of us occasionally note the metric markings on product packaging, few of us remember the metric weight of a five-pound bag of sugar or the liter amount printed on a milk carton.

There are more metric labels around than we realize. Suggest that students look for them in the supermarket and at home. Have students create a metric scrapbook with labels from packages used in their homes. See how many kinds of labels your metric detectives can find—labels showing metric units of capacity, mass and length as well as the standard English units. Encourage the class to search out variety both in kinds of products and in package sizes.

Suggest that students save the full label rather than a cutout portion. This

way the label will reveal something about the size of the container—how tall, for instance, a 1.36-liter (46 ounce) can of tomato juice might be.

Have students collect a sizable number of labels before they start the pasting-in process. With a large quantity of labels they'll enjoy the challenge of analyzing their holdings and deciding on a system of classification; e.g., by kinds of products (food, medicine), by

kinds of measure (mass, capacity, length).

As the scrapbooks grow, some of the metric quantities may become more familiar. Try asking students for estimates of an item's mass or length once in a while—just to see how the metric thinking is coming along.

Idea by: Kathleen Ann Kutie, Black Junior High School, East Chicago, Ind.

December 10

No. 126

WORLD OF BOOKS TOURS

Popular "use-your-library" slogans tout the ability of books to carry readers to far-flung lands. You can put this idea into more tangible terms with a "World of Books" center.

The center features a collection of books and a large world map with construction paper arrows on it. Cut out paper arrows and on each write the title of one of the books. Place the arrows on the map so that each points to the general area in which the story is set. (You may want to reinforce the geographical side of the project by writing the name of the country, city, island, etc., on the arrow.)

If *Charlotte's Web* and similar stories of unnamed or imaginary settings are in the book collection, you'll need to add a new continent — appropriately named — to the map.

Travelers need tickets, and so as travel agent, you'll need to have some ready. These can be a duplicated form with a place for the name of the passenger and, below that, three columns: "Flight Schedule," "Arrival Date" and "Departure Date." Place tickets in a packet attached to the map.

Student travelers browse through the book collection and then plan their tours. They write the names of countries to be visited (titles of books they'd like to read) under Flight Schedule. When a student finishes reading a book, he can write the date under Arrival Date. The Departure Date indicates the time when the student has finished an activity suggested as follow-up on the book. The travel agent punches the ticket for each leg of the tour (book and follow-up activity) a traveler completes.

New book collections mean new arrows, new ports of call. Students interested in visiting places not within the "itinerary" of the book collection may check with the librarian to see what books might fill the bill.

Although travelers through the World of Books won't have to contend with strikes, lost luggage or customs regulations, they may have to put up with standby status and schedule changes if they find some popular locations (stories) overbooked — or in this case, underbooked.

Set up your center before the winter holidays. Then kids can take home a book during the break and *really* go somewhere this vacation.

Idea by: Carol Pelletier, Burkland School, Middleboro, Mass.

No. 127

CLASS-TO-CLASS CATERING

Parties can mean both hilarity and hectic times in primary grade classrooms. Your students can come to the rescue of a first grade teacher and prevent party-poop symptoms from setting in.

Giving a party provides older students (say fourth graders and up) with experience in organizing, calculating, cooperating and sharing.

• *Gifts*. If this is a gift-giving occasion, the fourth graders might make gifts ahead of time for the first graders. Colorful homemade jigsaw puzzles can be made from large magazine pictures. Temporarily mount each picture on cardboard and trim the backing as close to the exact size of the picture as possible. Spread watered-down white glue border-to-border over the surface of the cardboard and carefully smooth the picture in place. Press under heavy books overnight. Then cut the mounted picture into large puzzle pieces, place it in an envelope or box labeled with the puzzle's title and wrap it as a gift.

• *Entertainment*. A group of students

can plan activities and gather equipment for several games that appeal to young children. "Pin the Nose on the Snowman" might be a good one. Another group might select a story to read aloud.

Some students may wish to work up entertainment using their special talents—magic tricks, a yo-yo demonstration.

All facets of entertainment will need to be coordinated and scheduled according to a time allotment.

• *Refreshments*. These may be planned by a small group. The class as a whole can determine whether bringing food will be a volunteer effort or snacks will

be bought with money provided by minor fund raising.

There might be an exchange of correspondence between the classes before the party date; e.g., letters from the first graders to the fourth grade "Santa's Elves," who will answer in carefully worded and artistically decorated messages.

On the big day, fourth grade crews set up game centers and refreshment centers while first graders are out of the room.

Idea by: Karen W. Gronau, Baltimore, Md.

Christmas and Hanukkah

No. 128

TRACK TRACERS

When a science class takes up tracking, the focus is usually on animal tracks—the trail of a deer, the travels of a mouse. But there are many other kinds of tracks to observe and learn from.

Suggest that children look for signs that indicate people and vehicles have passed by. Ask children to describe

what they see and to speculate about the track makers and the conditions when the tracks were made: large feet, ski boots, old tires, snow tires, sled runners; walking, running; deep tracks, blurred tracks; muddy, windy.

Sharpen track-observing skills by playing How Did I Move? This game can be appealing to young children and can be played in snow or sand. Establish a GO line and a STOP line. Have all players but one, the trailblazer, turn their backs to the GO/STOP course and close their eyes.

The trailblazer moves—using any sort of footwork he or she chooses—from GO to STOP.

The other children then turn and try to determine if the trailblazer hopped, ran, walked, galloped, etc. Have the children examine the spacing, depth and direction of the tracks. After the trail-making method is guessed—the guessers can show or tell the way they think the trail was made—another trailblazer is chosen.

Idea by: Frank Watson and Christian Watson, Underhill, Vt.

CRAFTS

No. 129

"STAINED GLASS" ORNAMENTS

Colorful and not so fragile as the ornaments they imitate, these creations are easily made from white glue. The project is carried out in three sessions.
Materials:
- white glue
- food coloring
- heavy cardboard cut into 8-by-10-inch pieces
- plastic wrap
- black rug yarn
- heavy-duty needle
- clear nylon thread
- plastic cups and spoons

- pencils, scissors, tape, toothpick
Session 1: Making the outline and frame:

Each child draws a design on a piece of heavy cardboard. The picture should be *very simple*, not too large overall, and composed of large, closed shapes.

Cover the cardboard *tightly* with plastic wrap and tape it securely on the back of the cardboard.

Follow the pencil lines — visible through the plastic — with glue and carefully fix rug yarn in place over all the lines. The yarn must adhere securely to the plastic wrap because the yarn forms the compartments into which a glue mixture will be poured.

Let designs dry overnight.
Session 2: Filling the stained glass:

To prepare the stained glass mix, pour white glue into several plastic cups. Drop food coloring into the glue to make each cup a different color. Mix each cup well but slowly to avoid bubbles; skim off those that form.

Carefully spoon the glue mixture into the compartments created by the yarn. Fill the compartments, making sure that the mixture touches the yarn all the way around. Gently push the mixture against the yarn walls with a toothpick. (Don't overfill, or one section will flow into another.)

When all areas are filled, let the ornament dry *away from the sun* for several days — until all areas become translucent and hard.
Session 3: Removing the ornament:

When the ornament is completely hard and clear, gently lift its edges and pull off the cardboard foundation. It should come off easily. If it sticks to the plastic, wait another day or two. Then trim off the excess plastic wrap with scissors.

Thread the needle with clear nylon and poke a hole in the ornament near the edge to make a hanger. Put the ornament in the window and let the sun shine through.
Idea by: Gwen Malamud, Des Moines, Iowa.

Christmas

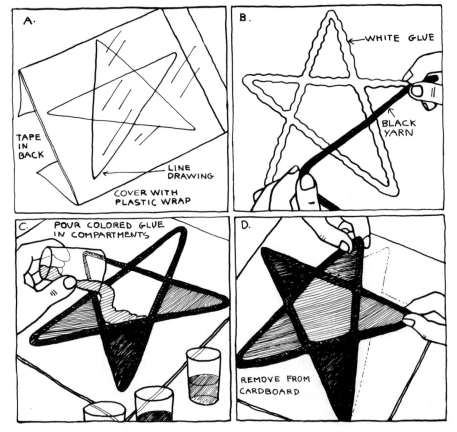

A. TAPE IN BACK — LINE DRAWING — COVER WITH PLASTIC WRAP

B. WHITE GLUE — BLACK YARN

C. POUR COLORED GLUE IN COMPARTMENTS

D. REMOVE FROM CARDBOARD

No. 130

CORK CRAFT

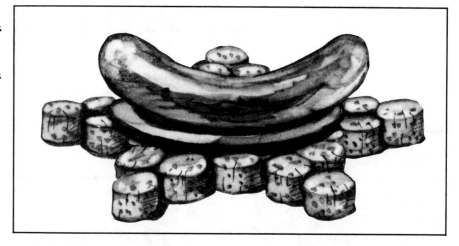

For this project you'll need three things: waterproof white glue, a sharp knife, and lots and lots of corks. And since the activity does depend on such a large supply of corks (about 15 per child), lining up likely sources is important. (Cork *does* grow on trees, of course, but you'll have to go about your collecting in a more roundabout fashion.)

Contact local restaurateurs about your project and, if they're sympathetic to the cause, supply them with collection containers (milk cartons decorated by members of the class).

The corks will be used to construct hot dish mats for the table. First, each cork must be sliced in half, crosswise, with the sharp knife. (You'll probably want to ask aides or older students to help with this, or you may develop cork cutter's cramp.)

The students can then arrange and glue together cork halves to make a geometric or free-form-shaped mat, being careful to keep the cork ends even for a flat-against-the-table surface. Allow the glue to set firmly.

And by the way, how much does your class know about this art material they're working with? You might have them do some research into how and where cork is grown, its processing and uses. (These investigations might go on during the cork collection phase of the project.) Students may decide to formulate a brief commentary on cork, to be included with the finished mats — after the fashion of discerning craftspersons.

As well as being attractive and intriguing, the cork mats have gift potential of a quite practical nature — much to the delight of the home-folk recipients.

Idea by: Vicki Briggs, Bitburg Elementary School, Germany.

Christmas and Hanukkah

No. 131

"STAINED GLASS" CANDLE HOLDER

For gifts or just for decorations that can be put together in a fairly short — though somewhat sticky — craft period or two, have the kids try making some candle holders in simulated stained glass. (The project calls for patience in dealing with gluey tissue paper and could be frustrating for "hurry-up" types.)

Materials:

1. Baby food jars — the small kind.
2. Scraps of colored tissue paper.
3. Elmer's glue, slightly thinned.
4. Brushes.
5. Black markers.
6. Candles — about ¾ inch, or 2 cm, in diamater, to be cut into short lengths.

Procedure:

1. Cut tissue paper into small, straight-sided pieces. Provide containers for keeping the various colors separate from one another.
2. Coat the outside of the jar with a thin layer of glue.
3. Apply a tissue piece and recoat the area with glue — for shine and to keep the paper smooth.
4. Keep applying pieces of tissue paper (they may overlap some) until the jar is covered.
5. To make a neat rim, wind string around the neck of the jar, fixing the ends in place with tape.
6. Allow to dry. Then trace each colored shape with a black marker to give the stained-glass effect.
7. Cut candles to a length that's no longer than half the height of the jar. Fix the candle upright in the jar by setting it into soft wax drippings.

The effect of the lighted candle is quite remarkable. The light glowing through the colors transforms the tissue-pasted jar into a fascinating and decorative display.

Idea by: Patricia E. N. Mays, Ridley Schools, Folsom, Pa.

Christmas and Hanukkah

No. 132

ANTLERS FOR ORNAMENTS

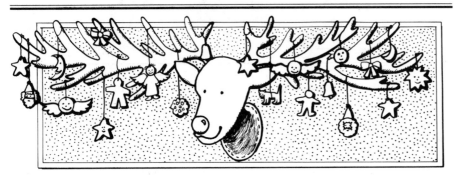

What more appropriate way is there to display your kids' holiday ornaments and winter snowflakes than to suspend them from Rudolph's sturdy antlers? Here's a bulletin board that does just that.

Rudolph's head can be little more than a two-dimensional construction paper facsimile with a small red tree ornament for a nose. But if you're more ambitious, make a three-dimensional Rudolph by covering a wire form with papier mache and painting the head when the construction has dried.

Whether Rudolph is two- or three-dimensional, you do want his antlers to extend out from the bulletin board so that ornaments hang freely. Cut out a set of branching antlers from heavy cardboard. Tape a long piece of curved wire across the back in several places so that the antlers curve toward you from the front. Either pad the antlers with papier mache and paint them, or bind them with closely wound ribbon. Yoke both sides of the antlers with fishline at points where the antlers fork. Slip the yoke over a large tack strategically placed so that the antlers will sit centered above Rudolph's head on the board. Have your kids decorate his antlers with crafted ornaments.

Christmas

No. 133

A QUILT THAT SPREADS THE WORD

Here is a plan that helps students keep track of their library reading, and at the same time encourages further reading by helping to spread the word about books students have enjoyed. Each book finisher gets a chance to create a "quilt" square to represent the just-read book, then adds the square to a growing patchwork reading quilt that covers up a classroom bulletin board.

Provide white construction paper cut into 9-by-9-inch squares. The block should be designed by the student in such a way that it can carry the book's title and author. But the major portion of the square will be devoted to an illustration or design that suggests what impressed the reader most about that book. The artwork can be done in crayon, tempera, or may be assembled from cut paper — for that authentic, pieced-together look.

Each student also prepares a paragraph or two telling about the book and perhaps explaining the symbolism used in his or her quilt block. These paragraphs, keyed to the appropriate quilt blocks by number, are collected into a reference notebook that should be stationed near the quilt display. These "reports" are for the benefit of others who, intrigued by some quilt block, may want to see what the book behind it has in store.

The ever-expanding quilt may occupy a fair amount of bulletin board space, something that needs to be planned for. But as a reference work, or even an open-house conversation piece, the patchwork reading quilt earns its territory.

Idea by: Dorean Kimball, Central Elementary School, Penacook, N.H.

No. 134

GRAPHIC HOLIDAY

Holidays often inspire stimulating reading, creative writing and art activities. Why not extend the holiday theme to include a graph-making project?

Use a small but festive sign to introduce a different holiday topic each morning: What is your favorite holiday _____ ? (song, story, food, etc.).

Show the class a ditto sheet with five horizontal bars, each divided into a labeling space on the left followed by about 15 measured blocks. As a class, decide on four or five choices as answers to the day's question. Print one choice in each labeling space. (If the children are beginning readers, include a small sketch beside each label.)

The ditto sheet should be centrally located so that each child can go to it sometime during the day and color in a single block on the bar of his or her choice.

Another approach is to have one student be in charge of administering the survey. This person must seek out and record classmates' opinions during lunch, recess or an activity period. At the end of the day, the student conducting the poll presents the finished graph and describes the results.

A bulletin board displaying the accumulated graphs will be sure to stimulate discussion. Students may also want to graph their own year-round survey ideas.

Idea by: Glenna Giveans, Sacred Heart School, Lebanon, N.H.

Christmas

RESOURCES

METRIC HEIGHT MEASUREMENT—What better place to begin thinking metric than with oneself? Students can use these two metric measuring tools to determine their own and each other's height.

Metric Height Measurement Chart. This is, very simply, a colorful, nicely designed chart made of glossy paper and measuring two full meters. (That's about six feet, six inches.) The chart is taped or tacked to a wall and a child stands with his or her back to it. The teacher or a student partner marks the student's height by holding a flat object on top of the student's head and seeing where it touches the chart.

The uncluttered chart is clearly delineated into centimeters and meters. It is also marked at every five centimeters and at each half meter.

Metrimeasure. A much more "official" type of measuring device, this one is similar to the kind you see attached to the scale in the doctor's office. It is a free-standing, hard plastic post with a slide that adjusts to sit atop a student's head. Small arrows inside a window of the slide point to the measured height. This measure is marked into meters (not quite two full ones), decimeters, centimeters and half centimeters.

Order from: Creative Publications, P.O. Box 10328, Palo Alto, CA 94303.
Grade Level: Primary–high school.

BOOKS FOR KIDS—
● *An Edwardian Christmas.* John S. Goodall. Illustrated by the author. McElderry/Atheneum. Recommended reading for the primary grades.
● *Christmas Crafts: Things to Make the 24 Days Before Christmas.* Carolyn Meyer. Illustrations by Anita Lobel. Harper & Row. Recommended reading and activities for the intermediate grades.
● *A Christmas Card.* Paul Theroux. Illustrations by John Lawrence. Houghton Mifflin. Recommended reading for the intermediate grades.
● *The Winter Bear.* Ruth Craft and Erik Blegvad. Illustrations by Erik Blegvad. Atheneum. Recommended reading for the primary grades.
● *The FunCraft Book of Magnets & Batteries.* Heather Amery and Angela Littler. Illustrated by Zena Flax and Pierre Davies. Scholastic. Recommended reading and activities for the intermediate grades.

SAFE AND SIMPLE ELECTRICAL EXPERIMENTS—*Safe and Simple Electrical Experiments*, by Rudolf F. Graf, provides 101 activities useful for introducing the concept of electricity.

The experiments fall into three areas—static electricity, magnetism and current electricity, and electromagnetism—with about 30 to 40 demonstrations in each area. Every experiment is illustrated and includes an explanation of procedures, materials and results.

The experiments can be set up simply and most require few materials. Many provide fascinating, often amusing, results. For example, "Making a Paper Spider," a magnetism experiment, uses a small piece of cut newspaper and a piece of polyethylene (or clear plastic). Rubbing the newspaper with the plastic gives the paper an electric charge, causing it to dance around like a spider.

Order from: Dover Publications, 180 Varick St., New York, NY 10014.
Grade level: Teachers of grades 3–junior high.

1

New Year's Day.

2

First rocket launched to the moon in 1959 by the U.S.S.R.

3

First attempt to measure an ocean's depth using deep-sea sounding, 1840.

7

The Harlem Globetrotters basketball team played its first game in Hinkley, Ill., 1927.

8

Elvis Presley, known as the king of rock 'n' roll, born, 1935.

9

Louis Daguerre receives France's Legion of Honor award for his work in photography, 1893.

13

14

Albert Schweitzer, noted humanitarian, born in 1875.

15

Martin Luther King, Jr.'s birthday.

19

Confederate army general Robert E. Lee born, 1807.

20

21

Nautilus, the first atomic submarine, launched in 1954.

25

Journalist Nellie Bly breaks the *Around the World in Eighty Days* record in 1890.

26

First electric dental drill patented, 1875.

27

In 1967, three astronauts killed in *Apollo I* fire.

SIX

DAY BY DAY

4
Louis Braille, inventor of the Braille alphabet, born, 1809.

5
Nellie Ross took office in Wyoming, 1925. First woman governor in U.S. history.

6

Three King's Day.

10
Oil discovered in Texas, 1901.

11
Alexander Hamilton, first U.S. Secretary of the Treasury, born in 1757.

12

16
National Nothing Day.

17
Benjamin Franklin born, 1706.

18

Boxing great Muhammed Ali's birthday. Born 1942.

22
First novel, *The Power of Sympathy*, published in America, 1789.

23

National Handwriting Day.

24
Discovery of gold at Sutter's Mill, Calif., 1848.

28
First Emmy Awards, 1948.

29

The Seeing Eye, a guide dog foundation, organized in 1929.

30
Anniversary of the first jazz record made in 1917.

N.J. court rules that girls must be admitted to Little League teams, 1974.

31

No. 135

HAPPY BIRTHDAY EVERYBODY!

What if all our birthdays were celebrated together on January 1 of each year? Ask your students that question and you are sure to arouse a lot of surprise and indignation. But that is what happens to Thoroughbred race horses. No matter when they were born, all Thoroughbreds automatically become one year older on January 1.

Have your students research to find out why Thoroughbreds have a collective birthday. Then, have them hold a classroom debate on whether a collective birthday would be a better system for people. An evaluative vote at the end of the debate will determine which side presented the most persuasive — and original — arguments. You might propose that the class choose a day in the school year on which they will celebrate a collective birthday for those students whose birthdays fall in the summer months.

Idea by: Linda Allison, author of *The Wild Inside*, Sierra Club.

New Year's Day

No. 136

CONTINUOUS CALENDAR

Calendar time, divided into weeks, months and seasons, can be a cumbersome concept for young children to grasp. After all, for kids time rolls along quite smoothly, and calendar months do such strange things as stop right in the middle of a week.

Starting with January you have a chance to help demystify the calendar for your class. You'll need a fairly large display space and a new calendar that you don't mind cutting apart. You'll also need four sheets of tagboard (in four different colors), each large enough to hold three calendar pages mounted one below the other.

Mount January, February and March on one sheet of tagboard, fitting the final week of each month directly into the first week of the month that follows. In this way, there's no break in the flow of days. (Trace over the lines dividing the months to indicate where one ends and the next begins.)

Mount April, May and June on another sheet of tagboard and overlap the tagboard sheets so that March is fitted into April.

Fit the next 6 months together the same way you mounted the first 6. You could run the 12 months as an unbroken panel, but the top might be out of reading range; so you might break the calendar in half — January through June and July through December.

Complete the calendar by writing the names of the months beside — rather than above — each month.

Once constructed, the continuous calendar can become the regular all-purpose date keeper for classroom events and holidays. Or it can be used as a learning center along with packs of days-of-the-week cards, month cards and season cards in a variety of sequencing and classifying activities involving calendar time.

Idea by: Dorothy B. Lundstedt, Lawrence Township, N.J.

New Year's Day

CALENDAR COVER

POSITIVE-THINKING CALENDAR

"Calendar Cover" is a game that recycles not only old calendar pages, but also old day-by-day appointment calendars. (You may need two of these appointment calendars if they are of the sort that has days backing on each other.) Use the appointment calendar to make a deck of date cards containing a card for each day of the year.

Take apart a large calendar. Each month becomes a playing board. Each player gets a board and a pile of chips or markers. Designate "free" spaces ahead of time, or before each game have players draw several date cards to establish free spaces. You'll also need to determine the winning pattern of squares (for example, four squares in a line in any direction, all odd-numbered weekend dates).

Play begins when the caller draws a date card and calls it out: "Tuesday, October 24." Anyone with October's page gets to cover that number. The first player to cover the designated pattern of dates is the winner. (Watch youngsters get speedier in locating numbers as well as in recognizing days of the week.)

Many everyday items easily take on alternative idenitities as learning materials. Look around for items that provide something to read, directions to follow, numbers and numerals to work with, organizational patterns for children to discover and use. The tie-ins to familiar, basic learning tasks become clear when you're looking for them: a telephone directory becomes a treasury of classification and alphabetical lists; egg cartons become number sets; an ice cube tray becomes a study in fractional parts.

Idea by: Belinda Zobre, Cincinnatus School, Cincinnatus, N.Y.

New Year's Day

It's new calendar time—time to turn over a new leaf, to look ahead and make plans, to fill in the calendar with things to do. But wait a minute. Sometimes a things-to-do type calendar becomes a record of things planned for and not completed, or perhaps not so successfully completed. What about a calendar of a more hopeful sort—one you can actually take pleasure in rereading.

Each month provide students with their own individual calendar pages. (Or students can make a monthly project of creating their own personally designed calendar pages.) The space for each day should be large enough to write a sentence in. And at the end of each week row there should be a longer box for an end-of-week wrap-up.

This calendar is for jotting down *good* things, *positive* thoughts. At some point in each day students write in something good about the day—something that happened, something they achieved, something that they noticed or observed. A little artwork may be included too, if that seems appropriate.

If it happens to be "one of those days," students might write about something they *wish* would happen, or something they intend to work toward.

At the end of the week set aside some time for individual reflection on the week's entries and provide opportunity for writing some impressions of the week as a whole.

These calendars deserve the same respect and privacy shown a journal or diary—though students may elect to share items. (Be mindful that appreciating someone else's good fortune can be a sensitive matter.)

Of course, everyone has both bad and good days, and sometimes feeling bad just seems to be right. Maybe on those days a child might just recall and name a favorite thing (banana split, sledding, *Star Wars*) and let that serve as the "good" for that day.

Perhaps later on at some low moment, reviewing some of the "goods" will raise some spirits just a little. It can't hurt to try.

Idea by: Jane Stenger, Gemini School, Simi Valley, Calif.

New Year's Day

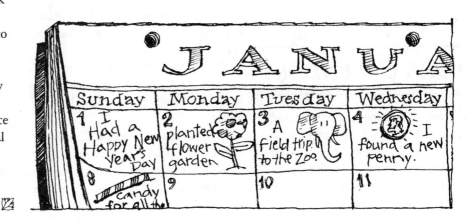

No. 139

PLANT PLANT

A greenhouse can bolster your winter science curriculum as well as brighten up your classroom. To create one, you'll need a tall bookcase (preferably taller than your students) with open shelves. Your room should have a large window located, if possible, near an electrical outlet and far from the classroom heat source. (If the windows are near the heat vents, try to divert the flow of heated air away from your greenhouse.)

Position the bookcase facing the window and about 4 or 5 feet from it. The window becomes one wall of the greenhouse; the bookcase, the opposite wall. You'll need clear plastic, 3 or 4 mils thick, to cover three walls and the top of your greenhouse. Leave the fourth side open for access and for air circulation, which will prevent mildew from forming. Before attaching the plastic to the window frame with small nails or staples, reinforce the edges of the plastic with cardboard. This should retard tearing.

The greenhouse will need continuous moisture. (Because a heated building is unnaturally dry, it is usually a poor environment for plants.) Moisture can be provided by a cold water vaporizer or humidifier. Or you may place plant pots in sturdy trays of gravel filled with water just to the tops of the stones.

Lights specially designed for growing plants or regular fluorescent lights installed over each shelf can extend the daylight exposure for the plants. Both lights and humidifier can be plugged into a timer to keep a stable environment during weekends, vacations and snow days.

Other equipment and supplies for the greenhouse might include: potting soil, vermiculite, peat moss, plastic pots in various sizes and — for students' individual projects — plastic or Styrofoam cups or foil-lined cigar boxes. Markers can be used to identify experimenters' cups and to record other pertinent data. **Idea by:** Julia Wood, McLean Elementary School, Wichita, Kans.

No. 140

ALIEN CALENDARS

The calendars of our planet are based on the trip the spinning Earth takes around the sun. For an out-of-this-world activity, have your students imagine that they are living on another planet in the solar system that has a very different orbital cycle. Have each kid design a calendar for his or her new home.

You might suggest that kids design a calendar that has a new shape, such as a circle or a triangle. Encourage them to invent special birthdays, anniversaries, events, names for the months, and so on for their planet calendars. Pose questions like these that will further tax their creativity and down-to-earth basic math skills:

How long — in Earth time — are your years?

How long are the seasons? How many are there?

How long is a day?

How old are you according to your planet's calendar?

Name some of the holidays you celebrate on your planet.

Idea by: Linda Allison, author of *The Wild Inside*, Sierra Club.

New Year's Day

No. 141

CANDY BOX COUNT

Here's an idea for recycling those left-over holiday candy boxes. A sectioned candy box makes an excellent gameboard that offers a variety of math activities. In this game it offers language practice as well.

Using a half-pound candy box with a stiff-sectioned paper divider (if no divider is available, make one with about 15 sections), glue the divider to the inside of the bottom of the box and label the bottom of each section with a letter, beginning with *A* and going as far through the alphabet as there are sections.

Next, cut a tagboard card slightly smaller than the box (for easy storage) and write on it three- or four-letter words spelled with letters that appear in the sections. After each word print an equals sign followed by a long blank. Laminate the card or cover it with clear Con-Tact paper so it can be written on with crayon and wiped clean with a paper towel. (A dittoed sheet can be used instead of a card.)

When the first child is ready to use the box, randomly distribute about 50 buttons (or beans or counters) in the different sections, put the top on and shake the box up and down. Have the student open the box and count the number of buttons in each of the letter sections that spell the first word on the card. Then have him add up all the buttons used in the word and write the total on the blank next to the word. Repeat the activity, going down the list of words on the card.

Children may wish to guess totals ahead of time, or shake the box, work the same words again and then compare the totals.

Idea by: Kathryn Kempf, Edgerton School, Roseville, Minn.

No. 142

SHAPE ORNAMENTS

Before you throw out all of this year's "Season's Greetings" cards, think about saving them for a lesson about shapes.

Collect ready-to-be-discarded cards and cut off the back panels (the part that contains the message). Have each student choose a card and cut it into the shape you are trying to reinforce: circle, square, rectangle, triangle, pentagon, hexagon, diamond, oval and so on.

On the back of the card, the student writes her name and the name of the shape. Then she punches a hole in the card and ties a length of colorful yarn through it.

The cutout shapes can be attached to a string that extends across the classroom. As new shapes are added, students can collect those they've already hung up and paste them into notebooks.

Idea by: Joan Sorensen, Sacred Heart/St. Anthony, Bridgeport, Conn.

No. 143

EXCUSES, EXCUSES

No teacher who listens daily to explanations about homework violations could ever doubt the inventiveness of kids. Just when you think you've heard every possible excuse, a gem shows up.

Because creating excuses for not doing homework is a task at which many students are already adept, why not propose a writing assignment that challenges students to come up with the most original, the most unlikely, the most fanciful, the most completely outrageous alibis for not getting homework in?

These excuses can take the form of several one-liners (you check your choice):

1. My brother has developed a rare disease, and all he can eat is fourth grade homework.

2. I turned my homework into a paper airplane, and the next thing I knew it had been hijacked.

Or a student may choose to tell the whole horrible story, starting the moment school got out (as many such tales of woe typically do) and describing the unfortunate, unhappy, troublesome or weird situations (throughout which the accused was heroically steadfast) that culminated in a missing paper.

If alibis seem to be a stimulating literary form for your students (particularly older ones), you might suggest that they write excuses for fictional characters or historical figures who slipped up. (They can lend authenticity to each person's alibi by incorporating appropriate details from the story or period.)

And at least you'll be somewhat prepared if some of these fabulous fibs show up in real-world homework confrontations.

Idea by: Trudy Whitman, St. Ann's School, Brooklyn, N.Y.

No. 144

COMMUNICATION WRITE-IN

A good way to practice writing skills is to take part in a write-in. What's a write-in? It's an entire class period when students communicate — with you and each other — only in writing.

The day before you hold your write-in, tell the students that they are not to talk at all once they enter the room the next day. Don't tell them any more than that. Then, before the next class, prepare and hang a number of quiet-inducing posters around the room: Silence Is Golden; Speak No Evil, Nor Anything Else. When the students enter the room, hand them each an instruction sheet with directions similar to the following:

1. Read all these directions before beginning.

2. You need at least three blank sheets of paper in addition to this paper.

3. Put your name at the top of each of those sheets of paper.

4. Do not write on *this* paper.

5. You will write to each person in your row at least twice during this class period.

6. Try to learn as much as possible about each person's interests, experiences and ideas. Write about something that interests you. Be imaginative in your questions. Try not to ask the same questions of each person.

7. Write as much as possible and still finish the tasks during this class period.

8. To begin, write a note to the person behind you. (If you are the last person in your row, write to the person in the front seat.) When you get a note from that person in return, write a second note to him or her to answer the questions and to react to the personal information that has been given. Then write to the next person in your row. Keep on until you have written and responded to every person in your row.

9. Write in full sentences.

10. On a separate sheet of paper, write something that you feel will be of interest to your teacher. You may write about yourself, about the class, about the assignment, about anything you would like her to know. You can work on this part of the assignment any time during the class period. Place the message on the teacher's desk.

11. Do not talk until ___. (*Give the time when period is over.*)

12. After the lesson, leave your notes on the teacher's desk.

13. If your teacher talks, you will have five minutes of visiting time in class tomorrow.

14. If something about this assignment is unclear, write your question on the paper on the teacher's desk. Begin.

A write-in provides an opportunity to practice following directions, writing for a specific purpose and self-discipline. It's great for those long winter days when something eventful is needed to break through the gloom.
Idea by: Jan Nielson, Coon Rapids Junior High School, Coon Rapids, Minn.

No. 145

RECIPES BY MAIL

January letters provide composition practice and bring materials for a springtime project by return mail.

Ask students to scan magazines and food boxes at home for recipe offers. Have them copy complete ordering information onto 3-by-5 cards. When you have one recipe offer for each student, distribute the cards.

Each student then writes a letter requesting a class quantity of recipes. Since some companies may not wish to fill requests for more than single copies (even though this may not be stated in the offer), a request including a polite "if possible" may help.

The second phase of the project takes place in spring. By then, students should have received a good supply of replies and recipes — which you will have stored away for safekeeping.

Have students clip pictures of luscious-looking foods from magazines and glue the pictures onto 12-by-18-inch sheets of heavy brown paper or oaktag. The bottom third of each sheet is folded up, and the two side edges are glued in place to form a pocket.

If possible, laminate the folders or cover them with clear Con-Tact paper. (Lamination seals the pocket, which then can be slit with a razor blade.)

Distribute the recipes for students to put into the folders. To finish the folder, fold the top down over the pocket and tie it closed with yarn or ribbon. The folders then become useful gifts for Mother's Day or can be presented to other favorite cooks in the students' lives.

What started out as a letter-writing project may lead to learning experiences in the kitchen too.

Idea by: Rosemary Stoelzel, Johnson School, El Paso, Tex.

No. 146

SEEDS OF SPRING

Nothing is more welcome on a gray winter day than the arrival of a bright (and free) seed company catalog bursting with beautiful pictures, plant lore and great expectations.

Just browsing through the colorful pages can be entertaining for primary grade children (and their teachers), but there are other ways in which seed catalogs can be useful.

1. *Learning about vegetables and fruits.* Have each child name a favorite fruit or vegetable and then look for it in the catalog. Why are some not listed in the catalog? What varieties are listed? How are the varieties different?

Children can add new names to the lists of fruits and vegetables they already know. The class might make a reference chart or booklet with names and pictures of fruits and vegetables.

Students can learn about colors as they learn about foods. Have them match colors with fruits and vegetables. Which fruits and vegetables come in several colors?

2. *Buying seeds.* Select a kind of plant that will grow well in the classroom. (What information does the catalog give about growing season, soil, light needs, watering?) Order seeds directly from the catalog. Have the children help complete and check the order. How long is it supposed to take for the seeds to come? Mark the date on the calendar.

3. *Word study.* Look through the catalog for useful and interesting words to study. The children might find words they'd like to know about: annual, perennial, mulch, cultivate.

4. *Plant lore.* As well as checking into requirements of plants for the classroom, children might investigate other plants' needs. Which plants grow well in shade? Which need lots of room? Which plants grow slowly?

What does the catalog tell about insect pests? See what other information about garden insects the children can find.

5. *Art.* After a catalog has been used for reading and research, it can be cut up for art projects.
- Cut out pictures of fruit to make a fruit basket picture.
- Cut shapes in many colors to use in a collage.
- Cut individual blooms to make a paste-on bouquet. Draw flower stems with a crayon and make a construction paper vase.
- Design a formal garden outlining shapes of flower beds on a sheet of paper and filling each with flower cutouts.

Idea by: Jo Fredell Higgins, Annunciation School, Aurora, Ill.

No. 147

HANDWRITING FRUIT BASKET

What's more sedentary than handwriting? Movement—other than from the elbow down—seems quite alien to the world of handwriting. But these unlikely partners can work together nicely, especially on a gloomy stay-inside January afternoon.

Simply write out a bunch of handwriting model cards—one sentence per card, one card per child. Make liberal use of whatever points of handwriting you're presently working on: special capital letters, joinings, loop letters, *a*'s and *o*'s—or perhaps it's time for some general review. It could be fun to slip in children's names, a joke or a riddle. If you are really inspired, you might write a series of sentences which, when properly sequenced, together read as a composite short story or coherent piece of narrative prose.

Tape one card to each child's desk. First, each child reads and copies down his or her own home desk sentence. Then comes the word: "Fruit basket's turned over!" Every child hurries to a different desk, just as in the familiar rainy-day recess game, except that in this case everyone carries along paper and pencil.

Once settled in the new desk, the child follows the same procedure as before, reading the sentence (and calming down a bit), then copying it.

Pencils down indicates that round two has been completed. Over goes the fruit basket again, and everyone is off in search of a new seat and a new sentence. Of course, nobody wants to have to repeat a sentence (it wouldn't hurt, but that's a different game), so each child needs to keep track of where he or she

has already been. If you have provided sentences, which together comprise text, have your students upon completion of the sentences try to correctly sequence them.

Movement and handwriting are both goals in Handwriting Fruit Basket, and as long as everyone remembers that, neither activity should overwhelm the other.

Idea by: Margaret H. Dabbs, N.H. Price Elementary School, Birmingham, Ala.

No. 148

CURSES!

Here's a handwriting game idea that should provide both practice and fun.

Materials: a large piece of tagboard for the gameboard; both white and colored tagboard or index cards (six colors are needed); a die; and markers or tokens (bottle caps work fine). Each player also must have writing paper and a pencil.

Preparation: Make a twisting pathway of blocks on the gameboard—125 blocks is a good number. Label about 10 blocks with the word "Chance." Leave room outside the pathway for six areas, each large enough for a pack of game cards. Number these card areas one to six.

The colored cards are for cursive writing tasks. Assign each color a number, one to six, and mark each card in a color set with its number. This color/number coding will show the level of difficulty of the tasks. Cards marked one, for instance, might call for writing a single letter; cards marked six might have a long word to write.

On one side of each card goes a letter or word printed in manuscript lettering. On the other side goes the same letter or word in cursive writing. (The cursive writing side of the card should be ruled off to resemble writing paper—for ease of checking letter position later on.)

The plain white cards are "chance" cards, carrying directions to go ahead or to go back. For example:

Nice note to Grandma. Go ahead three spaces.

Careless w's! Go back one space.

Super slant! Go ahead four spaces.

To play: Place colored cards on the gameboard, manuscript side up. Player 1 throws the die. The number that comes up indicates the number of spaces for the move and also the numbered card deck from which the player will draw. After drawing a card, the player must write in cursive writing whatever appears on the faceup side of the card. The player then turns the card over and compares his or her work with the cursive writing on the back of the card. The other players must agree that the writing is correct before the player may move down the pathway.

If in moving a player lands on "Chance," a chance card is drawn and its directions are followed.

The first player reaching the end of the pathway wins. Players may wish to add cards to the game, posing even tougher writing tasks to stump their worthy opponents.

Idea by: Gillian Quinby and Jill St. George, Shelburne Middle School, Shelburne, Vt.

January 23

No. 149

COLOR STROKES FOR LITTLE FOLKS

On charts that handwriting material companies provide for use as letter models there are often tiny numerals indicating the order in which pencil strokes are to be executed: (1) down, (2) around. Learning the steps in forming letters and numerals can be made a little easier if colors (rather than tiny numerals) are used to show the order of the strokes. Children soon associate red with the starting stroke, blue with the second stroke and so on.

Patterns can be introduced on the chalkboard with colored chalk or on an overhead transparency with water-base markers. Large charts can be used to reinforce the patterns. (You may want to include sets of objects on numeral charts to reinforce number concepts.)

You might also prepare smaller, laminated cards that children can trace over with wipe-off crayons. For another trace-over reinforcement, glue colored sand to individual blocks in the appropriate letter- or numeral-forming patterns.

Idea by: Marilyn Y. Doner, Syracuse, N.Y.

January 23

No. 150

STORIES-IN-THE-ROUND

Winter is traditionally a time for gathering around a warm fire for storytelling. Although you may not be able to simulate a hearth-like atmosphere in your classroom, you can create an atmosphere that is conducive to storytelling. These story-generating ideas are featured in *Creative Escapes: Adventures in Writing for Grades 7–12*, Pitman Learning.

Have the students arrange their desks and chairs in a close circle in the center of the classroom. In a clockwise direction, your students will spin a story-in-the-round, each contributing a few minutes worth of story elements — setting, conflict, action, climax, and resolution. Begin your story-in-the-round with one of your more inventive students. Provide some ground rules: No more than four individual characters may be included in the story, and only one character may be introduced to the story by an individual student. Each student may have two (or three) minutes to contribute to the story, or one minute if the story goes around the circle twice. Keep track of the story's progress so it doesn't bog down, and make sure all of the elements of a short story are present.

If you have a rather sophisticated group of students, you may want to try one of these variations. Discuss the literary scenarios for Chaucer's *Canterbury Tales* and Boccaccio's *Decameron* — a group of pilgrims setting out on a holy pilgrimage to Canterbury, and a group of young lords and ladies biding their time in the countryside as they await the liberation of their city from the Black Death. Encourage your class to create its own literary scenario or occasion for storytelling. Have each student assume the personality of a character in the given situation, and create a tale that the particular character would be likely to tell. Although this may initially be an oral storytelling activity, have the students write and refine their tales, and compile them in a classroom anthology.

Another literary variation will work well with your circular desk arrangement. Have each student write two or three paragraphs beginning a story, establishing the time, place, characters (no more than two), and initial conflict. The papers will be passed clockwise around the circle so each student can contribute to every other student's story. Establish a time limit within which students must add a paragraph to the story passed to them, then pass again until the stories have reached their originators. Have each student read a completed story-in-the-round during another class period.

No. 151

DREAM OR REALITY

As year after year we commemorate the efforts of Martin Luther King and other civil rights leaders on King's birthday, we begin to see that their dreams are coming true — to a degree. Perhaps this year, instead of that old standby, the "I Have a Dream" composition, you might have your students compare Martin Luther King's dream of the 1960s to the reality of the 1980s.

As a class, devise a list of social studies topics that are relevant to the examination of race relations in the United States today. Your list might include such topics as Supreme Court decisions on racial issues after 1968 (the year of King's assassination), blacks and employment, blacks in politics and government, and the issue of reverse discrimination. Have each student prepare a mini-report on some facet of a race relations topic. Keep the research simple — a recent magazine or news article should provide enough statistics.

On Martin Luther King's birthday, hold a class Civil Rights Forum in which students present their findings. Afterward, have one student read King's "I Have a Dream" speech aloud. Now ask — how much of King's dream has *really* become reality?

Depending upon the ethnic and racial make-up of your class, you may want to include other racial groups in the research topics and subsequent discussion.

Martin Luther King's Birthday

No. 152

BANKING CENTER

Taking care of student money matters can be an endless chore—for both students and teachers. Setting up a banking center can relieve you of one bookkeeping task while providing students the opportunity to learn real-world banking skills. Counting and other math operations come into play as students become responsible for depositing and receiving their lunch money, field trip contributions or other school-related finances.

Your banking center can be as simple as a desk for the "banker of the day" or as elaborate as a class-made cardboard bank—a huge box with a cutout window behind which the banker sits.

Students with money to turn in bring it to the banker (supervised by you initially), fill out a deposit slip (designed and dittoed by you), turn in the money and receive a receipt for it. Deposits can be listed alphabetically by depositor on a sheet of paper for reference. When money is to be withdrawn, the banker is responsible for receiving checks and handing out the cash.

Though the system may take some time to set up, it will eventually save you time and paperwork. Instructions for the center can be written out so that substitute teachers will be able to work with it too.

Idea by: Opal Star, Clark County School District, Las Vegas, Nev.

January 11

No. 153

LET'S HAVE
A GAME-IN

You've probably made up math games or reading games of one sort or another. You may have found that game making brought out new facets of the content you were working with. Game making could have a similar effect on students.

Staging an all-class game-in requires some preparation. Concentrating on a standard format may be the most productive procedure at first. You might suggest a gameboard with a track that has special spaces keyed (by color or labels) to cards of two kinds: question cards and "chance" cards. (If a roll of the dice lands a player on a question space he or she must answer a question card before that space can be occupied. Chance cards may send a player either ahead or back.)

Gameboard materials include: tagboard (or flattened cardboard boxes or an old white plastic tablecloth), markers or crayons, scissors and 3-by-5 cards.

Each game-making unit—a small group or an individual—first needs to decide on the subject matter area to be "gamed" and then on the kind of information within that area to be included—facts about food chains, addition facts, milestones in black history.

Making up the question cards—and the answer key—is the heart of creating the game, since this is where the review of subject matter comes in. (Remind students to key question cards to the answer key.)

After the basics are in hand, students can go ahead with making up the game itself—deciding on a name and the shape the game track should take, drawing the track and making appropriate illustrations or decorations. Individual creativity gets a chance to show its stuff—and such intangibles as satisfaction and pride begin to show through too.

Storing the games and providing dice or spinners may present some temporary problems, but ingenuity undoubtedly will triumph.

The learning and pleasure involved in creating, sharing and playing all these new games should make the game-in a very worthwhile project.

Idea by: Ruth Ann Keim, Memorial Park School, Fort Wayne, Ind.

No. 154

READ-A-THON FUNDRAISING

Following the lead of walk-a-thons and ride-a-thons for charity, the read-a-thon is springing up. Whether you're interested in raising money for a particular fund or for an outing for the class — or are just looking for a reading change-of-pace — a read-a-thon is worth considering.

Though a read-a-thon can take many forms, a kind that can encourage a high degree of participation is an all-day reading-activities carnival. If this event is to be a fundraiser, each prospective participant first tries to secure sponsors to pledge 10 cents or so for each hour the student engages in read-a-thon activities. (The "time spent" factor will be more relevant if read-a-thon events extend beyond the limits of the school day.)

Initial steps in read-a-thon organization include letters of explanation to be sent home, permissions to be returned and some footwork on the part of students getting sponsors.

The activities scheduled for the day will vary, of course, depending on the age of the group and your school situation. Here are a few ideas:

1. A tour of the public library with a focus on the kinds of services available and the many reading-related activities going on.

2. Word-game potpourri — a time for playing a variety of commercial and teacher-made games.

3. Story writing, followed by oral sharing of the works produced.

4. Verbal gymnastics — a gym period in which all activities (exercises, obstacle course, gymnastics) are written out on a schedule for each student to read, do and check off.

5. A treasure hunt in which students need to fill in crossword puzzles, unscramble words or solve riddles to get clues for finding the treasure.

6. Captioned silent movies — for a comic break in the day.

7. A rousing read-along sing-along. Words to favorite songs (or newly created words for old songs or perhaps even some new songs) are displayed, using the overhead projector, while music — taped or live — is played.

Of course, for students who want to extend their reading time even more, there's always the pocket paperback and silent reading. It's probably best to set a maximum limit too, before the overzealous come down with reader's red-eye.

Idea by: JoAnn Kraut, Bangor Central Elementary, Bay City, Mich.

Read-A-New-Book Month

No. 155

SAVE THOSE HOCKEY CARDS

Kids collect them, trade them and maybe even read some. Hockey cards — the wintertime version of baseball cards — are probably around your room, and they could be an asset to your math classes. Here are some activity-starting suggestions based on hockey-card data.

• Do you think centers and wings are generally heavier or lighter than defensemen? Test your answer by picking ten of each group and calculating the average weight of each group.

• Do you think that defensemen get more of their points from goals or from assists? Is it the same for forwards (wings and centers)? Test your answer by calculating the percent of points that comes from goals (1) for a group of defensemen and (2) for a group of forwards.

• Write down the names and birth dates of three of your favorite players. Calculate their ages today to the nearest month.

• Make a graph with weight on the horizontal axis and height on the vertical axis. Pick 15 players and mark their locations on the graph. Do you notice any pattern?

As a whole class activity you might prepare a large graph with a horizontal axis representing *points scored* and a vertical axis representing *penalty minutes*. The length (number of units) of the horizontal axis would be set by determining the largest number of points scored by any player represented among the cards held by the class. The height of the vertical axis would be set by finding the most penalty minutes accumulated by any player among the cards. Completed axes are then bisected, and from these midpoints the grid is to be divided into four sections. Students suggest which section would contain the most valuable player and which would contain the least valuable player.

Plot the records of a sizable number of players on the graph, identifying each point with the player's name. (On a bulletin board you might use pins that can be flagged.) It is important that goals and penalties for one full year (last full season) be used for all players and that all players used have played more than 65 games. Use the data to rule on the following hypotheses (or others the students may develop):

• Forwards have more points than defensemen.

• Defensemen have more penalty minutes than forwards.

• The "high goal, low penalty" section will be overrepresented in forwards and underrepresented in defensemen; the converse will hold for the "low goal, high penalty" section.

If your class isn't ready for this kind of math, they may enjoy using the cards for classifying into teams and for simple add/subtract activities.

Idea by: A.L. Titus, Pierre Laporte School, Mississauga, Ontario, Canada.

No. 156

CHECKING TWICE

For kids the checkbook can represent some exciting opportunities indeed. Before setting this money-go-round activity in motion, you'll probably want to do some work with the class on how to write a check correctly — using special check forms you've prepared.

Gather ten or more merchandise catalogs of various kinds. When all is ready, divide the class into groups: four bankers, four sellers, and the rest of the class buyers. Provide each of these groups with a job card that outlines what they are to do.

Buyers:

1. Deposit any amount of money up to $500.00 in the bank.

2. Sign your name at the bank for identification.

3. Check out a catalog from a seller.

4. Select items to buy and write a check for each (or all) of them. (You'll need to total the items if you write only one check.)

5. Be sure to keep a record of each check and keep your own balance.

6. Return check(s), list of items purchased and catalog to seller.

7. Make other deposits if you wish.

Sellers:

1. Check catalogs out to buyers.

2. Look over checks carefully for correctness as they are given to you.

3. Be sure buyers return catalogs.

4. Keep a list of things you sell and the prices paid. Total the money at the end of the period.

5. Take checks to the bankers as you receive them.

Bankers:

1. Keep track of the accounts of four of the buyers, each on a different sheet of paper.

2. Subtract each check carefully.

3. Add each deposit to the balance.

January 11

No. 157

SNOWBALL MOBILES

A snowball mobile in the classroom gives the cheerful impression of soft, white snowballs flying — none of that brown slush and icy crust that makes winter outside the classroom a hazard and a mess. Here's how you and your students can construct one together.

Bind two long dowels in a cross with strong cord. Tie an additional length of cord to the center; this will be your means of suspending the mobile when it is finished.

Provide each student with a small round balloon, a spool of white thread, and a baby food jar containing liquid starch. Have the kids thoroughly soak their spools of thread in the starch.

While spools sit, students blow up and knot the open ends of the balloons. Then, each child should begin to ravel a network of thread around the balloons, criss-crossing back and forth until the balloon looks like it has been wrapped in a web or a piece of lace. The thread should not be too densely woven. The easiest way to do this is to set the spool of thread on its side and roll the balloon over the thread as it unwinds off the spool. Admonish the kids to handle the balloons and thread gently so that the balloons won't break.

In a few days, when the starched thread has dried to stiffness, it's time to pop the balloons. Have a number of

straight pins handy for the noisy occasion. Also have on hand a lot of thread pre-cut to varying lengths. Once the kids have very gently removed the flaccid balloons from within the delicate balls, have them select a length of thread and tie one end to each snowball, knotting a loop at the other end.

Hang the balls on the arms of the crossed dowels. Once a balanced arrangement has been achieved, suspend the mobile from a fixture in the room and enjoy a continuous bombardment of snowballs.

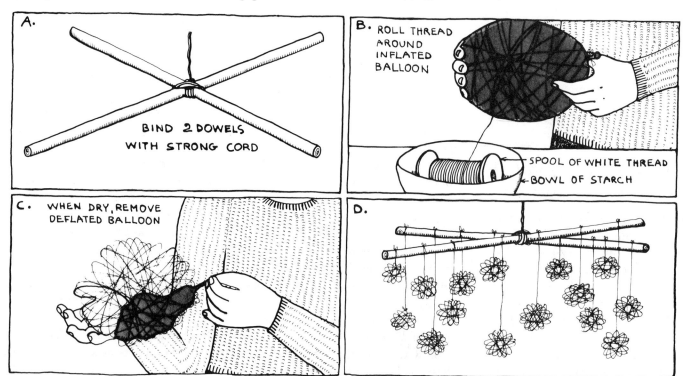

A. BIND 2 DOWELS WITH STRONG CORD

B. ROLL THREAD AROUND INFLATED BALLOON — SPOOL OF WHITE THREAD — BOWL OF STARCH

C. WHEN DRY, REMOVE DEFLATED BALLOON

D.

No. 158

SNOW SCENES IN A JAR

At nearly any major tourist stop you can purchase a sealed, water-filled glass globe with a figure of the local attraction set in place inside. When you shake the globe, a "snowstorm" takes place inside. The artificial snow is really no mystery. Here's how kids can make snow scenes of their own. (From *Creative Art Tasks for Children*, Love Publishing Co.)

Only a few materials are needed: a jar with a screw-on cover, small figures made of plastic or ceramic material, steel wool, waterproof glue, 1½ teaspoons of minute tapioca, a fine strainer and felt.

The directions for putting the scenes together are relatively simple.

1. Use steel wool to remove wax coating from inside of jar lid.

2. Glue figure(s) to inside of jar lid with waterproof glue. Set aside to dry.

3. Fill the jar with water and add 1½ teaspoons of minute tapioca. Allow this mixture to soak for two days. Then pour through a fine strainer.

4. Fill the jar with fresh water and replace strained tapioca.

5. Run waterproof glue all around jar rim. Close jar and allow to dry.

6. Glue felt on the jar lid.

The final product of these two craft projects (from *Do a Zoom Do,* Little, Brown) will be useful to kids in class. The situpon — or several of them piled on top of each other — makes a good cushion for a reading center. Kids can keep paperback bookcases at their desks, or these too can be used in a reading center.

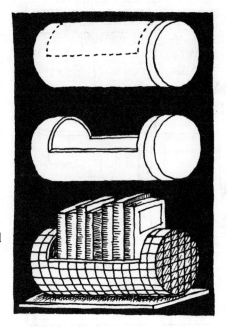

● *Situpon.* "You will need newspaper, scissors, tape. Here's what you do:

1. First, take a sheet of newspaper and fold it in half like a book. Fold it over again. Then fold it again; it should be about an inch and a half wide. Make about 20 such strips. (You can make more depending upon how large you want your Situpon to be.)

2. Place 10 or 11 of the strips of paper next to each other so they line up vertically.

3. Then take another strip and begin weaving it horizontally into the strips about an inch from the top. Do the same with 9 other strips. Make sure that the weaving is tight! You will have 10 back and forth strips which alternate under, over.

4. Then tape the ends down."

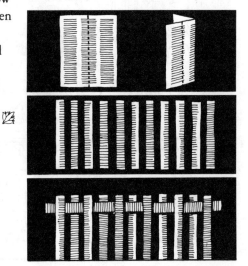

● *Paperback Bookcase.* You will need a round oatmeal or cornmeal box, white glue, a knife (a serrated one will make it easier) or scissors, self-sticking paper or poster paint, a piece of heavy cardboard or wood at least as long as the box. Here's what you do:

1. Make sure the box is clean. Then glue on the lid tightly.

2. Mark and "saw" out with the knife a section of the box. (Be careful. This is a slow process, and the box may slip out of your hand.) Scissors can be substituted for a knife.

3. Cover the edges and outside of the box with cutout pieces of self-sticking paper or paint the box with poster paints.

4. Glue the back of the box onto the cardboard or wood so that it won't roll.

When the projects are finished, stack the situpons in a corner of your reading center and let kids select books for their new cases.

Read-A-New-Book Month

No. 160

WHILE YOU WERE GONE

It's the cold and flu season, and you know what that means: absences and missed assignments. Keeping students informed about what went on during their absence can seem to be a never-ending task these dark winter days.

Establishing a While You Were Gone bulletin board may help take the chaos out of the makeup merry-go-round. One student in each class (or subject area) is made weekly chairperson of the board. For one week this student is re-sponsible for listing daily assignments, projects, test dates, etc. If notes were taken, the chairperson makes arrangements for the notes to be provided for absent students. If handouts are given to the class, the chairperson sees that one is labeled and tacked on the board for each absent student.

Sick-at-home students know that any assignments they miss will be on the board when they return. This eases worries about falling behind. Returning students also know that the chairperson will be available to help explain assignments and to discuss missed work.
Idea by: Sara Wetzel, Wallace H. Braden Junior High, Ashtabula, Ohio.

No. 161

CLIPPING FOR LITERARY TERMS

Literature incorporates many devices that help capture experiences in words and also add character and richness. But it's easier to appreciate the effects of simile and metaphor than it is to keep straight which is which. The following activity may help students to sort terms out.

The first steps are (1) students start keeping notebooks of literary terms; (2) you provide a stack of old newspapers and magazines. When a literary term comes up for discussion in a language arts lesson, students record the term and its definition in their notebooks.

Then each student finds and clips out two or three examples of the literary device as used in the magazines or newspaper headlines. The searcher initials each find and also copies it into his or her notebook near the appropriate definition. Then the examples are collected and stored. Clippings continue to accumulate as more terms are introduced.

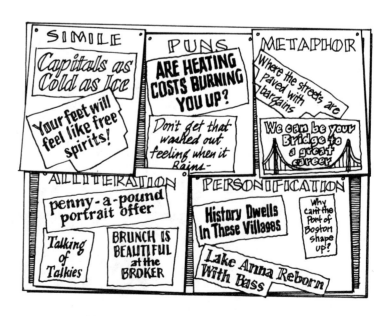

When clippings for five or six items have been collected in a box, poster making begins. You might set up a center with the box of mixed clippings and several shoe-box sorting bins, one for each term. Students can then work at the sorting process at odd moments. The final sort may be checked against notebook entries before the pasting starts.

Groups can be organized to assemble and paste up two posters for each term. The term serves as a title for the poster and should be prominent.

Finished posters can be displayed as reference models throughout the year. Then they can be saved and used to introduce terms to next year's students, who may reach their first understanding of certain literary terms by reading and analyzing poster material.

Idea by: Ann Goer, Miller Junior High School, Aberdeen, Wash.

RESOURCES

BOOKS FOR KIDS —
● *The Wild Inside: Sierra Club's Guide to the Great Indoors.* Linda Allison. Illustrations by the author. Sierra Club/Scribner's. Recommended reading for the intermediate grades.
● *The Assassination of Martin Luther King, Jr.* Doris and Harold Faber. Illustrated with photographs. Watts. Recommended reading for the primary and intermediate grades.
● *Connie's New Eyes.* Bernard Wolf. Photographs by the author. Lippincott. Recommended reading for the primary and intermediate grades.

EXACT CHANGE — Money, the root of all evil, is also the basis of Exact Change. This game for two or three players uses realistic cardboard coins and a gameboard format to give kids practice counting money and making change for amounts up to a dollar.

The goal is to be the first player to reach the finish of a highwaylike course. Along the way players must pay 11 tolls, the amounts depending on the correlation of the roll of a die with printed charts. The game can be played at three levels of difficulty. The main difference between levels is in the distribution of small and large change the players start with.

The package includes two complete games that consist of gameboards, dice, wooden pawns, play money and change trays, plus a set of large cardboard coins for classroom demonstration or display.
Order from: Educational Teaching Aids, P.O. Box 2643, Menlo Park, CA 94025. **Grade level:** Primary–intermediate.

POSTURE-RITE LAP DESK — The writer — seated at a desk, pencil in hand, studiously hunched over a clean sheet of paper — is a likely candidate for body fatigue if he or she remains in the same position too long. For those kids (or adults) who want to vary the writing posture, perhaps by sitting in a corner or lying down in the middle of the room, this Lap Desk might be the answer. Kids will enjoy using the Lap Desk for its practicality as well as for its novelty.

The Lap Desk is an improvement on stacking books on your knee and using them for a writing board. It is a wedge-shaped cushion attached to a hard, smooth top. The cushion is filled with foam beads, and when placed on a lap or across a leg, the cushion conforms to that shape, providing a comfortable angle for writing and eliminating the awkwardness encountered with makeshift surfaces. The cushion is covered with colorful fabric (which unfortunately cannot be removed for washing), and the desk top has a raised edge to prevent pencils from rolling off.

The Lap Desk can also be used on a regular desk top by the person who wants a comfortably inclined surface. And it's a natural for a creative writing center.
Order from: Hoyle Products, 302 Orange Grove, Fillmore, CA 93015. **Grade Level:** Preschool–high school.

1

Robinson Crusoe Day. Anniversary of the rescue in 1709 of a man whose adventures inspired Daniel Defoe's book.

2

Groundhog Day. Old belief that the groundhog emerges to look for his shadow, and thus predicts the advent of spring.

3

First paper money issued in America, 1690.

7

Author Charles Dickens born in 1812.

8

The U.S. President's salary was set as $25,000 in 1793. Today the President earns $200,000.

9

U.S. Weather Bureau established, 1870.

13

14

Valentine's Day.

15

Galileo, Italian astronomer, physicist and mathematician, born in 1564.

19

Copernicus, Polish astronomer, born in 1473.

20

John Glenn becomes the first American to orbit the earth in 1962.

21

Cherokee Phoenix published, 1828. First Indian-language newspaper.

25

Slavery abolished in England, 1807.

26

Grand Canyon National Park established in 1919.

27

In 1902, author John Steinbeck born.

4

Charles Lindbergh, great American aviator, born in 1902.

5

Weatherman's Day. Commemorates the birth in 1744 of John Jeffries, one of America's first weathermen.

6

Homerun hitter Babe Ruth's birthday. Born in 1895.

10

Anniversary of the first singing telegram, sent in 1933.

11

12

Abraham Lincoln, the 16th President, born in 1809.

16

17

National PTA founded in 1897.

18

22

George Washington's birthday, 1732.

23

First mass inoculations against polio in 1954.

24

Gregorian Calendar Day. The new calendar replaced the Julian calendar in 1582.

28

The Republican Party formed, 1854.

29

Leap Year Day, added to the calendar once every four years.

ACTIVITIES

No. 162

WEATHER PREDICTIONS

There is an old belief that the ground-hog emerges from his hole on February 2 to look for his shadow. If he sees it, he goes back down into his hole and six more weeks of winter will follow; if he doesn't find it, then spring has come early.

On Groundhog's Day, have your students make weather predictions just for the fun of it. Provide each child with a copy of the Groundhog's Calendar, a six-week calendar which begins February 2 and ends March 16 (or March 15 if it is a leap year). The calendar should have a small block of space for each day in which the children can write and/or illustrate a weather prediction for the day. Have a master calendar displayed on which you will record the actual weather pattern for each day as it passes. Have kids be responsible for recording the weekend weather and transferring their recordings onto the master calendar on Monday morning.

When the six-week period is over, check the students' predictions against the actual weather conditions. Determine which child's predictions were most accurate and award the winner a Groundhog Certificate. Six weeks of mounting suspense and, most probably, a continuing change of frontrunners ought to hold your students' interest. But, if you feel you need more immediate reinforcement, check predictions weekly for accuracy and honor several winners with Groundhog of the Week certificates. As a class, look at the overall weather picture and decide whether or not the groundhog saw his shadow way back on February 2.

Groundhog's Day

No. 163

A SHADOW OF ONE'S SELF

Groundhog's Day is a good time to have your students examine their own shadows — with a more scientific premise than the groundhog has in mind.

Shadows usually don't make lasting impressions. Here's a way to record shadows permanently and to observe their changes over the course of a school day.

Have a child stand in the sun so that her shadow is cast upon a long sheet of paper. (Black paper is best, but several sheets of newspaper taped together also will do.) Quickly outline the shadow with a contrasting piece of chalk. Then cut out the shape and label it with the child's name, the exact time and the date.

Repeat the activity once or several times during the day. Compare and discuss the results. You should discover that the children's shadows are longest in the early morning and late afternoon when the sun is rising or setting at the greatest angle. At noon, when the sun is directly overhead, the shadows will be shortest. Display several students' shadow outlines for each recorded time around the classroom.
Idea by: Patsy O. Williams, Alvin, Tex.

Groundhog's Day

No. 164

CLASSY VALENTINE CUT-UPS

Making your own valentine cards can be a fun, practical project. It can also be a way to reinforce the concept of word play.

Ask students to bring in department store catalogs and some of last year's valentines. Have the children sort through the old valentines for messages that show word play such as "It's time to be my valentine" with a picture of a clock and "You light up my life!" accompanying a picture of a lamp.

After taking in just a few such examples, students should be ready to find some message ideas of their own by meandering through the merchandise pictured in the catalogs:

(tire) "I'll never *tire* of you!"

(bathing suit) "You *suit* me fine!"

(hairdryer) "You *blow* my mind!" or "You've got *style*!"

(shoes) "You *stepped* into my heart!"

(lamp) "You *turn* me *on*!"

(glue or adhesive tape) "Stick with me!"

(stove) "You are hot stuff, kid!"

(radio) "I'm *tuned in* to you!"

(hangers) "*Hang* around with me!"

(typewriter) "You're my *type*!"

(TV) "Get the *picture* — I want you for my valentine!"

Have students jot down lines as they discover them. (Younger students may find it helpful to see some written on the board.)

Pictures can then be cut out and cards assembled. Some students may decide to try to keep their cards "secret" to surprise people on Valentine's Day, when excitement, fun and creative corn take over.

Idea by: Clara Statz Fairfax, R.B. Hayes Elementary School, Milwaukee, Wis.

Valentine's Day

No. 165

SHADOW-MATES ON THE MOVE

Personal shadows come in all sizes and shapes, and they're quite as active and versatile as the children they follow around. On your next sunny outing, have the children try experimenting with their shadows:

● How tall can you make your shadow?

● How short can you scrunch it?

● Can your shadow stand on one leg?

● Can you make your shadow's arms disappear?

● Can you put your shadow in back of you?

● Try to move around quickly without bumping into anyone else's shadow.

● Can you put your own foot on your shadow's head?

● Put your shadow on a wall.

● Get together with three others and make the biggest shadow you can.

After some shadow manipulation, suggest that children play shadow tag. Choose a few children to be shadow chasers. Rather than trying to tag others, the shadow chasers try to stand in or on someone's shadow. (Given the insubstantial nature of the basic equipment, this game requires some refereeing to settle "I stepped on your shadow, Jack" claims.)

Some of the following suggestions for varying the game may be adopted:

● Designate an area in which any player can be "safe."

● Declare a player safe unless a chaser has both feet in the player's shadow.

● Decide whether a tagged player becomes a chaser or sits out, counts to 50 and then reenters the game.

Of course shadows are good for math and science activities too — if you want to pursue them.

Idea by: Kathy Pattak, Foster School, Pittsburgh, Pa.

Groundhog's Day

No. 166

BROKEN HEART MENDERS

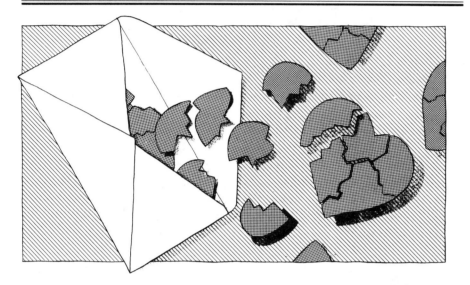

For a break in the Valentine's Day bedlam, try an activity that involves challenge, cooperation—and absolute quiet.

You'll need one construction paper heart for each child in the class. The backs of the hearts must be distinguishable from the fronts; you can accomplish this by making two-layer hearts—white on one side, red on the other—or you might mark the backs of the hearts with a distinctive pattern.

For this activity the class will be divided into groups of nearly equal size. For each group, prepare an envelope containing the same number of hearts as members in the group. Before distributing the envelopes, cut each heart into five pieces (no two cutting patterns should be alike).

Once the children are arranged in their groups, give each child five heart pieces from the envelope for his or her group. (The pieces should turn out to

be from assorted hearts.) The task now is for each group member to put together a complete heart. Members may give pieces to others in their group, but no one may take or ask for a needed piece. In fact, *no verbal communication at all is allowed*. Children may soon begin to tune in to the needs of others in the group, thereby expediting the heart-mending process.

If you wish to have a "winner," the group that gets its hearts together in the speediest manner qualifies. But, winners aside, most groups will want to continue working until everyone's heart is mended.

Idea by: Alison Wilbur, West Caldwell, N.J.

Valentine's Day 🌿

No. 167

BE MY FIRST LADY

Combining Valentine's Day with February's focus on presidents isn't so far-fetched an idea as it might sound at first. It can be a fun way to stimulate use of reference books, to promote sharing of information, and to invite creativity.

Initiate research about U.S. presidents. Have students note the accomplishments and the slipups of the various administrations, but ask them also to seek information about presidents' families, hobbies, physical appearance, characteristic dress, famous quotes and so on.

Now for the valentine connection: Conduct a presidential name draw or ask each student to pick a president. Each student then creates an appropriate valentine for that president to give to his spouse or other family member. Girls may prefer to give First Lady valentines to their presidential spouses instead. The message may be serious or humorous, but it should provide clues to the identity of the president involved. Clues may also be planted in the artwork of the valentine or on the envelope.

Finally, collect the valentines and plan a guess-the-president session. Have all the first-family valentines read aloud or displayed on the bulletin board.

Idea by: Shirley T. Shratter, Morningside School, Pittsburgh, Pa.

President's Day and Valentine's Day 🌿

No. 168

GOOD FORTUNE

Fortune cookies often contain thought-provoking statements about what the future holds. Why not have your class compose and then discuss a number of "fortunes" that deal with self-worth and positive thinking? You might ask a home economics group to bake cookies in which to enclose the fortunes.

Here are a number of fortunes to provide as examples (or for you to include for discussion):

All your nice dreams will come true, sometimes in parts, which makes them more fun.

Be kind and kindness will walk your way.

The best day of your life is coming.

You will inherit some happy feelings. Pass them on to others.

Today you will have a fortune if you make a new friend — or be one.

Memories are something to hold on to — be a neat memory for someone.

The road you take today will lead to the right turn.

This fortune will be anything you like if you believe in it.

If you give something today, you'll get something tomorrow.

Something nice will happen to someone you love, and you will be happy for that person.

Idea by: Peg Stapleton, Wilson Junior High, Yakima, Wash.

Chinese New Year

No. 169

HEART BREAKERS

Because the valentine "season" is a time for sending messages, it is often a time that's scheduled for reinforcing letter-writing skills. For a "something different" project, suggest that students dream up letters that rupture relationships (only temporarily) between famous couples in history or literature. Students may choose to be Romeo or Juliet, John Smith or Pocahontas, Marie or Pierre Curie, Victoria or Albert, Tom Sawyer or Becky.

To include "knowing" allusions and authentic details, students will need to research the quarreling couples — their period in history, significant events in their lives or, in the case of literary pairs, other characters in their stories or perhaps the lives of their authors.

For seasonal irony, the letters might be dated February 14 — in an appropriate year, of course.

(In the interest of fair play, the recipient of the "Dear John" letter should have an opportunity to reply. Students may volunteer for this extra letter-writing challenge on their own.)

Idea by: Trudy Whitman, Brooklyn, N.Y.

Valentine's Day

No. 170

PULSE TAKERS AND WATCHERS

How fast does the heart beat? Kids can find out by taking one another's pulse or by making a simple device that enables them to watch their own.

A pulse is the throbbing that's caused by the heart forcing blood through an artery. When an artery passes close to the skin, you can feel and sometimes see the pulse throb. With the pointer and middle fingers of one hand, have kids find their own pulse on the opposite wrist, just above the hand. Have them press down lightly with their fingers and count the beats they feel for 15 seconds, then multiply the answer by four to find out how many times their hearts beat each minute.

Sometimes it is confusing to try and take your own pulse. You can have your kids take one another's pulses using the same method. They might want to see if different kinds of activity cause changes in the pulse. Have them take one another's pulses after lying quietly for five minutes, walking the hallway and back, and running in place for one minute.

Although you usually *feel* your pulse, with a little ingenuity you can also *watch* it. Here's a device that requires only a short wooden matchstick and a small ball of clay. Have each kid put the ball of clay over the pulse point on his or her wrist, then flatten the bottom of the ball slightly and stick the matchstick into it. It is now possible to watch the pulse as the child's arm rests on a table. The throbs cause the matchstick to move in its foundation. Have kids count how many times the matchsticks move in a given period of time to determine the rate of their heartbeats. **Idea by:** Linda Allison, author of *The Wild Inside*, Sierra Club.

Valentine's Day

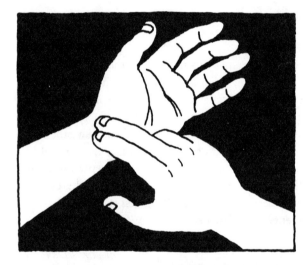

No. 171

MAKE YOUR OWN STETHOSCOPE

Lub-dub, lub-dub. That's the sound a healthy heart makes. It is the sound of blood rushing through the heart and the heart's doors, or valves, closing behind the blood. Doctors listen to our hearts through stethoscopes to determine whether there are any obstructions that block or slow up the free flow of blood. And with the help of a stethoscope your kids can make themselves, your students will be able to hear the heartbeat more clearly than if they put their ears to one another's chests.

You will need an 18-inch piece of rubber tubing and two kitchen funnels for each stethoscope you plan to have the kids make. It's wonderfully easy: Fit one end of the tubing over the narrow end of each funnel. A child holds one funnel to his or her ear and the other to a partner's chest.

Idea by: Linda Allison, author of *The Wild Inside*, Sierra Club.

Valentine's Day

No. 172

MY PUNNY VALENTINE

Most of the valentine greetings exchanged by students are of the humorous sort. And much of the humor comes from word play, puns in particular. Why not make use of these language nuggets before the valentines go home?

After the initial frenzy of the valentine exchange has abated somewhat, gather the group for some "serious" analysis of gag lines. Discuss the meaning of the term *pun* and have a few card messages in readiness to use as illustrations.

Suggest that kids explore their card collections for puns. Invite volunteers to take turns reading the jokes aloud and explaining the puns.

The kids will laugh (and groan) their way through the punniest Valentine's Day party they've had yet. And some may be inspired to create some messages for use next year. Be prepared!

Idea by: Virginia J. Osborne, New Miami Local School District, Hamilton, Ohio.

Valentine's Day

No. 173

FORCED FLOWERS IN WINTER

We live in eternal spring. The inside of your classroom may not smell like it, but for all practical purposes it's spring. And there are no doubt a lot of elaborate hardworking heaters and air conditioners at your school to make sure of this. In fact, plants brought indoors won't know the difference; you can fool them into spring flowers. The name gardeners use for this trick is forcing. Here is what happens.

Trees and shrubs in the late winter and early spring get buds, seen as bumps. These are leaves and flowers waiting to happen. Warm weather is their cue. If you cut some of these branches and bring them into a warm, winter-proof classroom, these branches think it is suddenly spring and they go into action bringing out the flowers. It's a good show.

In January or February, cut some branches from a flowering shrub or tree. If you are not a gardener, you might ask for some advice because you will in effect be pruning these plants. Bring the branches into the classroom and set them in a vase with water in a warm spot, but out of the direct sunlight. You will have flowers on these sticks in about two weeks.

If you can't wait, here are some tricks to hurry the flowers along:
• Soak the stems in warm water for 15 minutes before bringing them into the classroom.
• Soak a paper towel in a bit of household ammonia. Put it into a sealed plastic bag with your branches for about an hour. After exposure to the fumes, treat them according to the original directions.
• You can force flowers any time after a cold spell. Some plants need a bit of winter sleep, which comes in the form of cold winter weather. Branches that are cut in the fall will take longer to flower than ones in the early spring.

Just because a twig has a lot of promising-looking bumps doesn't mean that it will make flowers. Cut only those that are known for their spring blooms. It is sometimes difficult recognizing barebones plants, but here are the ones to look for: peach, quince, dogwood, apple, poplar, honeysuckle, hawthorn, pussywillow, lilac, pear, rhododendron, forsythia, witch hazel, azalea, cherry and crab apple.

And while your class is thinking about climate, you might throw out a few questions on the subject of indoor weather. Is there any part of your school where it is winter all the time? How about summer? What would happen if there were no heaters in your classroom? Can you think of some alternative climate controllers? What kind of climate control do kids carry arround with them?
Idea by: Linda Allison, author of *The Wild Inside,* Sierra Club.

No. 174

MONEY-WISE MATH

Dollars and cents are added and put in their proper places in these money counting and recognition activities from *Math Sponges* (National Institute for Curriculum Enrichment).

Name the Coins. Place a number of coins—nickels, pennies, dimes—in a container and tell the class the amount the coins add up to. Divide the students into two teams and then ask them to guess the combination of coins inside the jar (have them keep a tally or chart of their guesses). One point is given to a team that works out a correct but different combination from the actual one, and three points are awarded to a team that identifies the exact number of nickels, pennies and dimes in the container. After several rounds, declare the winning team.

Dollar Dash. Make a set of 14 cards: one each for the numbers one through nine, two zeros, one dollar sign, one decimal point, and one comma. Distribute the cards randomly to students, and then call out a dollar amount, such as $8.45. Students holding the cards involved arrange themselves in the right order to show the amount.

Variations: Have students play the game as a team relay (this would require two sets of cards) or ask the students to add a certain amount ($2.00, $.50 or whatever) to the sum you call out before displaying their cards.
February 3

No. 175

TURNING ON INVENTIVENESS

Insights tend to build on one another, expanding knowledge gradually; only rarely do they inspire an exuberant "I've got it!" And although students may well enjoy the excitement of an occasional "Eureka!" they will also find satisfaction in step-by-step, exploratory thinking that turns on inventiveness.

Most students have recycled newspapers into papier mâché; turned cans, jars and bottles into pencil holders; made Popsicle-stick trivets and so forth. Extend this kind of inventiveness with new challenges.

● Countless school projects involve pasting, gluing or in some way sticking things together with an adhesive. Suggest that students think of ways things can be joined or held together without stickum of any kind. Ask them to look around the room, find two things to join, think of a nonsticking way to join them and show the class. Depending upon the resources in the room, you may see demonstrations of clipping, tying, pinning, nailing, stitching, lacing, braiding, wedging, folding, mixing and dissolving.

● For a physical display of inventiveness, have your students demonstrate ways—other than walking—of crossing an open space. Have students stand in a circle and ask each in turn to cross the circle without walking and without repeating any mode already used. At first you'll probably see a variety of foot movements, but as the activity moves along, look for sliding, scooting, somersaults, crawling, handstands and other feats.

● Ask students to imagine that they must leave an important message for someone, but they have no pencils, crayons, pens or other writing utensils. How will they leave the message? Look for words in beads, glue trails, carvings.

● And while inventiveness is flowing, challenge students to produce a new way to exhibit examples of their work for visiting parents. Don't be surprised to find a work tree (a real branch decorated with papers) sprouting up, or perhaps you'll see a tower of cartons turned into display surfaces rising toward the ceiling.

Inventiveness is a valuable skill that should be exercised in all kinds of tasks. And once inventiveness is turned on in your class, expect the unexpected.

Idea by: Sharon Crawley and Lee Mountain, Department of Curriculum and Instruction, University of Houston, Houston, Tex.

National Inventors' Day

No. 176

A CHANGE IN INDOOR CLIMATE

Climate refers to long-term patterns of temperature, weather, smell, wind, light and, metaphorically, mood.

One way to compress the study of climate into a limited time frame is for kids to compare climatic conditions in various regions within the school: the classroom (bright, warm, sunny) with

the cafeteria (warm, steamy, fragrant) with the main office (noisy, frantic) with the boiler room (dark, hot). You might set up a chart listing different climatic elements across the top (temperature, smell, etc.) and different regions down the side; then have small groups of researchers be responsible for filling in the appropriate data for each site. Later, as an independent follow-up study, kids can do a similar survey of the rooms in their homes.

One of the oldest notions in geography is that climate has a direct impact on the way the inhabitants of a place live—how they work, play and live. To test out this hypothesis, let the class

conduct an experiment in which they systematically vary the climate of the room. They might at first change the temperature for a week (by opening a window or shutting off the radiator). Or they might bring vibrant color to the walls by adding several large wall-hangings. Or play background music during study period. If the classroom has a large expanse of windows, try blocking these off for a sunshineless, electric-light-only climate.

Each change should be discussed and evaluated in terms of productivity, mood or other physiological and psychological variables.

No. 177

COMPREHENSION THROUGH COMICS

The compact, humorous stories told within the frames of comic strips found in the daily paper can provide useful and appealing material for reading comprehension activities. Perhaps the following tasks will suggest ways that comic strips might work in your reading program.

● Use comics to check comprehension on several levels. Ask questions calling for factual, inferential or creative thinking.

1. What word does Peppermint Patty use that tells you her teacher is a woman?

2. What kind of test is the class taking? Name two other kinds of test.

3. What does Peppermint Patty mean when she says that this kind of test is "like giving a menu to a starving man"?

● Use comics to study double meanings. The point of many comic strips lies in the use of words with more than one meaning—punning.

1. What did Jughead mean to say to Veronica?

2. What did Veronica think that Jughead was saying?

3. Veronica's misunderstanding makes the story funny, but often it's important to make meanings very clear. How would you reword what Jughead said so that no one would be likely to misunderstand?

4. List five other double-meaning words that you might use in a comic strip. Try building a funny situation around one of the words.

● Use comics to teach students how to draw conclusions. Look for strips that invite discussion.

1. What do you think might happen next? Why?

2. How would you feel if you were Dagwood?

3. What would you do if you were Blondie?

4. Why do you think your chosen action would be the right one to take in this situation?

● Cut-apart comic strips are perfect for students to use to practice sequencing. Make the task more challenging by putting separated frames from three episodes of the same strip into one envelope for sorting out both by story and by sequence within each story.

With comic strips around, reading comprehension activities can provide laughs along with skill development.
Idea by: Jill Kaiserman, Princess Anne Junior High School, Virginia Beach, Va.

No. 178

ALIAS BIG DIPPER

The Great Bear, Orion the Hunter—astronomers long ago named these constellations according to pictures that the star configurations brought to mind. Science classes centuries later identify those star clusters with the same ages-old names.

Following a study of constellations, your students might enjoy taking the role of ancient astronomers and renaming some star patterns. What pictures—animals, birds, people (even machines or TV characters)—might modern-day children see in the stars?

Prepare a constellation configuration sheet (using gummed stars) for each student. (Older students could do their own.) Ask the children to look at the patterns and try to imagine pictures in the stars. Then have them draw and label the pictures with their new names for the constellations. Some children may even decide to make up myths about how the star groups got their new names.

Idea by: Wilhelmina Lucille Lewis, General Nash Elementary School, Harleysville, Pa.

February 15 and 19

No. 179

SOLAR WALK

How far is it from the Earth to the sun? How much farther is Pluto from the sun? These distances can be shown with diagrams and models, but they come into more dramatic focus when the class goes on a solar walk.

First prepare labels for the sun and each of the planets. Then assign the tasks of "planet markers" and "distance pacers" to various students and move the class out to the playground. The sun label is placed at the farthest corner of the playground. (Labels can be held or chairs brought out and used as temporary signposts.) The first distance pacer begins moving away from the sun using baby steps. Explain that each baby step represents one million miles. After 36 baby steps, the student holds his position while another student posts the Mercury label. Thirty-one baby steps from Mercury is Venus. From there, it's 26 steps to Earth. Use the

following chart as a guide to solar walk distances:

Distances from the Sun in Millions of Miles	
Mercury	36
Venus	67
Earth	93
Mars	141
Jupiter	484
Saturn	887
Uranus	1780
Neptune	2794
Pluto	3658

At Mars, you may wish to speed the process along by switching to the "giant step" mode, with each step representing ten million miles. If your playground is small, students may wind up pacing into a nearby neighborhood to cover the distance to Pluto.

Although this project is hardly compact, neither is the solar system. Perhaps the vastness of space will become more real as children pausing on Saturn find themselves nearly 90 giant steps from neighboring Uranus along the pathway of their solar walk.

Idea by: Beverly J. Anderson, Concord, Calif.

February 15 and 19

No. 180

SOFT BAT BALL

If you're short of play equipment, improvise. You might start out with some stocking bats. Since the materials are just ordinary wire coat hangers and stockings or pantyhose ready to be discarded, you probably will be able to collect enough for a class size number of bats—which the children can make themselves.

The hanger is bent into a diamond shape with the handle at the bottom. Then the stocking is drawn over this frame with the toe positioned at the top point of the diamond. Pull the stocking taut and secure it with a rubber band at the handle end of the frame. Cut off the excess.

To make a ball, stuff stocking scraps into a stocking toe and tie it tightly. Or make balls out of crumpled newspaper—which will be slightly heavier than the nylon.

Pairs of children can bat a ball back and forth. Or children may try a kind of free-form softball. Or a child may play alone, bouncing a ball on the flat surface of the bat.

Soft bat/soft ball is ideal for those indoor play periods that seem to be the rule this time of year.

Idea by: Eleanor P. Anderson, Levittown, Pa.

February 6

No. 181

A CLASSROOM-SIZE TIME LINE

There are so many events and figures in history—even in our personal histories—that kids often confuse the order or place in time of occasions. An illustrated classroom time line can straighten things out, and the events it notes are likely to stay in kids' minds better than memorized dates from a book will.

At the first sign that it's needed—perhaps during January and February, when Washington, Lincoln and Martin Luther King, Jr., get jumbled into one time period, or when kids are arguing about which month the class went to visit the chocolate factory and which month they went to see the fire station—begin constructing your time line. Choose a time span that suits your purpose best and list events that occurred during that period on the chalk-

board. Ask each student to choose one event to illustrate and hand out drawing materials. Then have the children read about their events in history or reference books (if the event is a personal one, they may need to contact friends or relatives) before completing their drawings. If the children use pencils, you may wish to have them trace over the pencil lines with black markers and color their pictures to make the drawings more visible once they are hung. Have each child write the name of the event and its date in bold letters on the picture and frame the drawing with white construction paper.

To hang the pictures in their proper order, run a length of string high on a wall from corner to corner (use two adjacent walls if you have the space) and tack it in place. Then hang the drawings in sequence, using clothespins or tape to attach them to the string. You can encourage children to add to the time line by posting an event sign-up sheet, putting out a stack of blank paper and making a box where kids can deposit finished drawings.

Idea by: Sue Hahn, Concord Elementary School, Concord, Va.

President's Day

No. 182

FUN FRIDAYS

The Februarys—the insidious will-spring-never-come? malaise that brings out the grump in practically everybody—is going around again. While spring is taking its sweet time in coming, look to Friday afternoons for a midwinter reprieve.

Turn over an hour of Friday afternoon to the creative resources of your class. Prepare kids for this responsibility by asking them to be thinking of activities, games, entertainment (native talent), demonstrations—whatever (reasonable) they'd like to see featured in a one-hour slot on Friday afternoon.

The class votes in an activity committee—which should be changed periodically—to handle the initial screening of ideas. (It might be wise for the committee to be exempt from contributing ideas during their tenure.)

On a Monday morning have kids submit their activity ideas—written up in brief—depositing them in an idea box. The committee goes through the suggestions and announces about five finalists, which the class gets to vote on toward the middle of the week. Ask the committee to handle bids for leadership and to assist in organizing the event.

Post-activity feedback sessions might be helpful in the planning for subsequent Fridays. New ideas can be submitted weekly; old ideas can be held for reconsideration.

Encourage students to seek out activity resource books and to brainstorm for ideas, working for a variety of experiences in many areas and an ever-expanding roster of leadership.

Friday activities may be effective right through the epidemics of spring fever that are sure to come—soon.
Idea by: Byron Pegram, Port Edwards, Wis.

No. 183

POSITIVE IDENTITY

Perhaps you've set up a "Student of the Week" series in your room, or maybe you've initiated other think-positively-about-someone projects. Such activities have very likely pointed up the problems we all have in delivering compliments to others. But there's another side of the situation that may not have received much attention. Have you noticed how vague and impersonal the compliments often are? "He's nice" or "She's a good friend"—however true and sincerely meant—are pretty general statements applying to quite a number in the class. Could your students come up with some positive statements about a fellow classmate that would be somewhat more specialized—data from which others might actually be able to identify the student?

Try the project on a group basis first. Select a person from the faculty or staff who's well known to the children. (It doesn't have to be the person most likely to be named "most popular.") Ask students to think about this person and contribute to a list of ten specific and positive observations about her or him. You might suggest that students think of things that they personally find appealing about the person or of some specific instances when this person was kind or helpful to them. When you have the ten items, invite students in from another class to put the positive profile to the test. Can the staff person be identified from the observations?

Now have students turn their attention to their own class. Ask them, working in pairs, to compose a ten-item listing of positive thoughts about their partners that will be likely to identify the person being complimented. Expect a somewhat lengthy composition period, with numerous trips to the dictionary and the wastebasket. When the listings are completed, try a guessing game with the class to see if the statements serve to identify the students. (Since each person being read about already knows from working with his or her partner what statements will be included in the positive profile, there should be no surprises and little embarrassment over the readings.)

Discuss the effects of using specifics as compared to generalities—and also discuss situations in which one type of comment is preferred over the other.

And allow some time too for everyone to enjoy the rarified atmosphere of honest, custom-styled compliments.
Idea by: Nora Mitcham, Albuquerque, N.M.

No. 184

CARTOON COLLABORATION KITS

The cartoon can be a most effective means of making a point. Many profound ideas have made a lasting impact when expressed in a cartoon format. Your upper intermediate or junior high students may enjoy portraying their ideas on current events or other concerns through cartoons and captions.

But wait — yes, there is a rub. Even if children's artistic efforts have ever and always been treated with utter respect, there seems to come a time when groans of "But I can't draw" are heard in the land. At the same time, some of your students just seem to sketch perpetually — they can't seem to help themselves.

Try a little collaboration, cooperation, synergistic effort. Enlist the aid of student artists in making up cartoon kits. Put artists to work outlining head shapes, as well as some pages of features — eyes on one page, mouths on another, etc. (Have students try to keep features in scale with the heads, so the parts will fit together.) Another artist might draw torsos; another, arms and legs.

When the artists are satisfied that they have a sufficient variety of components, have them outline all their drawings with felt-tipped markers or flow pens. Then duplicate the prepared pages in class-size quantities. Staple the pages together and everyone can have a do-it-yourself cartoon kit that can be used over and over. Cartoon makers simply trace and combine whatever parts they select.

To introduce cartoon making, you might display and discuss some good examples from magazines and newspapers, pointing out the various aspects of life being portrayed and poked fun at. Invite students to suggest areas for cartooning, such as school, politics, family life, TV.

The cartoons themselves may also be prepared by team effort (pairs or small groups). Humorous lines for captions often come more easily through interaction.

Students who never considered cartooning may surprise themselves by turning out some really satisfying work, with the help of cartoon kits.
Idea by: Doris Miller, Rutland Junior High School, Rutland, Vt.

No. 185

STRING PAINTING

Paintings that help paint themselves can be fun for both the eager artists and the reluctant Rembrandts in your class. String-board art has that quality.
Materials (per artist):

1. a sanded rectangular piece of wood, approximately 8 by 10 inches (or fiberboard or heavy corrugated cardboard, though it tends to warp).

2. twine or light cord; a 4-foot length should be enough.

3. tempera paints (if possible, in squeezable containers).

4. shellac or varnish.

5. brush. The size depends upon how large a board you're covering.

6. lots of newspapers to protect the work area.

No. 186

WEAR YOUR HEART ON YOUR SHIRT

Has this ever happened in your class? You introduce the systems of the human body, the kids laboriously draw diagrams of the heart, lungs, etc., the drawings are put into notebooks—and they're never seen or thought of again. If that's the way it's been, here's a project to warm your auricles and ventricles. What if, instead of filing away those diagrams, the kids got a chance to see them walking around—on T-shirts!

Why not start with the heart. You'll need some tracing paper, fabric crayons or iron-on transfer pencils and an electric iron. (Fabric paints for coloring in the diagrams are optional.) Another requirement is a heart diagram for tracing. It should be as simplified as possible without damaging scientific believability. (Also see the note in Step 2 following.) You may want to run off several copies of the pattern so a number of tracers can work at the same time.

Students follow these steps:

1. Trace the design and labels onto tracing paper. (A little reinforcement is tucked into this step.)

2. Turn tracing over and retrace the lines with special transfer pencil. (Note: When you "print" a transfer, everything comes out in reverse, of course. You'd save the kids a step if you provide a pattern that's in reverse already; but since there isn't much reinforcement in tracing backwards labels, you have a choice to make.) Check directions with fabric pencils, crayons or paints for procedures to ensure washability.

3. Place tracing color side down on the shirt.

4. Press slowly with medium-hot iron. (Check to see if the lines are transferring before removing the paper.)

5. The diagram can now be painted with fabric paints for a bolder effect.
Idea by: Lynne B. Baines, Rappahannock Elementary School, Washington, Va.

Valentine's Day

Procedure:

1. Paint the front of the board with a thin coat of two or more pale colors in irregular strips. Let the board dry.

2. Wrap string around the board in a crisscrossing, spiderweb design. Tie the string securely at the back of the board. Strings should be taut but in contact with the surface of the board as much as possible. If strings tend to slip and loosen, suggest that students wrap shorter lengths and tie each in place. Some spots may need taping (on the back). If students are using cardboard, they can cut small notches in the edges to keep strings in place.

3. Have several paint colors ready. The consistency should be such that the paint runs—but not too fast. Squeeze a color (or two) onto the string pattern. Tilt the board and let the paint follow the strings. This is when the painting process goes off on its own. Changing the tilt controls the flow somewhat, but the design can be something of a surprise. Let the first color dry a bit before adding more paint.

4. Squeeze on a few spots of a contrasting color. Tilt the board again—if you wish—but stop the process before the colors become homogenized.

5. Let the paint dry. Protect the painting with one or two coats of shellac or varnish.

The string-board painting can be framed and given as a special gift.
Idea by: Judy Dahl, Salt Lake City, Utah.

No. 187

WALL ONE-LINERS

In Beijing, China, people once wrote messages on a wall. These messages, which were usually one-line slogans, let people know what the writers think about important issues.

Post a large sheet of paper on a wall in the classroom. Invite students to write one-line messages on the paper. The messages should be serious and tell the writers' feelings about something important — in your school, town or state, or the world.

Chinese New Year

No. 188

VALENTINE POST OFFICE

Here is a new kind of valentine mailbox in which kids post hearts and greeting cards on February 14. This year, convert an entire bulletin board into a valentine post office. The dividers from cardboard cartons that hold wine and beverage bottles provide a post office box for every student in your class.

Before February, visit a local liquor store and request three or four relatively lightweight cartons that contain sturdy corrugated cardboard dividers. There are twelve compartments in each carton, so you can easily determine how many cartons you need. But ask for one more than you need to ensure against mistakes.

Remove the dividers carefully so they maintain their 90° angles. One false move and you may have to negotiate with a lot of collapsing parallelograms! Cover the empty cartons with red wrapping paper or paint them red with tempera. Then, with a heavy duty stapler, staple the backs of the boxes to the bulletin board, punching the staples into the board within the open fronts of the boxes. Arrange the cartons so they are stacked or touching side-by-side.

Reinsert the dividers. Number a small cutout heart for each student in your class and tape the hearts so that they hang *over* the post boxes they belong to. Assign each kid a post office box number and post a list of names and numbers for the class's reference.

Now no one needs to shake the valentine box to ascertain how full it is. Everybody can watch the valentines accumulate together. You may run into two problems, however, that you can avoid beforehand. If you are fearful that less popular students will suffer to see the post office boxes of their more popular classmates pile up with valentines, arrange to have flaps that close over the boxes rather than numbered hearts. If you don't want to discourage students from designing and posting oversize cards, you can staple an empty carton to the bulletin board and label it "bulk mail." Keep a mail sack on hand to store valentines if the post office boxes begin to overflow. A volunteer postal person can deliver them to the desk tops on February 14.

Your post office may be so successful that you may want to keep it up for the remainder of the year. It's a good vehicle to encourage letter writing, and to discourage the furtive passing of personal notes during class time.

Valentine's Day

RESOURCES

TEACHERS & WRITERS COLLABORATIVE COMICS — One medium that even reluctant readers will at least pick up and browse through is the comic book. So if they are willing to read comics, why not have them write their own? Kids already know quite well the comic-book language and format.

The Teachers & Writers Collaborative, which is responsible for producing many useful teacher resources in language arts, has published several student-made comic books that were developed in one of their classroom projects in New York City.

Stories involve monsters, crime, mystery and so on. Some of the student author-illustrators show an amazing sophistication in their mastery of the comic-book idiom. Others have eked out some often unintelligible stories. Both good and bad examples will serve as models to learn from.

Teachers who make requests will receive one of the first two issues, either *Pest* or *Bang!* Each issue contains a few pages that give brief instructions on several aspects of comic-book making, which will be useful to teachers and students who decide to make their own comics. They will also supply useful ideas for topics, formats and lengths.
Order from: Teachers & Writers Collaborative, 186 W. Fourth St., New York, NY 10014. **Grade level:** 3–junior high.

ODYSSEY — *The Young People's Magazine of Astronomy and Outer Space,* as this 32-page publication is subtitled, arrives at a time when space-age technology and information are growing by leaps and bounds.

Odyssey, a monthly magazine for students in intermediate through junior high grades, treats astronomy and outer space seriously; early issues present no science fiction. There is an interesting mix of articles — from lengthy pieces about Jupiter, asteroids and conditions for life on Mars to a short, newsy item about a class's star chart to a cutout solar system mobile.

Odyssey is richly and colorfully illustrated with pictures that will intrigue kids.
Order from: AstroMedia Corp., 411 E. Mason St., P.O. Box 92788, Milwaukee, WI 53202. **Grade level:** Intermediate–junior high.

OUTER SPACE — Studying the stars in class? Then write to the Harvard-Smithsonian Center for Astrophysics, Publications Dept., 60 Garden St., Cambridge, MA 02138, and ask for copies of *Meteorites* and *Comets*, two excellent introductions to space phenomena. You might also ask for *Life in the Universe*, which discusses the question of whether or not we really are alone. You shouldn't have any trouble getting a discussion going on *that* topic!

In addition to explorations in astronomy, an interest in the stars can lead to lessons in math, physics and geography. For the younger set, a good starting point is "What Do You Know About the Big Dipper?" a free reprint from *Ranger Rick's Nature Magazine.* The article tells how to find the Big Dipper and how to pronounce the names of other constellations you can locate using it as your point of reference. The reprint is available from the National Wildlife Federation, 1412 16th St., N.W., Washington, DC 20036.

1

Yellowstone becomes the first national park in 1872.

2

Theodor Geisel, otherwise known as Dr. Seuss, born 1904.

3

Author J.R.R. Tolkien born in 1892.

7

8

International Women's Day.

9

Russians launch first canine space traveler, Blackie, in 1961.

13

First earmuffs patented, 1877.

14

Albert Einstein, the great theoretical physicist, born in 1879.

15

The buzzards return to Hinckley, Ohio today.

19

The swallows return to San Juan Capistrano, Calif. today.

20

21

25

26

Poet Robert Frost born, 1875.

27

First coast-to-coast color-TV broadcast, 1955.

4

5

The Boston Massacre, 1770.

6

Davy Crockett dies at the Alamo, 1836.

10
First telephone message transmitted by Alexander Graham Bell in 1876 — "Mr. Watson, come here, I want you."

11

Johnny Appleseed Day.

12
In 1789, the U.S. Post Office established.

16
First downhill ski races, 1866.

17
St. Patrick's Day.

18

First walk in space, 1965.

22
The Equal Rights Amendment (ERA) submitted to the states for ratification, 1972.

23
Patrick Henry says, "Give me liberty, or give me death!" in 1775.

24
First American-made car sold, 1898.

28

29

Coca-Cola invented, 1886.

30 Doctor's Day. Anniversary of the first use of ether as an anesthetic by a physician in surgery.

Cesar Chavez, farmworkers' leader, born in 1927.

31

No. 189

WAYWARD WIND CORRESPONDENCE

The Beaufort Wind Scale

Beaufort Scale Number	Wind Description	Miles Per Hour	Wind Effect	Beaufort Symbol Used on Weather Maps
0	calm	0-1	Smoke goes straight up	○
1	light air	2-3	Smoke drifts in wind direction	
2	slight breeze	4-7	weather vanes turn; flags flutter; leaves move	
3	gentle breeze	8-12	flags blow out; small branches move	

Weather reporting has an "alphabet" all its own. Your class can explore the ABCs of wind speed in a learning center that also provides practice in map reading and perhaps some writing too.

For this center you'll need to make a chart of the Beaufort Wind Scale, which can be found in children's books about weather and in some science texts. Next, run off copies of a U.S. map with states outlined but not named.

The task cards for the center are postcards. They're written as if sent from various places in the United States. You might prepare a set of cards with appropriate pictures — cars for Detroit, the Maine seacoast — or shop around for some that depict seasonal changes.

On each card, write a message describing the weather:

Dear Tina:

I'm having a great time in Texas. It's hot, but there's a gentle breeze (8 to 12 miles per hour) today. See you soon.

Your friend,
Jay

Each center user takes a postcard and a map, reads the message, selects the correct wind symbol from the Beaufort Scale chart and draws the symbol on the state from which the postcard was "sent."

Children may enjoy adding postcards to the collection, making sure that the "wayward wind" gets a chance to blow through all 50 states.

Idea by: Deborah Beaucaire, East Bridgewater Intermediate School, East Bridgewater, Mass.

No. 190

ALL STEAMED UP

Why do geysers shoot water into the air? *Earth Science* (activity cards published by Educational Insights) provides the following experiment to help answer that question.

When underground water boils and makes enough steam, pressure forces the water and steam to the surface. The size of the passageway to the surface as well as the shape and kind of opening help determine how often the geyser will erupt.

To create a miniature Old Faithful in your classroom, you will need a saucepan, a funnel, water and a heating element.

Place the funnel in the saucepan, wide end down, and fill the pan with water, leaving just the tube of the funnel above the water. Bring the water to a boil and ask students to observe and comment on the results.

Here are discussion starters: What happened when the water began to boil? How can you compare a funnel in a saucepan to a geyser? What heats the water for a geyser? Why doesn't the geyser erupt continually?

You might also bring in and demonstrate the use of a coffee percolator, which works in much the same way as a geyser.

March 1

No. 191

WHICH WAY DOES THE WIND BLOW?

The wind is an ever-changing part of nature. Your class can study its caprices by constructing a wind vane and using it to chart wind direction. (From *OBIS Trial Edition*, Set I, University of California.)

To make a wind vane, cut a 15-by-2-cm piece of heavy-duty aluminum foil. Bend the foil in half around a 6-cm piece of drinking straw. Press the ends of the strip tightly together and tape them near where they wrap around the straw. Also tape the foil to the straw to keep the strip from sliding off. Put a nail (small enough to allow the straw to rotate) through the straw and push it into the center of a rectangular cardboard base. Spread the two foil ends slightly.

When the wind vane is ready for use, place it outdoors in an accessible area and note the direction in which the aluminum foil pieces swing. Since winds are named for the direction from which they *come*, a wind blowing from the north is a north wind; a wind from the south, a south wind; and so on. Your class can chart wind direction for a specified length of time, perhaps a month, or simply note wind direction at different times of the day.

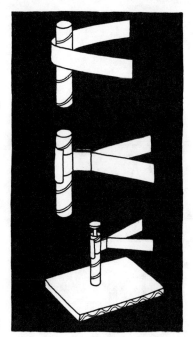

No. 192

BAROMETER FROM A BOTTLE

Air pressure is a key ingredient in predicting the weather. Amateur forecasters can make this barometer from *Ten-Minute Field Trips* (J. G. Ferguson Publishing Co.).

"You can make a simple barometer from a bottle, a tight-fitting cork with one hole, two two-inch pieces of glass tubing, rubber tubing, wax, and cord. Fill the bottle with colored water. Fasten the two pieces of glass tubing together with the rubber tubing. Insert one piece through the cork. Put the cork in the bottle securely. Seal with wax. Invert the bottle. Suck the water into the tube. Tie the tubing to the neck of the bottle so that it forms a U. Hang the bottle in an inverted position in a cradle knotted of cord.

"When air pressure is high, it will push on the colored water in the glass

tube and the water will rise in the bottle. When air pressure is low, the water level in the bottle will drop.

"With this barometer, a thermometer, the Beaufort Wind Scale, and the school flag to tell wind direction, a daily weather report can be written. As data is collected, weather prediction may also be tried. If the class feels the need for more information, they can obtain a cloud chart from the United States Weather Bureau or build additional equipment as described in some reference books on weather."

No. 193

WIND EROSION RECORDER

TAPE WITH STICKY SIDE OUT

Milk

When most children think of wind erosion, they probably think of exotic cliff faces in the Southwest or the great winds that make desert sands shift and slide. But wind erosion takes place all around us, constantly, as students will discover by making and using this device from *Science in Elementary Education* (John Wiley & Sons).

To explore the phenomenon of wind erosion, students will need to make a wind erosion recorder. This is done by cutting two narrow slots in the top of a small milk carton and sticking two rulers through the slots, as shown in the illustration.

When the rulers are in place, fill the carton with sand or soil. Then cut two 30-cm (12-inch) strips of tape and put one strip, sticky side out, on each ruler. Approximately 15 cm of tape should cover each side of the rulers. Fasten the strip ends to each ruler with additional tape. Draw an arrow on the carton top with crayon.

Place the recorder outside in a spot where the wind is blowing loose soil. Point the arrow north and leave the recorder for 30 minutes. When you return, notice how windblown soil bits have become attached to the tape. Examine the recorder and discuss some of the following questions: Which side of which piece of tape collected the most soil? From which direction did the wind blow most?

Where do you think the most wind erosion takes place around the school? Where does the least wind erosion occur? (You can make more recorders and test your hypotheses.)

You may want to run the test again, this time comparing different areas — one grassy and one with bare soil, one dry and one damp. Expose identical recorders in these areas at the same time and for the same amount of time. You may also wish to collect windblown bits each day for a week, changing the tape each day and comparing the results.

No. 194

SEND-AWAYS

A quiet spot stocked with letter-writing supplies can easily become a Send-Away Center; just add a file of "live prospect" addresses. Look in magazines for offers of booklets and pamphlets, clip the information and mount it on cards. Also make cards that will enable students to write to their favorite authors. Head each card with popular titles followed by the author's name and

MAIL TO SENDERS

the name and address of the publisher.

Because students want their Send-Away letters to be in the best possible form, they'll probably welcome checks for grammar and spelling.

The Send-Away Center may also open up opportunities for public speaking. Every proud letter receiver is eager

to share a response with the class. And every letter shared is instant motivation for new letter writers to try out the Send-Away Center.

Idea by: Sandra Markle, Dunwoody, Ga.

March 12

No. 195

PERSONALIZED LETTERHEAD

One way to get kids more interested in practicing letter writing is to have them use personalized stationery. Final drafts of letters can be written on these sheets of paper. (From *Basic Skills in the Content Areas: The Arts*, The EdCo Learning Center.)

Materials: scrap paper, ditto masters, paper, pencils and envelopes.

Students design their own letterheads on scraps of paper and then transfer their sketches to ditto masters. Run off 10 to 15 copies of each master on white or light-colored 8½-by-11-inch paper so that each student has a set of personalized stationery.

Teachers exchange class lists and pair students, or students themselves select names. If students need assistance in getting started writing, the class can discuss possible topics for letter writing (what children might say about themselves, what questions they might want to ask and so on). Letters can include such things as photographs, drawings, favorite jokes and school news.

When letters are completed, students address the envelopes to their pen pals. Each teacher puts all the letters in a large envelope for sending to the cooperating class.

Students can also use their stationery to write letters to friends and relatives.

March 12

No. 196

CLASSROOM ADDRESSES

It's always somewhat surprising to rediscover that the classroom is a microcosm; much of what we teach about the "outside world" is found in some form in the classroom itself. Being sensitive to this phenomenon enables us to bring real-life excitement to routine tasks. Suppose, for instance, you're about to focus on the capitalization of street names. If everyone uses a little imagination, each child can have a street address right in the classroom.

Each aisle becomes a street. The children will very likely have an abundance of possible street names; so you may have to put the favorites to a vote. Then a little research — conducted on neighborhood walks or field trips (group or individual) — will reveal that in most communities there are even numbers on one side of the street and odd numbers on the other. The children will also discover that directions determine the size of numbers: Numbers may, for example, grow larger as you go west on an east-west street and as you go south on a north-south street.

With this information, children can come up with a system of classroom addresses. A directory might be prepared — with all streets carefully capitalized, of course.

The project may not stop there. Children may decide to put their "return addresses" as well as their names on papers. They may want to correspond with each other at their "business addresses." Mailboxes and mail carriers may appear on the scene, and tips about letter writing and envelope addressing might be in order. Perhaps an energetic young entrepreneur will send out a mass mailing to the "occupant" at each address.
Idea by: Michèle Beal-Evans, Bush Elementary School, Salem, Ore.

March 12

No. 197

SAVING ENERGY MAKES CENTS

Computation and conservation go together in this activity. The format is a basic follow-the-path gameboard with students using a die or spinner to find the number of blocks to advance. The skills used are the four fundamental arithmetic processes. The content — cents saved or spent in relation to energy-using equipment — can very likely be obtained from publications of your local utility company.

The game goes like this: A player advances according to the number on the die or spinner and reads the directions in the ending block, e.g.: "Hang clothes on the line instead of using the dryer. Save 17 cents for each of four loads." The player does the computation, writes down 68 cents saved and then Player 2 sets out. Players keep a cumulative score of gains and losses.

Here are more label examples:
- Use a wind-up clock. Save 6 cents a month for eight months.
- Use electric coffee maker each day for the month. Spend 2 cents a day.
- Wash dishes by hand. Save 3 cents a day for a week.
- Turn off attic fan. Save 2 cents an hour for 12 hours.
- Broil some steaks. Spend 4 cents for using the broiler 15 minutes.
- Big savings! Car-pool with a neighbor and save 50 cents on gas each day for two workweeks.

- Hair dryer burns out. Save 4 cents every day for two weeks.
- Big savings! Cut down on TV. Save 1 cent per hour for 2 hours a day for a whole year.

Information on amounts saved (or spent) may be hard to keep up to date. But the idea of energy conservation is current even if the exact cent amounts are not.

Idea by: Shirley Heck, Ohio State University, Mansfield, Ohio.

Earth Day

No. 198

RETURN TO RECYCLING

Earth Day is celebrated in the United States on the vernal equinox, or the first day of spring. It is a time for concerning ourselves about the need to conserve

the world's waning resources, and therefore a good opportunity for raising some consciousness about recycling.

Each year American consumers pay more than $25 billion for packaging, 90 percent of which is discarded. From food and beverage consumption alone, more than 5 billion cans and 26 billion glass bottles and jars are thrown away. A change back to returnable bottles could save consumers $1.4 billion annually.

These and other facts lend force to the recycle movement. Locate recycling centers in your area. Have students prepare a recycling booklet for parents urging them to separate cans and bottles from the garbage for return to recycling centers. Finally, conduct a brainstorming session on ways to reuse old packages around the home and in the classroom.

Earth Day

No. 199

NO-PAPER DAY OBSERVANCES

Doodling, spitballs and origami-style airplanes are out when "No-Paper Day" is declared. So are ditto sheets and crayoned manila masterpieces.

No-Paper Day is simply a reflection of the times — with rising prices, numerous consumer products periodically coming up short, and various conservation efforts afoot. Doing without paper for one school day could be a revealing experience in creative coping. (Note: In the interest of health, No-Paper Day refers to the instructional phase of the day only; creative coping has its limits.)

Work with the children to establish alternative ways of handling the usual paper-dependent activities. Games may come in for increased use. The chalkboard may take center stage for more events. A spelling bee may be suggested. Science explorations will likely go on without a hitch, while paperless art projects may take some thought.

Each new task becomes a subject for analysis and cooperative planning as children discover new — and old — ways to do things. A sense of appreciation for the convenience that paper represents should be a valuable by-product of the project. And the sight of a less-than-overflowing wastebasket at the end of the day may carry a message of its own. **Idea by:** Phyllis Fox Stump, Richmond, Va.

Earth Day

No. 200

GARBAGE BALL

Storm, thaw; the weather's blah, and it's down to the gym in shifts. Running out of calisthenic capers, rousing relays, games and patience? You may be ready for garbage ball — especially if you teach primaries.

The rules are simple, and the game doesn't require the players to be particularly agile, or to be able to throw a basket, or to be able to hit a target with a ball. The game does require a goodly number of balls — playground balls, volleyballs and the like.

Divide the players into two teams and station them at opposite ends of the gym. Scatter the balls at random over the gym floor. Try to have an equal number on each side of the center line.

At the starting signal, players from each team try to get their side of the floor completely clear of balls by sending them over the center line. Kicking the ball and stepping over the center line are prohibited.

Children soon learn that it makes good sense to aim away from players on the other team; if a ball goes right toward an opposing player, it's apt to be returned that much quicker.

At another signal the game ends. The scoring system is up to you. You might assign differing point values to the various kinds of balls, or you might just have each ball worth one point. Now total up the points; the team with the low score wins.

Some variations:

1. Have teams move the ball only by rolling it.

2. Blindfold teams and see how many can find a ball and roll it across the line.

3. Have players pass the ball to a member of their own team first before sending the ball across the line.

4. Suggest using using only volleyball-style passes in handling the ball.

5. Have them pass with one hand only — the nondominant hand.

6. Specify parts of the body that may (or may not) be used in trying to get the ball across the line.

You may find more children are active in garbage ball than in some other games because more balls are in play, and children don't have to fear being hit intentionally as in dodge ball. And since it's a new game, everybody starts out closer to being "even." **Idea by:** David L. Wooster, Kenmore Public Schools, Kenmore, N.Y.

No. 201

WARM WEATHER WINDOW WATCHERS

Spring is in the air, and staring out the window is fast becoming the most popular pastime in the school. It is exciting to see the changes spring can bring, so instead of drawing the drapes, shades or blinds, why not help the class share what they're looking at.

Suggest a few guidelines for sorting out and listing some observations. These suggestions can be written on the chalkboard or appear at some "observation post" learning center. And since the possibilities in "look fors" are endless, the list can be changed often.

Students record observations for listing at random moments during the day—and should, of course, be able to point out any of the observations that are of a concrete nature. And if they're supposed to be looking for "something yellow," "the sun" doesn't qualify if the skies have been cloudy all day.

Here are some look-for starters:
1. What can you see that's hard?
2. What can you see that's red?
3. Look for something beautiful.
4. Look for something that begins with the /b/ sound.
5. Look for something that makes you unhappy or angry.
6. Look for something taller than you.
7. What can you see that moves? (You'll have to take students' word on this one, since whatever it is may have just moved on.)
8. What can you see that's round?
And for a little vocabulary enrichment:
9. Look for something *stationary*.
10. Look for something that would interest an *arboriculturist*.
11. What would an *entymologist* look at?

12. What do you see that is *ambulatory*?

The look-fors might involve math, art, creative/critical thinking, as well as other skill areas, depending on the level of the class and what seems appropriate to your current program.

Some kinds of observing have the potential for developing into discussions, more extensive writings or science activities. Gazing out the window can be more productive than it appears at first glance.

Idea by: Deborah Saunders, Cookson Elementary, Troy, Ohio.

No. 202

LOOKOUT BINGO

Lookout Bingo is a quick and simple way to help organize a field trip and to lend a sense of productivity without spoiling the fun. Bingo cards (standard format, five rows of five cells each) can be set up with content that will encourage students to use several senses as they explore, or the game can be designed to concentrate on one sense only. The cells describe (with pictures or words) objects, places, processes, even people for the explorers to find during their visit. Sample items might be: a spider web, rough bark, a seed, a sign of erosion.

All cards may be alike, or you may list items and let students fill in their own cards randomly. You may want to prepare a list of items on a large master sheet that can then be duplicated and used to construct "equivalent form" cards. Cards can be laminated for reuse, or small, self-adhesive labels can be placed in the corners of cells to be marked and covered over for the next game.

To play the game, students mark their individual cards as they discover the various items. "Finds" in a straight line score a Lookout Bingo.

Idea by: Charlie Rathbone, Living and Learning Center, University of Vermont, Burlington, Vt.

No. 203

A POND IN THE CLASSROOM

Without too much trouble, you can create a balanced mini-pond in the classroom. You can do it with or without plants and animals collected from a living pond. The following guidelines describe a balanced mini-pond that requires no outside maintenance once it is established.

In this sealed mini-pond, plants produce oxygen by using sunlight and animal waste materials for nutrients. The animals obtain food from the self-perpetuating community of organisms and oxygen from the plants. Observation of water samples under a microscope will reveal the presence of many plants and animals in your pond.

Initially you will need a clean gallon-sized jar with a tightly fitting top (or a small aquarium with a glass top that can be taped in place), several kinds of pond plants (collected from a pond, if possible, or purchased from a tropical fish store) and clean white sand.

Place two inches of sand on the bottom of the jar. Add pond water to within one or two inches of the container's top. If pond water is not available, use tap water that has been allowed to stand for at least 24 hours.

Introduce two or three kinds of aquarium or pond plants to the jar. Include small floating, rooted and submerged plants, and take care not to crowd them.

After allowing the jar to stand for several days in indirect sunlight, introduce animals to the mini-pond. A small quantity of *Daphnia* may be added first. They can be obtained from a pond, from a tropical fish store or from a biological supply house. A few small snails should also be added.

Seal the jar and let it stand in indirect light for several weeks, during which time it should develop a balance of plant and animal life. If the temperature of the mini-pond is allowed to become too warm (above 70 degrees), algae will form along the sides. To correct this condition, the pond should be placed in a spot with less light, or more algae-eating snails should be introduced. If the plant population becomes depleted, there are probably too many snails, and some should be removed.

Idea by: Will Kirkman, a freelance writer.

No. 204

POTATO DAY

Were it not for the potato — or more correctly, for the lack of potatoes during Ireland's Great Potato Famine in 1845 — there would be a lot fewer Irish people here in America. The famine forced the Irish to emigrate. So why not celebrate the Irish holiday, St. Patrick's Day, with potatoes?

Talk to your class about the plans for Potato Day. Ask what they like about potatoes and how many ways they can think of to use a potato. Make a list of activities and events for a Potato Party. Here are a few to get you started.

1. *Potato History*

The potato comes from South America where it was called by an Indian word that the Spanish explorer heard as "batatas." The Spanish brought some of these strange batatas along with them to Florida. When the British raided the Spanish colonies in Florida they carried off some batatas which to them sounded like "potatoes."

The traveling tubers were shipped to Britain where they were grown and fed to pigs at first because it was rumored that potatoes caused disease. (In fact, the green parts of the plant are toxic, but the tuber is good food.) The potato grew so well in Ireland that it became the main crop. People in America were introduced to potatoes in 1719 when Irish settlers came to Londonderry, New Hampshire.

There is more to the potato story. Kids in your class may want to do some research on the potato's travels, or more tangentially, on the origin of the potato chip.

2. *The Great Potato Feed*

French fries, hashbrowns, baked, stuffed, mashed — there must be a million ways to eat a potato! Have each student write out a favorite recipe, then assemble the recipes into a cookbook. Now kids can cook their potato favorites at home or, if facilities permit, at school.

3. *Potato People*

Kids can make vegetable sculptures using potatoes for the heads and assorted sliced vegetables such as carrots, celery, olives, radishes, turnips and carrot curls for the features.

Wash and set out the materials. You may prefer to slice the vegetables yourself. If so, use your imagination!

Each sculptor gets a potato and a handful of toothpicks. Show them how to stick on the features with the toothpicks. Stand up the potato people in cardboard collars assembled by stapling cardboard rings and setting them on their sides.

4. *Potato Prints*

This is a classic art project because it works so well. Each kid will need a potato, a knife, ink and paper.

These are the directions: First cut the potato in half to reveal a smooth white surface. Engrave a design with the point of the knife into the surface. Cut away the background to the depth of one-half inch, leaving the design area in

relief. Coat the design with ink and stamp it on paper.

5. *Potato from Outer Space*

If you leave a potato in the dark it will grow long white sprouts. A potato is actually a knob of stored food in the form of starch and sugar which grows from the roots of the potato plant. The proper name for the knob is a tuber. If planted, a tuber can produce a whole new plant.

Sponsor a "Weirdest Potato" contest. Give each child a potato and a plastic bag to see who can grow the most bizarre-looking crop of tuber sprouts. Let each kid experiment with the best sprout-growing conditions. After a few weeks you might want to commission some portraits of the contest winners.

6. *Potato Culture*

Those ominous fuzzy growths on foods left around the kitchen for too long are actually wild micro-gardens seeded by invisible airborne spores. The starch and sugar content of a potato make it a great place to grow such tiny mold gardens.

Cut some slices of baked or boiled potato and lay them in a plastic margarine tub with a lid. Expose the slice to the air for an hour, then cover it up and put it in a warm, dark place. In a few days you should see the dark signs of a colony of molds. Ask your micro-gardeners to speculate how the mold got there. Try growing mold on un-cooked potato slices. Why doesn't it work as well? Use a magnifier for an up-close look at the micro-plants. Request drawings of the little colony.
Idea by: Linda Allison, author of *The Wild Inside*, Sierra Club.

St. Patrick's Day

No. 205

MAKING RESEARCH A TASTE TREAT

A fruit-, vegetable-, and cheese-tasting party is a natural springboard to any number of health-related or food-related studies. You can plan research projects before your smorgasbord, or see what projects develop afterward.

Before the party is to be held, students can discuss which particular food each will contribute from home, and committees can be formed to prepare and arrange foods brought in. A buffet-style presentation may make for easy sampling and attractive display, or students may decide how they wish to have foods tasted. Post- or pre-nibbling projects may include such things as researching the nutrients beans supply, finding out where various fruits are grown, learning about how cheese is made or surveying how many students like rutabagas.
Idea by: Nancy Farrell McCarthy, Buffalo Public Schools, Buffalo, N.Y.

National Nutrition Month

No. 206

ARCHAEOLOGY DIG

Now is the time, right in the middle of the mud season, for you and your social studies class to start planning and preparing for an archaeological adventure that won't reach its culmination until next fall. (This is a "half and half" project: this year's class does the first half and next year's class does the other.)

Whatever part of the world you've been studying in social studies, it's bound to have a certain amount of historical diversity. Even the U.S., while a relatively young country, has seen Indian cultures, early settlements and modern civilization. Select an area of the world to focus on, and ask students to speculate on what items might be found if an archaeological excavation were to be undertaken at that place. Review and research each historical period or civilization related to the chosen area. Then make or collect items for "artifacts" representing the various cultures — pottery fragments, rope, food bones, scraps of documents (fixed with spray varnish), etc. Some evidence of the modern era should be collected too.

When the weather improves, organize the digging of a "dig" — about two meters wide, two meters deep, and long enough to accommodate a small plot for each student to work on (or limit the length to ten meters and plan to divide next year's archaeologists into groups of diggers, photographers or artists, catalogers, reporters, etc.).

Seed the dig, starting with artifacts of the earliest civilization in the bottom layer and interspersing succeeding layers with dirt. Then leave the completed dig over the summer for the "next generation" of archaeologists.

Before excavation begins next fall, you may want to provide the new class with some orientation in archaeology and archaeological methods.

It is quite likely that the class that does the seeding will want to be kept informed about next fall's "discoveries." This may be added motivation for the new archaeologists to do an especially thorough job of digging and reporting.
Idea by: Eileen Cooper, Cross Street School, Oxford, Conn.

No. 207

FOOD FOLK

A picture-cutout project gives visual reinforcement to the theme "We are what we eat" and reminds kids of important nutrition lessons.

Collect magazines with food-focused advertising and have the children cut out as many food pictures as they can. Have the kids separate the pictures into food groups.

Now invite the children to use the pictures to create food folk—characters composed of food pictures that represent a food group or a special nutritional problem, such as junk food. The children might decide to create a Sweet-tooth Sam or a Debbie Dairy, a meat muncher or fruit-and-vegetable twins.

Have the children draw outlines of characters on tagboard (or the backs of binders) and then fill in the outlines with food pictures, arranging, trimming and rearranging for the best effect. Some children may want to add features in black marker or construction paper.

When the figures are finished, you might ask the children to provide captions for their food-fashioned characters. The captions, which reinforce nutri-tional messages and describe personality traits, might be in the form of direct quotations or a dialogue.

Displayed around the room, the food folk are friendly reminders of good nutrition.
Idea by: Donna Anderson, Churchville-Chili Elementary School, Churchville, N.Y.

National Nutrition Month

No. 208

MATH FACTS HOT LINE

For kids having trouble mastering and remembering the multiplication tables (or any other math facts), a student-support telephone network might be the answer.

Ask students in need of motivation and assistance to agree to study math facts flash cards via the telephone. Parental permission will be necessary for these students to call each other several times an evening for short periods (two to five minutes) to drill each other on their work: "Hey, Greg, it's Sue. What's 9 times 6?"

Children will also have to agree ahead of time not to rely on answer sheets or cards while being drilled. With newfound support as well as an unusual study technique, frustrated students may find themselves on a direct line to success. They may also strengthen friendships along the way.
Idea by: Jeanne F. Turney, Gila County Schools, Globe, Ariz.

March 10

No. 209

EDIBLE ALPHABET

Young children may find it easier to remember the letter *j* if they associate it with the taste of jelly beans (or Jell-O or jelly rolls). And the same goes for the letter *i* (ice cream) or *y* (yams). In fact, with a little imagination (and indispensable aid from some parents—a room parent plus a volunteer crew, perhaps) you can make letter learning much more fun.

Make out your food lists and then schedule the foods in the order you wish to introduce the letters. After your own favorite letter-introduction activities—tracing, writing, forming in clay—it's on to eating.

(You'll notice that in the following list of suggested edibles there are both nutritious foods and popular "junk" items. These choices, as well as your own selections, will provide opportunities for discussions about nutrition.)

A — apples
B — bananas
C — coconut cookies, Coke
D — doughnuts
E — eggs
F — fudge
G — garlic bread
H — hamburgers
I — ice cream
J — jelly beans
K — Kool Aid
L — lemonade
M — marshmallows
N — nuts
O — oranges
P — pickles, popcorn, potato chips
Q — Quik (cocoa mix)
R — raisins
S — saltines
T — toast
U — upside-down cake
V — vanilla pudding
W — waffles
X — mystery food
Y — yams
Z — Zingers (cream-filled cakes)

To reinforce the food-letter association, you might prepare a large picture of each food labeled with its letter.

While letter recognition grows, children become aware of food preparation procedures and storage requirements as well as experience a variety of flavors and textures.

Idea by: Jennifer L. Fletcher, Ridgecrest Elementary School, Phenix City, Ala.

National Nutrition Month

No. 210

COMPLIMENTS OF THE CHEF

Nutrition can be a bore, but eating certainly isn't—especially eating out. And although a make-believe restaurant is not nearly so stimulating as the real thing, it beats a basic foods chart for excitement.

Suggest that each student is about to become owner and head chef of a new restaurant. Each palace of gastronomic delights will, of course, be needing a suitable name and an impressive menu of mouth-watering meals.

The emphasis is to be on serving the ultimate in nutrition—to keep those crowds of eager customers in top shape and coming back regularly; this is the prime responsibility and the creative task of each chef. Using the four basic food groups, each chef should come up with two or three (or more) full breakfasts, lunches and dinners—meals with variety and good taste. (Pricing of meals will add another dimension to the project.)

Some restaurateurs may want to develop a special atmosphere or carry out a particular theme in their establishments—reflecting this in the name of the restaurant, the look of the menu and the wording of the meal descriptions. If the specialty is to be some national or international food, research may be required, for authenticity as well as good nutrition.

Since these restaurants are to be designed to serve the public's need for good nutrition, not to cater to individual whims, no allowance will be made for placating picky people—no à la carte dinners of apple juice and chocolate mousse.

Idea by: Elise Wolcott, Marina Del Rey, Calif.

National Nutrition Month

No. 211

CREATIVE JUNK

Although your students may not solve the nation's trash disposal problems, they may surprise themselves with the number of ideas they generate for using trash items constructively. Most of the class will have come into contact with games, crafts, constructions that utilize bits of junk. Invite students to share their information and challenge them to come up with still more possible uses.

Have each student bring in some clean throwaways: egg cartons, plastic tubs, bottles, tubes, cans, aluminum pans. Your contributions to the project will consist of string, tape, glue, staplers, paint, brushes and other such fastening and decorating agents.

A trash renewal center can be established. Post suggestions students have already shared along with other idea starters. List materials needed and include illustrations or models if possible.

● *Egg cartons:*

1. seedling planters. Use the pulp kind so that seedlings can be planted outside right in the container.

2. artificial flowers. Cut slits in cups to form petals and attach the cups to pipe cleaners.

3. caterpillar toys. String cups together and decorate.

● *Milk cartons:*

1. bird feeders. Cut out one side and insert Popsicle sticks for perches.

2. desk organizers. Cut tops off cartons and staple several together, side by side or stacked.

3. pencil organizers. Cut off tops, invert, punch holes of appropriate sizes for pencils (or scissors).

● *Cans:*

1. hanging planters.

2. pencil holders.

3. kitchen containers.

● *Newspapers:*

1. fireplace logs. Roll newspapers tightly and secure with string. Newspapers can also be used in constructions of all kinds (papier-mâché, sit-upons, etc.).

Provide plenty of space for your inventors to use while creating, to set up displays and to post directions for their new craft ideas. A bulletin board devoted to construction instructions is an incentive for polishing clear, step-by-step descriptive writing. The bulletin board also provides a home for a reminder list of trash items you and the students will use as raw materials.

When you've collected a good supply of ideas, you might have students compile a *Creative Trashcraft* booklet to share with other classes.

Idea by: Jane Sammis, New London, Conn.

Earth Day

No. 212

MIGRATION MOBILES

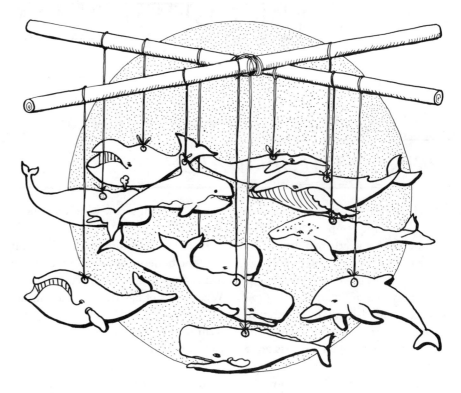

March is the month when the swallows return to Capistrano and the buzzards return to Hinckley, Ohio. In many other areas of the country, animals arrive punctually according to their migratory schedules.

Have your class make a study of animals whose migratory paths cross over the United States and its territorial waters. Include the whales who sound off the Pacific Coast, the sea lions whose spring mating on the beaches of Anno Nuevo, California attracts spectators, and the monarch butterfly whose arrival is celebrated in Pacific Grove, California.

When you have compiled a long list, ask each child to select a favorite species to suspend from a migration mobile. The construction of a suspension crosspiece is simple: Bind together with string two wooden dowels (or two sticks salvaged by the child) at right angles in the center. Provide lots of colorful poster board, heavy construction paper, or felt from which the kids can cut out at least five of their chosen species. They should first design a simple pattern so the cutouts will be consistent.

Let the kids punch holes in each of their cutouts, and then snip varying lengths of thin string and tie a string to each animal shape. At the other end of the string should be a small loop which slides onto the crosspiece.

When the animals dangle together from the mobile, they will look like a very colorful migratory group making its way back to its spring home. And with all those mobiles hanging at once, your room looks very well traveled!

National Wildlife Week

No. 213

BOTTLE CAP DOORMAT

You may have been recycling the bottles all along. Now, *Good Cents: Every Kid's Guide to Making Money* (Houghton Mifflin) suggests a project for reusing the caps.

"If you can collect enough of them, bottle caps make a doormat perfect for scraping the mud off dirty boots or shoes. It takes about 300 of them to make a mat 16-by-20 inches. The best place to get caps is anywhere there is a soft-drink machine. Any kind of cap works, even the twist-off kind."

Get a board about 16-by-20 inches. Plywood works best if it is exterior-type plywood, the kind that withstands water. It should be at least 5/8ths inch thick. Make rows with the caps (upside down) just touching each other. Drive a nail in the middle of each cap. After the caps are all nailed in place, spray paint the mat.

March 29

_____

No. 214

SPRING WEATHER WATCH
_____

March, with its roaring winds and its promise of rising temperatures, is a good month for weather study.

Eventually it's bound to get warmer. As a keep-up-your-courage measure (and for science and math learning too), start recording daily high-temperature readings and continue collecting them until spring's official arrival. Assign responsibility to students for recording the readings from weather wrap-ups on radio or TV or from newspapers.

Children can keep individual data sheets and graphs, but for maximum interest organize the class for the construction and daily updating of an impressive and colorful bulletin board bar graph. Appoint a new weatherperson each day.

As the temperature readings accumulate, the bulletin board can become the focus of discussion and speculation: What kinds of patterns do you find in the temperatures? Do the temperatures seem to go up and down with no pattern?

What was the average temperature during the first week of recordings? How does that compare with this week's average temperature? Were any temperatures exactly the same as the average?

On Wednesday and Thursday of this week the high temperatures were simi-

lar. What was different about the weather on Thursday that made it feel colder that day?

Share your "Hurry Spring" temperature graph by putting it on a hallway bulletin board, and it can spread spring — and graph awareness — to other classes too.

Idea by: Lois Smith, Conger Elementary School, Delaware, Ohio.

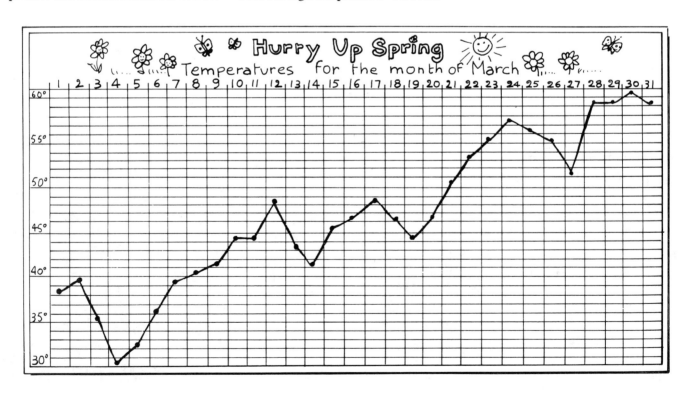

No. 215

WEEKLY BEASTIES

Animal life takes many forms — some of them quite fantastic. There are animals that puff up, animals with armor, and animals whose claws grow so long that walking is difficult.

Construct a "Beasts of the Week" bulletin board. Each week post three pictures of unusual critters (the more bizarre the better for older students), and assign each a number. Include three questions as a permanent part of the display: (1) What is the animal? (2) Where does it live? (3) What does it eat?

Provide 3-by-5 cards for students to write their speculations (and researched conclusions) about each question and staple a pocket at the bottom of the bulletin board to receive the responses over the week's time.

On Friday (happy Friday) the pictures can be taken down and some of the speculations can be discussed. Reasoning behind some of these guesses can be quite revealing; students may be noticing adaptations that suggest certain food habits or probable habitats. Correct answers can then be revealed.

National Wildlife Week

RESOURCES

MIGRATION STUDY MATERIALS—
● *Animal Migration* (BFA Educational Media, 2211 Michigan Ave., Santa Monica, CA 90404). An 11½-minute film describing animal migration patterns and reasons for migration.
● *Butterflies*, in the Wonder Starter series (Grosset & Dunlap, Inc., 51 Madison Ave., New York, NY 10010). A fine primary level introduction to butterflies. Colorful illustrations.
● Butterfly Garden (Nasco West, P.O. Box 3837, Modesto, CA 95352). A kit for raising your own painted lady or buckeye butterflies. Comes with food, display box and coupon for just-hatched caterpillars. (Class-size kits also available.)
● *The Year of the Butterfly* by George Ordish (Charles Scribner's Sons, Bookstore, Mail Order Division, 597 Fifth Ave., New York, NY 10017). An anthropomorphic description of a year in the lives of a pair of monarchs. So clear and descriptive a "story" that many intermediate grade children will be able to read it independently.

BOOKS FOR KIDS—
● *Elephant Seal Island*. Evelyn Shaw. Illustrations by Cherryl Pape. Harper. Recommended reading for the primary grades.
● *Evening Gray, Morning Red: A Handbook of American Weather Wisdom*. Barbara Wolff. Illustrated by the author. Macmillan. Recommended reading for the primary grades.
● *Wild Animals, Gentle Women*. Margery Facklam. Illustrations by Paul Facklam and photographs. Harcourt. Recommended reading for the intermediate grades and up.

RECYCLOPEDIA—A not-quite encyclopedic collection of recycled games, crafts, musical instruments, and science and math equipment is presented in *Recyclopedia*. Written by Robin Simons, this 118-page book contains about a hundred things to make and do that were developed by the author and the staff of the Recycle Center of the Children's Museum in Boston.

The projects are perfect for kids to work on either in classrooms or at home. Intermediate students can use the book independently while teachers can introduce the projects to primaries. The final products are either permanent learning tools (balance scales, word games, etc.) or one-time arts-and-crafts projects (weavings, sand castings, etc.).

Each project is described very simply and is accompanied by one or several line drawings that make the steps or the final products easy to visualize. Project descriptions run from a few lines to several pages. As the book title suggests, materials needed for the projects can almost always be scrounged for free.
Order from: Houghton Mifflin Co., 1 Beacon St., Boston, MA 02107.
Grade level: Primary–intermediate.

1

April Fools' Day!

2

Children's storyteller, Hans Christian Andersen born 1805.

3

Pony Express run between Sacramento and St. Joseph, Mo., begins in 1860.

7

World Health Day.

8

9

The American Civil War ends, 1865.

13

Thomas Jefferson, third President of the U.S., born 1743.

14

The *Titanic* strikes an iceberg and sinks in 1912.

15

Income taxes due today.

19

First battles of the American Revolution in Concord and Lexington, 1775.

20

21

John Muir's birthday. Father of our National Parks born in 1838.

25

Automobile license plates required for the first time in the U.S., New York, 1901.

26

Naturalist and artist, John James Audubon, born in 1875.

27

Ulysses S. Grant, Civil War general and U.S. President, born in 1822.

4

Martin Luther King, Jr. assassinated on this day in 1968.

5

Indian princess Pocahontas marries American colonist John Rolfe, 1614.

6

First modern Olympic games opened in 1896.

10

Humane Day. Celebrates the chartering of the ASPCA in 1866.

11

Jackie Robinson is first black to play major league professional baseball in 1947.

12

Russia launched the first person into space in 1961.

16

Silent film star Charlie Chaplin born in 1889.

17

Giovanni da Verrazano discovers New York harbor in 1524.

18

Paul Revere made his midnight ride tonight in 1775.

22

23

William Shakespeare's birthday. Best-known English-language playwright and poet was born in 1564.

24

First soda fountain patented, 1833.

28

James Monroe, fifth President of the U.S., born 1758. His policy toward Latin America called the Monroe Doctrine.

29

Huntingdon, Pa., becomes the site of the world's biggest Monopoly game, 1967. The gameboard was 550 square feet.

30

Formal end of the Vietnam war, 1975.

No. 216

EASTER INCUBATOR

While your students have their minds on chocolate Easter eggs and marshmallow chicks, why not introduce them to the real thing? Here is a project featured in *Science Projects for the Intermediate Grades* (Fearon Pitman) which shows you how to build an incubator, and how to incubate and hatch some eggs.

You will need a heavy cardboard box with a lid, a sheet of glass smaller than the side of the box, masking tape, a sixty-watt light bulb, a socket with a plug-in cord, a thermometer, a small pan of water and a number of fertilized chicken eggs (available at poultry supply houses).

"Cut a hole in the side of the cardboard box slightly smaller than your piece of glass. Tape the glass in the box so that it covers the hole. The edges should be sealed so no air can escape. Wire the light-bulb socket into the back of the box (opposite the window). Tape the holes so the box is airtight. Affix a thermometer to the back so that it can be seen through the window. Now you are ready to put the eggs in. Place the eggs on the bottom of the box with a pan of water beside them to keep the air moist. Put a sixty-watt bulb in the socket and plug the socket in. This will keep the temperature between 103° and 106°. Place the lid on the box. It should fit as tightly as possible, but don't seal it, because you will have to get into the box every day.

"Each day you should check the temperature to make sure it is within the proper limits. If the temperature is too low, the lid is not tight and air is entering. You may also need a higher watt bulb. If the temperature is too high, use a lower watt bulb.

"You will have to turn the eggs at least once a day, but not more than twice. This turning action keeps the baby chicks from being deformed by having their heads or feet stick to the shell. You may sprinkle water over them periodically. The eggs should hatch in 22 days."

If you want the chicks to hatch for Easter, be sure to plan in advance so that the 22-day period ends just before the beginning of Easter vacation.

Easter

No. 217

EGGSHELL MOSAICS

Chickens may have to start working overtime when the children in your class discover the fun in this art activity from *Easy Art Lessons* (Parker).

Before you begin, you'll need to assemble a few materials: eggshells; pans or jars; thinned-out food coloring or assorted paints; pencils; colored rug yarn (black looks best) or heavy cord; white glue; and heavy cardboard or thin wood panels.

Crush the cleaned eggshells and distribute them among several containers. Tint the eggshells with food coloring or paint, and spread them out to dry. Draw a design on the cardboard or wood. Glue yarn or heavy cord over the lines of the design. Spread glue in areas surrounded by yarn and cover the glue with tinted eggshell bits. Repeat until the picture is complete.

Any of the following may be substituted for the eggshell bits: pebbles of different colors and shapes; rice tinted with paint or food coloring; macaroni in various shapes and sizes (spray-painted gold or silver); dried peas, beans and corn (spray-painted or shellacked).

Easter

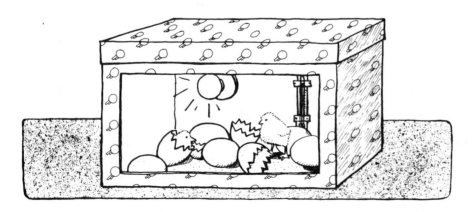

No. 218
EGGWORKS

Tie dyeing is a striking way to decorate fabric. In this simple dyeing project from *Time Out for Art* (Book B, Harcourt Brace Jovanovich), students use leaves, dye, dental floss and fabric to decorate hard-boiled eggs.

Each student will need two 4-inch (about 10-cm) squares of nylon stocking, a small leaf, waxed ribbon dental floss, two eggs, cooking oil and string. For the dye bath, you'll need water, vinegar, tea bags, a pan, a slotted spoon and a heat source.

When everything is assembled, have children place a leaf in the center of one of their two nylon squares and place one of the eggs on top of it. They should pull the nylon tightly over the egg, twist the ends of the nylon together and tie them tightly with string.

Have the kids wind as many pieces of dental floss around their second eggs as they like. They will have to tie knots in the pieces to fasten the dental floss, which creates designs on the eggs when they're dyed. Parts of the eggs should remain uncovered. Students should pull their second squares of nylon tightly over the eggs, twist the ends of the nylon together and tie them tightly.

To make the dye bath, fill a pan with water, adding three tea bags and half a spoonful of vinegar for each cup of water. Place the pan on a stove or hot plate and heat the solution until it boils. Now place as many eggs in the pan as it will accommodate, cover the pan and cook the eggs over low heat for 30 minutes. Remove the eggs with a slotted spoon and allow them to sit in cool water for about a minute. When the eggs are cool, have the children unwrap their creations and rub a small amount of cooking oil on them to make them shiny.

Easter

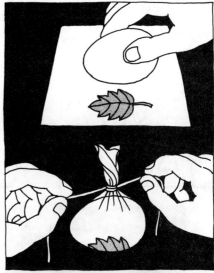

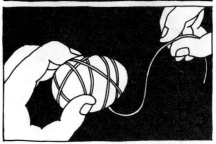

No. 219
EGGS AWAY!

"How can you drop an egg without breaking it?" The question comes from the writings of Tsiolkovsky, Russia's great rocket scientist. The answer is given in the following demonstration from *Science Teasers* (Harper & Row). Have students speculate before they try this solution.

"In Verne's book *From the Earth to the Moon* water was placed under the spaceship floor to serve as a shock absorber and to protect the space traveler from injury. Tsiolkovsky wondered if water could be used in this way. When he experimented with eggs in containers of water, he found he could drop them without breaking them. The trick was to keep the egg from floating to the top and from sinking to the bottom of the container.

"Can you think of a way to do this?

"Here is Tsiolkovsky's method: Put an egg in a glass that is half full of water and add salt until the egg floats.

Then pour in fresh water slowly, so that it forms a layer on top of the salt water. Since the egg sinks in fresh water but floats in salt water, it stays at the meeting place of the two layers. 'Now,' wrote Tsiolkovsky, 'strike the glass against the table as hard as the strength of the glass will permit, and you will observe the egg will not stir.'" (If students are to carry out the experiment, make the following adjustments in Tsiolkovsky's procedure.)

"Put an egg in a plastic tumbler. Add food coloring to the fresh water to see the separate layers form. Cover the tumbler with plastic wrap . . . and hold it in place with a rubber band. Then drop the tumbler outdoors. Even if it falls from quite a height, the egg will not break."

Easter

No. 220

INVESTIGATING CITY BIRDS

"Fewer kinds of birds live in the city than in the country. But the kinds that live in the city are found in great numbers. How do the nesting and feeding habits of pigeons, starlings, and house sparrows enable them to survive in cities?" begins this activity from *Investigations in Ecology* (activity cards published by Charles E. Merrill).

Choose one kind of city bird to study, such as the types mentioned previously or other birds particular to where you live. "Where do they nest and rear their young? Where do they roost at night and in cold weather? Look in the ivy vines that cover the walls of some old buildings. Look at the trim around doors and windows and under the eaves.

"Watch the birds eating. Make a list of the foods you see birds eating. In what kinds of places do you see most birds? When you go to the zoo or the park, notice where you see the pigeons, starlings, or sparrows. What are they doing?

"These birds are said to be *man-tolerant*. After you have watched them, try to explain what man-tolerant means. How do man's buildings and man's activities improve the environment for these birds?

"There are fewer birds around some of the newer buildings. Compare these new buildings with old ones. Try to explain why fewer birds are found there."

Do research to compare the city birds you have observed with their country brethren. Make a list of differences in their living habits.

April 26

No. 221

PINE CONE FEEDER

Here's a bird feeder that takes just minutes to make from all-organic ingredients. You will probably want to hang only a few in view from your classroom window, but you might want to provide additional materials so your kids can make their own feeders at home.

You will need a pine cone, a long length of string, two bowls, some peanut butter and bird seed for each feeder. Circle the string once around the pine cone, tucking it under the overlapping scales of the cone, then tie it securely. Put a generous portion of peanut butter in one bowl and a good handful of bird seed in the other. First roll the pine cone in the peanut butter, coating all of its shingles. Then roll it in the bird seed.

Suspend the bird feeder where you and your students can watch the birds that flock to peck at it. Repeat the rolling process whenever it becomes necessary to replenish the seed. That should be quite often!

April 26

No. 222

JOGGERS EXPRESS

Jogging is good exercise, but almost everyone agrees it can be boring. Setting a goal toward which to jog may help. And a really ambitious goal may be just the challenge some kids need to start taking jogging laps in earnest.

How about trying a reenactment of the Sacramento to St. Joe pony express trip. The distance for that run — which started on April 3, 1860 — was 1,980 miles (traveled in 75-mile segments by 80 riders with a change of horses every 10 miles, just for the record).

Plot out a track and set the number of laps that will represent the pony express run. (One lap might stand for 10 miles.) The class can combine laps run by individuals to achieve the goal. "Riders" may sign up to jog for the

pony express during their recess periods — volunteers only, of course — and report their laps to a recorder. Five might be set as a maximum "ride" per period. And since this is to be a jog, not a race, riders who get tired may walk.

Math comes into the process as the daily lap totals, the representative mileage and the laps-to-go are figured. A map of the U.S., circa 1860, can be

drawn, marked with the pony express route and used to plot the progress of the class riders.

When the class completes the route, a celebration might be in order, with awards and "decorations" for all participants — riders, recorders, map tenders, as well as cheering section. **Idea by:** Frank Sellers, Halls Hill School, Colchester, Conn.

April 3

No. 223

INTERNATIONAL BREAD TASTING

Spring is ushered in by two very important religious holidays, Passover followed by Easter. Like many other holidays, Passover and Easter feature traditional, symbolic breads — matzoh and hot-cross buns. Discuss the symbolism of the breads with your class. Extend your discussion to include other holiday breads and traditional ethnic breads. Then, propose an International Bread-Tasting party at which your students can sample many of the everyday and special-occasion breads eaten by different peoples of the world. You can tie in such an event with a social studies

unit on immigration or international relations, or you can incorporate it into a "discovering your roots" project.

Most metropolitan areas cater to different cultural eating groups, so if you live in such an area you won't have too much trouble finding a good variety of breads. If your class can afford a class trip, visiting local bakeries in the different ethnic neighborhoods of a city can be quite a culinary as well as a cultural learning experience. But, if your school is located in a more provincial area, you may have to find volunteer parents and grandparents to bake your class samples.

Here are some of the breads you might offer at your bread-tasting party:
knacker brod (Swedish)
pita (Mideastern)
scone (Irish)
stollen (German)

pumpernickel (Russian)
bagel (Jewish)
croissant (French)
corn pone (southern U.S.)
challah (Jewish)
sour dough (San Franciscan)
chapatti (India)
bruschetta (Italian)
tortilla (Mexican)
brioche (French)
rye (German)
You may also want to splurge and serve a few sandwich spreads — cheese, peanut butter, butter, or jam — and some fresh milk or juice. If you do, hold your International Bread-Tasting Party during the school lunch hour when appetites are biggest. Then you'll be sure to make adventurous eaters out of your students.

Passover and Easter

No. 224

REAL ESTATE MATH

Those outrageously expensive prices for homes can be used for outstanding and inexpensive activities for math. Start clipping real estate ads from newspapers or check with local realtors for castoff listings. Mount the ads on index cards for easy handling, sorting and distributing. Then use this costly collection to prepare math tasks that will give students a chance to wheel and deal with large numbers.

Some sample tasks:
● Pick ten real estate cards and put them in order from the cheapest to the most expensive house.
● Pick two homes for Richie Richman. Add the prices together. Then exchange your work with a friend who's also figured the combined price of the two homes. Check each other's work.
● Draw ten cards and quote the prices aloud to a few friends, who will write out each price. Compare the prices they write with the figures on your cards.
● Find one or more homes that will fit the Fosters' price range: $45,600–$52,900; the Pratts' price range: $86,400–$89,000.
● Fill in the blanks using the prices you find on the real estate cards: *The Kramers are considering buying a house. Should they spend as much as _____, or should they economize and look for a house in this range: _____ to _____?*

After handling a few real estate "deals" of this sort, students may come up with more ways of using the cards — a real estate card game, perhaps. And as prices continue to soar, at least there'll be no end of exciting activities for big number math.
Idea by: Kathy Newcaster, St. Mary's School, Herman, Pa.

No. 225

TAXING COSTS

"We all help to pay for government and its economic activities because, in one way or another, we are all taxpayers." And that includes kids. Let them find out for themselves just how much they personally contribute to keeping Uncle Sam solvent. (From *Government and the Economy: A Resource Unit for Grades 7, 8 and 9*, Joint Council on Economic Education.)

Have pupils keep records for a week or more of all their expenditures and the purposes of them, making special notation of the taxes included in the price. If no taxes are charged, pupils should attempt to find out if there are any "hidden" taxes, such as the entertainment tax often included in the cost of admission to a movie.

At the end of the accounting period, each student should compute the amount that was paid in taxes. What percentage of their allowance or earned income is this?

Next, see if they can figure out what they are getting for their tax money. If they are at a loss, point out such things as schools, police, public health facilities, parks.

April 15

No. 226

MONOPOLY WITH A LOCAL FOCUS

How about giving your class the opportunity to conduct business on a Monopoly-style board that has familiar landmarks — the opportunity to try their wheeling and dealing, their buying and selling in a distinctly local setting?

To set up such a game you'll need a supply of play money in various denominations, tagboard "deeds" for the properties shown on the gameboard, markers and, of course, the gameboard showing a pathway of local landmarks.

When preparing the gameboard, include a number of multi-block sections that reflect urban centers, neighborhoods, enclaves within the area. Label and color each section. Within each section mark businesses, such as hotels and restaurants, as well as libraries, schools, churches and city and community buildings. (Properties that will not be for sale should be distinctively marked.) Color railroads and utilities so that they contrast with the sections in which they're located. Add

parking lots (for free and for a fee), include a few "Pay the bank $20" and "Bank pays you $10" blocks, and set aside a jail as well as a couple of "Go to jail" blocks.

When the gameboard is complete, prepare the deed cards for the salable properties and color-key them to the appropriate sections of the board.

Turns are taken as in Monopoly, with players moving according to the pips on dice — buying available properties as they wish and paying rents as they must. For younger players you may want to simplify the transactions by making all property prices $10 and rents $2 ($10 if all the properties in a

section are owned by the same player). For more challenge, introduce such complexities as taxes and assessments.

In moving through the various sections, students may be introduced to landmarks or areas they've never seen and may want to visit. Research and field trips may be generated.

Many places shown on the board will, of course, be well known and popular "buys." Students should find it much more satisfying to "own" a local movie theater than to purchase hotels for a faraway Park Place.
Idea by: Quennie Ezelle, Prattville, Ala.

April 29

No. 227

GAME OF CHECKS

To provide easy-to-take practice (or review) of money-handling procedures — filling in deposit and withdrawal slips, writing checks and keeping a balance sheet — set up a special game of Monopoly. The rules will be the same as for the regular Parker Brothers game,

but all the paper money is to be removed. This version of the game also calls for a supply of checks for each student, along with deposit slips, balance sheets, etc., which you and the class may want to design especially for the game — carrying out the Monopoly mood.

Divide the class into playing groups of four or five with one member designated as banker. After the basic starting accounts have been duly recorded in the bank's ledger, all transactions — buying

property, making improvements, paying rents and fines, as well as collecting for passing "Go" and other such bonuses — are carried out with checks or deposit slips. The banker inspects all documents for accuracy. Each player keeps his or her own balance sheet.
Idea by: James D. Weaver, Hollansburg Middle School, Hollansburg, Ohio.

April 29

No. 228

BALL PARK MATH

If you're looking for an offbeat way to liven up math class, choose up sides and take over the baseball diamond.

But before you and your teams adjourn to the playing field, prepare two ditto master forms, one for each team, to use in keeping score and collecting math data. Head each "stat" sheet with the name of one team. Then make a six-column chart with the headings inning, single, double, triple, home run, total runs. Rule off nine rows across the sheet to accommodate nine innings. Don't duplicate the masters until after the game is over and you've recorded the data on the forms. Now gather up your equipment for math baseball.

As each player bats, fill in the statistics on the appropriate ditto master.

After the nine innings have been played (this may take several play periods), run off enough of both dittos for everyone in the class and create some story problems using the data:

● Based on the total number of home runs for *both* teams, what percent of the home runs did Team A make?
● Team B made what fraction of the total runs scored in the fourth inning?
● What was the average number of runs per inning for each team? for both teams together?

You can use the stats to review just about any math area you've been working with, from long division to metrics (using meter distances around the bases). At the lower grade levels the stats can be used to review addition and subtraction. Students seem to enjoy working with data that they've had a part in making. Stat data could make math a whole new ball game.
Idea by: J. Caldwell, Our Lady Help of Christians School, Los Angeles, Calif.

No. 229

AMERICA: THE BABY YEARS

Children can look at pictures of themselves to see what they were like as babies. But what about a country? What was America like when she was a "baby"?

To help your students better understand America's birth and growth as a nation, prepare a picture of the U.S. at her birth (perhaps in the form shown in the illustration), showing the 13 original states, the capital, major water routes and so on. You can discuss the early days of the country and put up a new illustration from time to time to show changes and growth over the years. Interest in the nation's development should heighten, and may produce such questions as, "What will America look like as she ages?"

Compared to other countries of the world, isn't America still a baby?
Idea by: Sue Morrow, Amqui School, Old Hickory, Tenn.

April 18 and 19

No. 230

RAIN GAUGE

How many inches of rain have to fall before puddles form? before water runs down the street? before there is "enough"? To get these answers, you might like to keep a running total of the amount of precipitation falling in your area. *Science 1: Observation and Experiment* (Holt, Rinehart and Winston) gives directions for making a rain gauge.

You'll need a funnel, a can, a jar, water, fingernail polish and a ruler. The diameter of the can should be slightly smaller than the top of the funnel so that the funnel can rest on the can without falling into it. The jar should fit inside the can.

"To make a rain gauge, first pour water into the can to a depth of 1 inch. Then, pour this water into the jar and mark the jar to show the level of the water. Use the fingernail polish to make the mark on the jar. Be sure the top of the mark is even with the top of the surface of the water in the jar. Now, pour the water out of the jar. Measure the distance inside the jar from the bottom to the top of the water-level mark. Mark off the rest of the height of the jar in lengths equal to this distance. Thus, all of the marks will be the same distance apart. Place the funnel in the jar and place the jar and the funnel in the can. You now have a rain gauge. Put the gauge in an open spot outdoors where it will not be upset.

"A light rain can be measured by means of the jar alone. A heavy rain will overflow the jar and be caught in the metal can outside the jar. This overflow can be measured by pouring it into the jar. The total rainfall will be indicated by the contents of the jar plus the amount of overflow."

No. 231

FACT AND FICTION

A good way to find an idea for a story is to go back into history, pick an interesting event and change it around a bit. Two writing activities from *Composition Workshop* (Yellow Level, Oxford Book Co.) help students do just that.
● "Everyone knows about Paul Revere's ride through the streets of Boston to warn of the British. However, little is known about how Paul managed to borrow a horse at such a late hour. Of course, Paul probably had his own horse, but we are going to change that for the sake of a novel approach to a story.

"Imagine that Paul Revere comes knocking on a neighbor's door about midnight and excitedly asks to borrow

No. 232

RAINY DAY RELAYS

Look no further for two great rainy-day or sports-alternative activities. (From *500 Games*, Grosset & Dunlap.)
● "Lemon Roll. Ever tried to roll a lemon across the floor using the pointed end of a pencil? Well, this game gives everyone a chance to see how difficult it can be. Form two teams with the players lined up behind one another. On the starting signal the first player of each team tries to poke his lemon across the room and back with a pencil. Then the second team member repeats the procedure and the relay game goes on until one complete team has finished the course. . . .

a horse. The neighbor, who was fast asleep, is both drowsy and angry. Therefore, he is slow to understand Paul's request, suspicious of Paul's intentions, and somewhat unwilling to lend the horse. Using dialogue whenever possible, relate what you think the conversation will be. Do not be afraid to use your vivid imagination."
● "We all know the legend about how George Washington chopped down a cherry tree, and how he later displayed his honesty by readily admitting the deed to his father. However, Mr. Washington's reaction to his son's mischief is not recorded in history.

"Imagine that it is a summer afternoon. George is busy sharpening his ax. His father enters, holding a few broken cherry branches. He is quite upset because he has just discovered that someone destroyed his tree. You write the conversation for this scene."

April 18

● "Blow the Cup Relay. A little preparation is needed for this team game, but the fun makes it well worth the trouble. You will need two plastic or paper drinking cups and plenty of garden twine or strong thread.

"Stretch two lines of twine across the room, and thread one end through a small hole in the bottom of the cup. Each cup should move easily on the twine. Tie the ends of the twine to sturdy furniture, and choose two teams to line up at one end of the room. The first player of each team must *blow* the paper cup to the other end of the twine. When he reaches the end, he slides it back with his hand and the next player in the team begins. The first team to complete the course will be out of breath, but they will have won the game."

No. 233

PARK PLANNING ON A SMALL SCALE

Combining a little science with some creative thinking and a bit of writing — all in an outdoor setting — could be an ideal way to channel energy often lost to the spring fidgets. Materials for this venture consist of paper, pencils, clipboards, hand lenses, an outdoor area with vegetation, and lots of imagination.

Each student is to select a spot — an area no larger than can be encircled with the arms — as a park site for the use of persons two inches tall. The student park planners then reconnoiter from the vantage point of two-inch-tall park visitors by getting down to ground level and using hand lenses to check out the landscape.

Suggest that students jot down "landmarks" that enhance their parks. They should try to imagine how these sights might appear to tiny people: Twigs might seem like fallen trees, pebbles might loom as if they were boulders, and one might come face to face with an ant the size of a dog!

In describing their parks, students may include not only what a visitor might see but also what a visitor's reactions, feelings and experiences might be. Students might try writing about "A Walk Through the Park" — an account by a diminutive park visitor who describes scenic spots along a particular footpath. Another project could be the designing of illustrated advertising brochures that list and describe the parks' attractions and recreation possibilities.

And looking ahead to next year's class, you might try sponsoring park tours in the fall, winter and spring, with students noting seasonal changes — as viewed from two inches above the ground.

Idea by: Don Englert, Woodstock, Ill.

No. 234

PLANT MAZE

A plant will go far in its search for light. In this easy-to-do experiment, a plant will demonstrate its tenacity by wiggling its way around obstacles in a closed box. Its goal? A hole at the opposite end of the box through which natural light shines.

You will need a three-inch-long stem of a Wandering Jew (genus *Zebrina*) or one sprouted white potato, a baby food jar if you're using the Wandering Jew, a shoe box, and masking tape.

Cut 4 cardboard rectangles using end of box as pattern. Cut each exactly as high as box, but 1½ inches less wide.

Tape cardboard into box to form baffles as shown. Spaces should alternate side to side. At one end of box, cut a slot as shown near bottom corner about ½ inch wide and 2 inches high. Cut the slat opposite space left by baffle. At end opposite slot, place either cut stem in jar full of water or sprouting potato (potato needs no water).

Cover and tape box lightly. (You will remove cover to observe.)

Place box so slot points at a strong light source. Observe the plant every 3 days.

Idea by: Will Kirkman, a freelance writer.

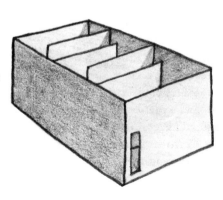

No. 235

A SCIENTIFIC SCAVENGER HUNT

A science scavenger hunt can be more than a simple shopping list of objects to locate. Try investing the listing with a little mystery — some items that require the application of some science knowledge or creative thinking. Here are a few for instances:

● an animal that has its own oars
● a forest dining table
● togetherness
● a tree that would be in sixth grade
● an insect apartment
● something invisible
● a predator-prey relationship
● a traveler without feet
● a highway

With this sort of list, many of the "finds" will require some explanation and justification as the scavengers check in. A "dilly" adequately justified is a dilly duly credited.

Idea by: Bebe Sarcia, Glastonbury, Conn.

No. 236

DISSECTING A DAFFODIL

While frogs in formaldehyde seem to have a distinct fascination for upper elementary kids, dissecting a flower can be equally "scientific." Plan your unit on flowers to culminate about the time those bunches of daffodils start arriving in supermarkets or when gardens begin overflowing with them. Provide each student with a daffodil and a labeled diagram of a flower. Have a sizable number of hand lenses available and a microscope for use when the task indicates a need for it.

Tasks and investigation questions such as the following can guide the dissecting process and flower study. (If it looks as if the project may take more than one period, flowers can be kept reasonably fresh in plastic bags with a few drops of water added to ensure adequate moisture.)

1. Make five good observations about the flower using four of your senses. (DO NOT TASTE.)

2. Describe the stem.

3. List some of the important things the stem does.

4. Describe the area between the end of the stem and the beginning of the flower.

5. According to the flower diagram, what is inside this part and what develops there?

6. Open this part and describe it.

7. Observe the inside of the flower with a hand lens and describe it.

8. Rub your finger in the middle of the flower and describe what you see on your fingers. What is this substance?

9. Observe this material through the microscope and describe it.

10. How does this substance (pollen) get from one flower to another?

11. How do you think pollen gets to people who are allergic to it?

12. Remove the outer petals and, using a hand lens, describe how they are attached.

13. What is the purpose of the brown leaves you see below the flower? Use the diagram to find and name this part of the flower.

14. Using the diagram and the flower itself, explain the development of seeds in the flower.

The budding botanists will no doubt find some satisfaction in carrying out their investigations — especially since each person gets to operate on his or her own specimen. And students can take heart in knowing that quite likely there'll be frogs in their future.

Idea by: John P. Martin, Anna P. Mote Elementary School, Wilmington, Del.

No. 237

UNDERGROUND SURVEILLANCE

Leaves stretching toward the sun and blossoms unfolding are only part of the plant-growth picture. Important action is going on out of sight below the ground. Spying on this interesting activity can be a bit tricky, though. (Pulling up the plant periodically to inspect the roots is not a recommended procedure.) What you need is a root view box. Make six or so; they'll come in handy for controlled experiments.
Materials:
• quart milk cartons
• heavy acetate or other stiff, clear plastic
• utility knife or sharp scissors
• rubber bands
• masking tape
• ruler
• seeds and soil
Procedure:
• Cut top off carton.
• On one side of the carton, draw a rectangular window measuring about 2½ by 4 inches.
• Cut across the top and down both sides of the window to make a flap that's still attached at the bottom.
• Working inside the carton, cover the window area with clear acetate and tape the acetate in place.

Now the root view box is ready to be filled with soil for planting. When you plant the seeds, be sure some seeds are close to the window side of the carton. Keep the window flap closed and secured with a rubber band most of the time because the roots will tend to grow away from light. Also tilt the box toward its window side so that gravity will encourage the roots to grow where they can be seen easily.

Use root view boxes to explore plant behaviors. Discover how roots develop in various soils (potting mix; potting soil with fertilizer; schoolyard soil; schoolyard soil with fertilizer; schoolyard soil with other additives, such as peat moss, perlite, sand, potting soil, etc.). Use the boxes to investigate how water moves through various soils. Think of ways to find out how roots respond to light and gravity.

Students may suggest other factors they would like to investigate in their root laboratories.
Idea by: James E. Abbott, Los Angeles Unified School District, Los Angeles, Calif.

No. 238

DESIGN A DAM

If rivers, ponds, streams or water in general fascinates your students, you might suggest a project that promotes inquiry into the design of dams.

Provide groups of four students with metal trays or pans with sides, modeling clay and, of course, water. Challenge each group to construct a clay dam across the tray (dams should be no more than ¼ inch thick), then to add water in back of the dam to see if it can withstand the pressure. As the experimenting gets under way, students should check with other groups to see which dams hold and which do not. Encourage inquiry into design features that hold back water more efficiently.

Suggest that students search reference books for pictures of famous dams, checking their configurations and noting whether dams are usually straight or curved. (Do curved dams bend toward the contained water or away from it?) This research may suggest new designs for the damming project. Students might also try experimenting with reinforcement materials.

This activity also has outdoor possibilities—if the class and the climate are favorably disposed.
Idea by: Barbara Clary, Columbia, S.C.

HAPPY TRAILS

One way to deal with spring fever is to take to the trail. Suggest to your restless students that together they work on compiling a Class Trail Guide. This will require some hiking and biking during out-of-school hours, and some publishing production during in-school time.

Have the kids independently retrace a favorite trail on bike or on foot, mapping the route carefully as they proceed. Ask them to note distances precisely if they have an odometer or pedometer, or relative to one another if they have no measuring device. They should also note the time it takes to follow the trail. Each kid should write in "landmarks" and identify interesting sights along the trail. If some kids are really in the mood to explore, then this activity may be the impetus for finding and mapping a new trail.

When the due date arrives, have the students bring their trail maps to class. Distribute dittos to everybody. Then have the kids redraw their maps onto the dittos. Duplicate all the pages so that all students will have copies of their own and everybody else's trail maps. Have them compile these in any of the following ways:

1. by mode of travel (bike or foot)
2. by distance of one completed loop (there and back)
3. by estimated time it takes to complete a loop
4. by location
5. by degree of difficulty (flat, lots of hills, etc.)

BEST BOOK OF THE YEAR

Suppose your class was asked to choose the best books for its grade level. How would students begin? What criteria would they use? "You don't want to put it down until you've finished." "You want to tell everyone about what's happening." "It's as if you were living in it."

Collect students' comments and ask the kids to keep these criteria in mind as they select and read books over the next couple of months. At the end of this time the class will hold a best book rally. At the rally, another class, basing its opinions on your students' campaign presentations, will vote for a best book.

As students read books that they feel meet the I-couldn't-put-it-down criteria, each submits an official nomination paper listing the title, author and reader's name — along with places for supporters (people who've also read the book and agree that it's worthy).

The official papers are posted. As students choose books to read, they may note nominated authors or series, or they may decide to read a nominated title to see if they wish to become supporters.

At the end of the campaign period, advise each nominator to select one of his or her nominations as most favored. Each nominator then prepares a campaign speech extolling the winning qualities of the book. The speeches can be presented in groups of four during a series of book rally sessions. Strive to keep these sessions focused on the books rather than on the presenters. Following these sessions, have the class select eight official candidate books and form committees to promote each one. The committee decides how best to campaign for its book and works with the nominator to develop a more elaborate presentation. (Committees also plan for a reasonable amount of pre-rally campaign activity — buttons, posters, etc.)

On book rally day the committees make their presentations before another class of students, who vote for "the book I'd most like to read." At the rally you might also display the complete list of books nominated. These, though not voted-in favorites, were greatly enjoyed by their nominators and represent a wide selection of good reading fare. The best book, after all, is the one you enjoy, regardless of what the critics and surveys say.

Idea by: Rosalind Engel, Iowa State University, Ames, Iowa.

No. 241

BASIC BASKET WEAVING

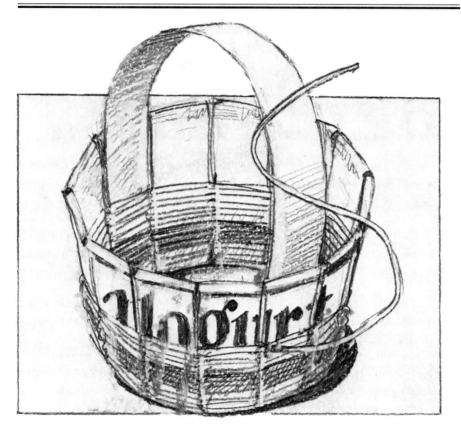

Since this craft activity calls for cartons that once held cottage cheese (or sour cream or margarine) in the quantity of one per basket weaver, you may need to rouse the recycling spirits of your class a bit in advance to assure an adequate supply. You'll also need quite a lot of yarn. But here again, calling in and recycling partially used skeins is a good beginning. (A variety of colors is desirable anyway.) As the children work, you may discover that additional yarn is needed, but the residue from everyone's winter handicraft projects can go a surprisingly long way.

Procedure: Measure the circumference of the container. (A one-pound cottage cheese carton will be in the neighborhood of 14 inches or 35.5 cm.) Divide this measurement into an *odd* number of segments of roughly the same width and mark the intervals along the rim with a felt pen. (For a 14-inch circumference you might have 13 sections of about 1-1/16 inch or 2.8 cm each.)

Slice the container sides at the segment markings from top to base. If the container is plastic, the edges may be a bit sharp, something to keep in mind as you collect containers. There's a problem with paper containers too. Their construction is such that you won't be able to slice all the way to the base, so you may want to cover the lower rim with Con-Tact paper—a 1-inch or 2.5-cm strip—before making the slices.

Pushing down and out on the sections from inside the carton will help separate the sections for easier weaving. This action can also be used to widen the circumference of the basket.

For a handle, securely anchor a strip of tagboard or cardboard in several spots down the length of two sections that are approximately opposite each other.

Tie the end of a hank of yarn around the base of one section, knotting it inside, and begin to weave it in and out of the sections. Push initial rings of yarn well down into the sections all the way to the base. When a new color is started, tie off the preceding color and knot the new one inside the container as before. Weave the colors until the entire container is covered. Wrap the handle.

The finished product, no longer resembling a dairy-case castoff, is ready for Easter goodies or, looking ahead, May flowers.

Idea by: Marlene Rorke, Garfield School, Yakima, Wash.

Easter

No. 242

APRIL FOOLS!

April Fool's Day is a creative holiday. A person has to invent a new way to celebrate it each year. In England it has been celebrated for a long time and in times past it was called Feul Gawk Day. The victims were called *gawbys* or April *noodies*.

Here is a box your kids can make with a fool inside to fool a friend outside of class.

Each kid will need a small box (the Styrofoam kind that comes wrapped around a fast-food hamburger is fine, or any small cardboard box will work), some big sheets of fairly heavy paper, crayons or markers and glue.

Here are the directions:

1. Cut out the fool according to the pattern, or draw one of your own about the same size. Color it in with wild, crazy colors. The kids in class might pose for each other looking as foolish as possible.

2. For a paper spring, cut two strips of paper at least 20 inches long and 1½ inches wide. Put the strips at right angles to each other. Fold the under-strip around and over the top strip keeping them at right angles to each other. Repeat the process for the entire length. Tape the ends together.

3. Glue the fool to the end flap.

4. Glue or tape the end of the spring to the bottom of the box.

5. Shut the lid taking care not to crush the little fool.

6. Present the fool to an unsuspecting noodie.

Idea by: Linda Allison, author of *The Wild Inside*, Sierra Club.

April Fool's Day

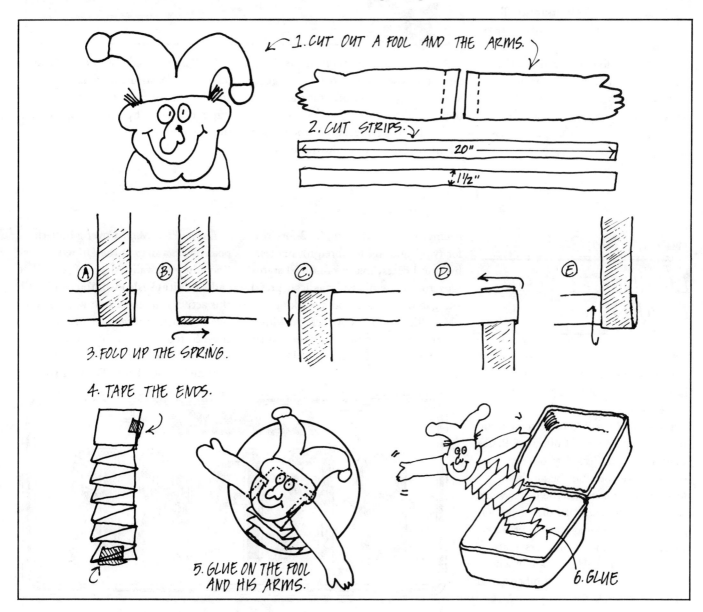

1. CUT OUT A FOOL AND THE ARMS.

2. CUT STRIPS. 20" 1½"

3. FOLD UP THE SPRING. A. B. C. D. E.

4. TAPE THE ENDS.

5. GLUE ON THE FOOL AND HIS ARMS.

6. GLUE

No. 243

BULLETIN BOARD NUMBER TOSS

Kids will get practice in both mental and physical skills in this game from *Pin It, Tack It, Hang It: The Big Book of Kids' Bulletin Boards* (Workman). To work well, both types of skills must be exercised accurately.

1. Cut and fold a long strip of oak-tag to make a number toss game.

2. On the front face of the game cut out circles large enough for a Ping-Pong or a four-inch foam ball to pass through.

3. Write in numbers below each hole. Use lower numbers for younger kids and higher numbers for the upper grades.

4. Tack the back flaps of the game to a bulletin board. (See illustration.)

5. Players should decide how many tosses will constitute a game. No points are given if the ball does not go through a hole. If played competitively, the highest score wins.

No. 244

LICENSE PLATE BOARDS

Original and personalized license plates are the basis for two bulletin board activities for your road-happy students.

Collector's Plates. Allocate some bulletin board space for a "Collectors' Plates Exhibit." For at least a two-week period, have your kids be on the lookout for unusual license plates when they're on the road with their folks, or during their everyday busride or walk to and from school. Collectors' plates can include those which contain whole words, rebus letters and numbers (such as EZ for easy, MT for empty, NME for enemy, DV8 for deviate, T42 for "tea for two," and 4N for foreign), names, historical dates, marks of official status (government, embassy, medical, press) and gag frames. Run off a stack of blank "license plates" which the kids can use to make replicas of their collectors' plates. Display them on the bulletin board.

License Plate Map. Cover a bulletin board with a map of the United States (including Hawaii, Alaska, Puerto Rico and the Virgin Islands). You can handle this activity in one of two ways. If you live in a metropolitan area or a well-traveled tourist town, have your students keep their eyes open for out-of-state license plates. The first student

RESOURCES

BOOKS ABOUT PLANTS AND PLANTING—
● *A Gardening Book: Indoors and Outdoors* by Anne Batterberry Walsh. From Atheneum, 122 E. 42nd St., New York, NY 10017.
● *Grow a Plant Pet* by Virginia Fowler Elbert. From Doubleday & Co., Inc., 245 Park Ave., New York, NY 10017.
● *House Plants for the Purple Thumb* by Maggie Baylis. From 101 Productions, 834 Mission St., San Francisco, CA 94103.
● *Kids Gardening* by Aileen Paul. From Doubleday & Co., Inc., 245 Park Ave., New York, NY 10017.
● *Look, Mom, It's Growing* by Ed Fink. From Countryside Books, 200 James St., Barrington, IL 60010.
● *Vegetables in Patches and Pots* by Lorelie Miller Mintz. From Farrar, Straus & Giroux, Inc., 19 Union Square West, New York, NY 10003.
● *Watch It Grow, Watch It Change* by Joan Elma Rahn. From Atheneum, 122 E. 42nd St., New York, NY 10017.

BOOKS FOR KIDS—
● *What's Hatching Out of That Egg?* Patricia Lauber. Crown. Recommended reading for the primary grades.
● *How to Play Baseball Better Than You Did Last Season.* Jonah Kalb. Illustrations by Kevin Callahan. Macmillan/Collier. Recommended reading for the intermediate grades.
● *Baseball: A Game of Numbers.* Addison-Wesley. An activity book recommended for the intermediate grades and up.
● *Tree Boy.* Shirley Nagel. Illustrated with drawings and photographs. Sierra Club. Recommended reading for the intermediate grades.

TEN-MINUTE FIELD TRIPS—
Ecology is an everywhere happening, and everywhere includes even the playground of your city school. If you're a doubter, or if you're a believer and want a little guidance, Helen Ross Russell's book is for you.

Subtitled "Using the School Grounds for Environmental Studies," the book's six main chapters deal with various aspects of the environment: plants, animals, interdependence of living things, physical science, earth science and ecology. The chapters are divided into sections, each of which provides teacher-preparation guidelines, in-class activities, possibilities for field trips outside of the classroom and a good deal of background information. The chapter on plants, for example, has sections on trees, leaf coloration, buds, seeds, grasses and dandelions.

While not all the activities can be performed by teachers everywhere, most can—either as is or with some adapting. For city teachers, there is a special section that cross-references the field trips for hard-topped school grounds. In addition, the book includes an index and bibliographies of supplementary materials for teachers and students (with appropriate grade levels and keyed to the chapters of the book).

Order from: J. G. Ferguson Publishing Co., 6 N. Michigan Ave., Chicago, IL 60602. **Grade level:** Teachers of primary–junior high.

---

to spot an out-of-state plate gets to pin a miniature replica (the student's own) on the map. Only one plate for each state is permitted. Keep the map up for quite a while if you want your students to come close to finding a plate for each state.

If you live in a less-traveled part of the world, have your students turn to the encyclopedia or an almanac to find pictures of the state and territorial license plates. If possible, cut up the pictures so that you have separate plates, or write the names of the states and territories on individual scraps of paper. Have the students randomly draw (probably twice each) to find out which license plates they are responsible for replicating and pinning on the map. Provide small rectangular cards and color markers for their construction.

April 25

CHAPTER

MAY

1

Law Day.

2

Louisiana Purchase from France in 1803 doubles the size of the U.S.

3

Sun Day. Celebrated since 1977 to promote solar energy.

7

The *Lusitania* torpedoed and sunk by a German U-boat in 1915.

8

World Red Cross Day.

9

Admiral Richard E. Byrd and Floyd Bennett are first men to fly over North Pole, 1926.

13

Jamestown, first permanent English settlement in America, founded by Capt. John Smith in 1607.

14

Lewis and Clark start cross-country expedition, 1804.

15

First baseball stadium opened in Brooklyn, N.Y., 1862.

19

20

International Bureau of Weights and Measures established in 1875.

21

Lindbergh makes first solo transatlantic flight and lands in Paris, 1927.

25

Star Wars released by 20th Century Fox in 1977.

26

27

San Francisco's Golden Gate Bridge is opened to traffic, 1937.

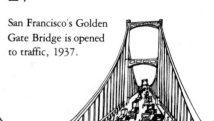

TEN

DAY BY DAY

4

5

Cinco de Mayo. Mexican and Mexican-American holiday celebrating the Battle of Puebla.

6

The first postage stamp is issued in Great Britain in 1840.

Golden Spike Day. First transcontinental railroad completed in 1869.

11

Station in Schenectady, N.Y., became first television station to begin regularly scheduled broadcasts.

12

Florence Nightingale, the founder of modern nursing, born 1820.

16

Congress authorizes first five-cent coin in 1866.

17

Supreme Court rules that racial segregation is illegal in public schools, 1954.

18

Mount St. Helens erupts, 1980.

22

National Maritime Day. First successful crossing of the Atlantic by steamship, 1819.

23

Ben Franklin invents bifocals, 1785.

24

In 1844, Samuel Morse sent the first telegraph.

28

Sierra Club founded, 1892.

29

Edmund Hillary reaches the top of Mt. Everest in 1953.

30 First auto accident, New York City, N.Y., 1896.

American poet and author, Walt Whitman, born in 1819. **31**

No. 245

COLLECTION, CLASSIFICATION AND MORE

When good weather beckons everyone outside, go on a collection walk.

Although the destination may vary — a park or nearby woods, a meadow or the schoolyard — the project is the same: each child is to collect ten natural items of a size that will fit into a small plastic bag. A collection might be several small stones, some twigs, seeds, leaves and a feather. (Because of their zeal for collecting, children may need to be reminded that they ought not to tear up plants, peel bark or terrorize tiny creatures.)

Wide variety in kinds of items is not necessary; you might even suggest that a child "specialize," collecting ten pebbles, ten leaves, etc.

Back in the classroom distribute large sheets of paper and have each child spread out his or her collection. Have the children study their items and try to separate them into several categories. Next have children study these primary categories for further sorting possibilities. They will be looking for likenesses and differences in color, texture, shape, size, pattern, weight, etc. On their papers the children may draw boxes or circles in which to house the various groups. Each set of items is then given a descriptive label. A child whose collection is of leaves might organize the specimens into long leaves, roundish leaves and big leaves.

As children do this sorting, they may discover problems, such as where to put a leaf that is both round and big. They may see the need to establish more discriminating categories.

Before the children get too technical in their sorting (or too frustrated by it), call a sharing session. Discuss and record some of the vocabulary they've been using in the grouping process: *same, different, group, set, match*. Were some items "left over" or in a set of one? Were any of the items they found *exactly* alike? What would it be like to try to put the children in the class into sets in the same way the children had classified their leaf and stone collections?

Help the children see that although grouping things is often useful for study purposes, uniqueness and diversity are important. These discussions may make this collection walk a little different from the usual nature excursion.

Idea by: Connie Zane, Azusa Unified School District, Azusa, Calif.

No. 246

CLAIM IT, NAME IT

The next time you schedule a field trip to a meadow, forest or seashore, suggest that children look for plants they especially like and would enjoy naming. Ask each student to select one plant as his or her own — preferably one not selected by someone else. In the process of avoiding plants already claimed, students must observe carefully and make comparisons to determine whether the samples they've chosen are the same species or simply similar.

When a student has claimed and verified his or her own plant, the naming can begin. Some plants will be named for their appearance: "hairy carrot," "green arrow." Other names may refer to locations where plants are found: "dune topper," "swamp beauty." Or the plant finder may decide to claim the plant as a personal prize: "Brandt plant."

Individual plant samples can then be mounted on posterboard and labeled with the newly created names, along with the plants' common names.

Discovering a plant, examining it and then naming it on the basis of its special characteristics is a sure way to sharpen observation skills while strengthening awareness of common plants. Students who encounter plants in this way may show more attention to details of plant structure and habitat than they would if you tried to teach them. They may also develop a sort of kinship with the plants they've claimed and named: "That's one of *my* plants."

Idea by: Larry Guthrie, Indiana University Northwest, Gary, Ind.

No. 247

NATURE MOBILES

Any sharp-eyed naturalist who goes out on a field trip can't help filling his or her pockets with specimens on the way home. Kids are no exception. Why not have your class convert those pocket natural history museums into a hanging display. You could pool the specimens and make several large class displays or have the kids make individual mobiles.

You will need some clear fishing line, a branch or piece of driftwood for the anchor piece, and natural history specimens from your collection, such as shells, feathers, seeds, stones, insect bodies, claws, bleached bones, leaves, pods, and cones, rusty and weathered things.

1. First, use a slip knot to attach the objects to 15 varying lengths of string.

Or, wrap the cord around the object if it is something as bulky as a rock. In the case of a shell, try drilling a hole to slip the line through.

2. Tie a string to the center of the anchor branch so that it balances. Hang it up while you attach the hanging museum pieces.

3. Tie the specimens onto the anchor branch. Work to achieve a balanced arrangement. Lengthen and shorten the strings so items don't bump into each other. You can slide things a bit at the last minute to fine tune the balance.

If you want a more learning-oriented project, have the students make identification tags for each of the things on the natural history mobile. Suggest various field guides to plants and minerals if your students get stuck.

Idea by: Linda Allison, author of *The Wild Inside*, Sierra Club.

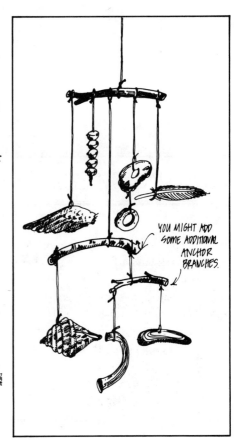

YOU MIGHT ADD SOME ADDITIONAL ANCHOR BRANCHES.

No. 248

VASCULUM

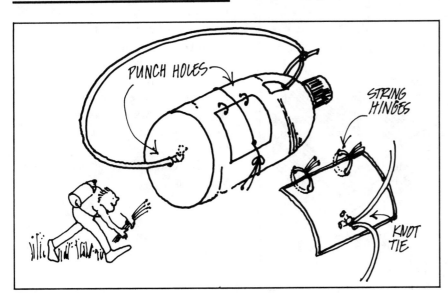

PUNCH HOLES

STRING HINGES

KNOT TIE

A vasculum is a bottle a botanist uses for collecting plants. It helps keep the specimens fresh and uncrushed until you get them home to your plant press. It's especially good for kid botanists who seem to have uncanny talent for smashing and crunching almost everything they touch. It's handy to take along on a hike if you think you'll be climbing cliffs and crawling along creeks. And it can always double as an emergency carrier for a toad.

Here's how to make one:

1. Cut a square door out of the side of a bleach bottle.

2. Punch holes in the door and the bottle for hinges.

3. Tie the door on with string or wire.

4. Add a long string onto the door. Wrap it around to shut the bottle.

5. Tie on a long rope for a carrying strap. Put a damp sponge or wet newspaper inside to keep specimens fresh.

Idea by: Linda Allison, author of *The Wild Inside*, Sierra Club.

No. 249

PRESSING MATTERS

When people traveled for pleasure back in the old days, they often packed a sketch book and a flower press. These were standard vacation equipment, much like an Instamatic camera is today.

If you know something about botany, collecting flowers can tell you a lot about a place. But you don't have to know a thing about botany to enjoy flowers. Pressing them is a way to get them home so you can study them or just look at them. Here is a simple press you and your students can make to take along on your next field trip.

You will need some corrugated cardboard, newspaper, and strong rubber bands.

1. Cut about five rectangles of cardboard the same size. An 8½ by 11 inch size is good. Or, if you'd rather, cut half-size boards for a more compact traveling press.

2. Cut about 40 sheets of newspaper the same size as your boards.

3. To press, lay your plant on several sheets of newspaper. Arrange it. Cover it with another couple of sheets, then a cardboard. Repeat until all your flowers or boards are used up.

4. Bind the press with rubber bands.

5. If possible, weight it with heavy books or bricks.

Idea by: Linda Allison, author of *The Wild Inside*, Sierra Club.

No. 250

HOT/COOL COLORS

Does color affect temperature? You can help your students find out the answer with a simple experiment involving water, sunlight, test tubes and colored paper.

Fill several test tubes with water and seal them with corks into which thermometers have been inserted (you'll probably have to drill a hole for each thermometer). Put a different colored sheet of paper behind each test tube and record the temperature of each vial of water.

Now expose all the test tubes with their colored backings to sunlight for five minutes. Read the temperatures again and record them. Are there any differences? Continue the experiment a while longer (up to 30 minutes), recording the temperatures every five minutes. Then ask students what they can say about how color affects temperature.

You can also try the experiment with test tubes completely covered with colored paper, leaving them wrapped and in sunlight for half an hour and then comparing temperatures with initial readings. Ask the class again to consider how the individual colors affect temperature.

Idea by: Carol Whiteley, Mountain View, Calif.

Sun Day

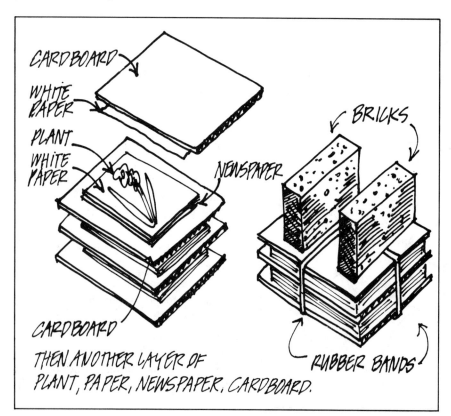

CARDBOARD

WHITE PAPER

PLANT

WHITE PAPER

CARDBOARD

THEN ANOTHER LAYER OF PLANT, PAPER, NEWSPAPER, CARDBOARD.

NEWSPAPER

BRICKS

RUBBER BANDS

No. 251

PHOTOGRAMS

Making photograms is a fine activity for a bright May day, for any day when there is a lot of available sunlight. It involves a photographic process on light sensitive paper. Making a photogram is sort of like taking a picture directly on paper, skipping the film step and all the fuss with the lens. The results are simple silhouettes that are quite attractive and a lot of fun to make.

You will need: (1) A package of Studio proof paper, also known as contact printing paper; 8 by 10 inches is a good size. (2) A box of fixer (sodium thiosulfate). You can buy this and the paper at a photographic supplier. (3) A sheet of clear glass. (4) A glass or plastic pan slightly bigger than your paper. (5) A sheet of cardboard.

1. Start by mixing up the fixer. ¼ cup of sodium thiosulfate crystals dissolved in two cups of warm water should be enough to start with. Set it aside to cool.

2. Now is the time to test the light. Cut a sheet of paper into quarters. (In fact, you could quarter all the sheets to stretch the paper.) Do this in a place away from direct light and return it to its envelope. Remember that the paper is sensitive.

3. Set up your sample. First, lay down the cardboard, next, a sheet of proof paper. Find something you want to print, such as a grass or a handful of paperclips. Arrange your items on the paper and place a sheet of glass over the whole setup.

4. Take the whole thing out into the sunlight and expose it until it turns dark purple. Don't move it or you'll have blurry edges. (You can vary the exposure time for a lighter or darker background—the longer the time, the lighter the background.)

5. Move the proof paper to the shade. (Hey, it already looks like you've got yourself a photogram!) Drop the picture into the fixer and swish it around for about two minutes.

6. Rinse it in running water for 8 to 10 minutes.

7. Hang it up to dry.

8. Before it is completely dry, press it between some heavy books to flatten it out.

You might try making photograms of leaves, grasses, insects, keys, paper cutouts, chains, feathers, clips; all are materials for photograms. Finding subjects is not the challenge; it's providing enough photopaper that is the hard part. Photograms are a project that kids dearly love.

Idea by: Linda Allison, author of *The Wild Inside*, Sierra Club.

Sun Day

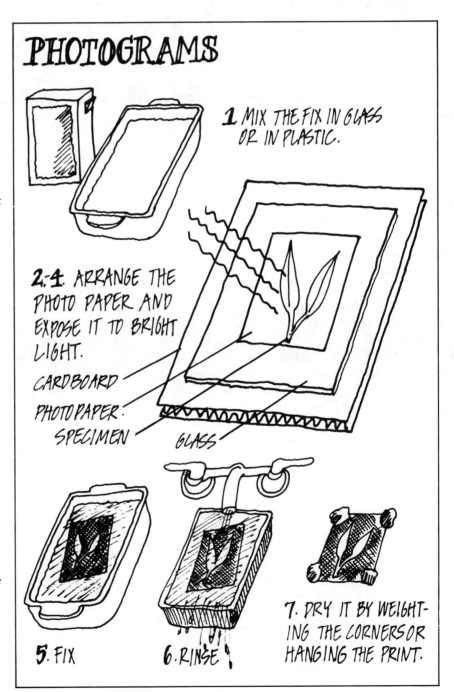

PHOTOGRAMS

1. MIX THE FIX IN GLASS OR IN PLASTIC.

2.-4. ARRANGE THE PHOTO PAPER AND EXPOSE IT TO BRIGHT LIGHT.

CARDBOARD
PHOTO PAPER
SPECIMEN
GLASS

5. FIX

6. RINSE

7. DRY IT BY WEIGHTING THE CORNERS OR HANGING THE PRINT.

No. 252

GET IN GEAR

Many science principles, such as the action of simple machines, can be demonstrated through model-making activities. Making working models of gears, however, can be a bit tricky because cogs must be uniform in size and regularly spaced, and the gear wheels must be securely positioned so that contact is maintained without the cogs missing or jamming.

Materials:
• lids (Collect container covers, jar lids and shallow cans of various sizes. Experiment to find pairs of lids that will nest — one lid fitting inside the other.)
• corrugated cardboard
• fiberboard or other board to serve as a foundation for mounting gears

Procedure:
• Select two pairs of nesting lids. The larger of each pair will be a gear wheel.
• Cut strips of corrugated cardboard in widths to match the heights of the gear wheel sides.
• Test wrap a strip of cardboard around each of the gear wheels. The strips should fit in such a way that the cogs

mesh when the two wheels are brought side by side and rotated. If the strips fit well, glue them in place. If they don't, try other pairs of nesting lids until you find a good match.
• After gluing a cardboard strip onto both gear wheels, you're ready to position the gear wheels over their smaller "partner" wheels. Glue or nail one of the small lids onto the foundation board and place its gear wheel over it. Carefully position the second pair of lids — gear wheel on top — so that when the small lid is glued down, the cogs of the two gear wheels will mesh.
• Put a dot or arrow on top of each gear wheel to help you keep track of the revolutions.

Now set the wheels in motion. You might suggest some of the following inquiry activities:

Turn one gear in a clockwise direction. In which direction does the other wheel turn?

Turn one gear wheel so that it makes one complete revolution. How many revolutions does the other gear make? Note the number of revolutions made by the second gear when the first gear makes three complete revolutions.

Compare the circumferences of the gear wheels. Compare the diameters.

What kinds of gears are involved in our daily lives? Examine a working clock. Try to arrange for a visit by an auto mechanic instructor who can explain about gears in cars. And don't overlook the bicycle!

Idea by: Karen E. Reynolds, Havenscourt Junior High School, Oakland, Calif.

American Bike Month

No. 253

SPICE PAINTINGS

Pictures usually delight the eye. These odoriferous paintings will surely delight the nose as well. (From *Developing*

Human Potential, ERA Press.)

To produce delicious-smelling paintings, provide the kids with a variety of aromatic spices (marjoram, thyme, mint, garlic powder, basil, nutmeg and the like); construction or drawing paper; paints or felt markers; white glue diluted with water; small paintbrushes. Have the children paint their designs

on pieces of paper and then paint over portions of the artwork with the glue solution. Before the glue dries, have the kids sprinkle a variety of spices on the sticky areas.

Specific themes — spring, flowers, landscapes — can guide the odoriferous artwork, or the paintings can be abstract.

No. 254

A BUBBLE YOU CAN KEEP

Is there such a thing as a bubble you can keep? How can you make a bubble with tougher skin? Gelatin bubbles — though not indestructible — are quite a bit more durable than ordinary soap-and-water ones. And although making gelatin bubbles is somewhat complicated and messy, the results are interesting and fun.

You'll need boiling water to dissolve the gelatin, and you'll also need to set the gelatin bubble mixture in hot water to keep the mixture free-flowing and blowable.

The gelatin bubble mixture contains 2 cups water, 8 tablespoons (packages) unflavored gelatin, about 2 tablespoons glycerin and 1 tablespoon liquid dish-washing detergent. Dissolve the gelatin in very hot water, then stir in the glycerin and soap. Set the container of bubble mixture in a larger pan of hot water on a hot plate or in a hot-water bath in an electric frying pan. You might prepare a double batch of gelatin bubble mixture and keep it simmering over water; this way you can dip out a small portion into a Styrofoam cup for each child. Children can come back for fresh warm mixture when their supplies begin to thicken. (The cooling gelatin can be poured into a second pan and subsequently reheated.)

Children will notice a marked difference in these bubbles. Freed bubbles of this mixture may float away on the breeze until they are too distant to be seen. Outdoor use is advised because of the greater floating space for bubbles and because the bubble skins stick tight wherever they land. Drippings congeal quickly too, so keep a cloth handy to wipe off spots on clothing.

Children may want to save gelatin bubbles by catching them on paper towels. The more patient and steady-handed among your students may try gelatin bubble "sculpture" by arranging bubbles and piling them into satisfying shapes. For sculpture, blowing bubbles with straws gives better control. Building with bubbles requires consideration of weight and balance as students perfect techniques for controlling bubble size and for placing bubbles for minimum sag or deflation.

Because gelatin soap bubbles are less likely than other soap bubbles to disappear, they're ideal for observing the beauty of bubble colors. Children can look for rainbow swirls and peaks-and-valleys patterns. Colors can be compared in sunlight and under artificial light, with naked-eye viewing and with lenses.

No. 255

BUILDING DEMOLITION STUDY

Renewing a neighborhood usually means tearing something down. Some of your students may be directly affected by this sort of face-lifting.

Students probably have not considered that whatever is torn down becomes a part of history with a reality only in the past. Students themselves can be firsthand observers and recorders, and through these means, participants in this kind of history.

Find out about a building scheduled for demolition and have students make sketches of it or photograph it to establish a record of its existence. Then help the class look into the history of the building — when it was constructed; what other buildings in the neighborhood, or in the city at large, are of about the same vintage. Note the ways in which the design of the building differs from newer buildings.

Research national and world events that occurred during the lifetime of the building. Try to find photos of the neighborhood when the building was new. Speculate about how and when the building began to go "downhill." Try to find out how the decision was made to replace it, and what will happen to the land. Help the class record information in different styles, from factual data to "reminiscences," integrating photos and illustrations.

Arrange for the class to observe the site during demolition to record some more history through photos or sketches. A variety of feelings beyond the sense of historical consciousness you've been building may be expressed in student accounts and follow-up discussions.

The demolition study may help the class to appreciate history as something ongoing, and an experience that they are all a part of. At the same time, they will preserve a little history for those who come after the physical traces are gone.

Idea by: Diane Kemble, North Street School, Claremont, N.H.

No. 256

WHAT DO YOU MEAN WHAT DO I MEAN?

A law cannot be obeyed if people don't understand it. Complex language and ambiguity are the most common pitfalls. Consider the following example:

No person riding or operating a bicycle shall perform or attempt to perform any acrobatic, fancy or stunt riding upon any public highway or street.

On the surface, the statement seems perfectly clear. Your students could easily draw a picture of a bicycle rider breaking this law.

The problem is that we can think of a number of behaviors that might or might not be in violation of this law. Does the law tell us whether or not riding with no hands is unlawful? For some people, riding with no hands might be a wonderful trick mastered only after weeks of practice. To others, it is the ordinary way to ride.

Suddenly we are confronted with the question of interpretation. We may think that only judges have to interpret laws, but in fact, everyone who lives under a system of laws or rules must constantly decide whether his behavior is permissible in the given context.

Poll your class and see how many students think that riding with no hands constitutes a violation of the law as it is stated above. If there is disagreement, let the students justify their various interpretations.

If possible, locate a similarly ambiguous law on the books in your city. Let students collect interpretations of the law from neighbors, police and judges.

Lest your students think it is easy to write a perfectly clear law, try the following: First, have your students

prepare a set of directions telling how to do some familiar activity — tying a shoelace or playing tick-tack-toe. As each student gives the instructions aloud, the teacher or perhaps another student should try to follow the directions as literally as possible. In most cases the results will be disastrous and will serve to demonstrate the difficulty in creating complete, unambiguous directions.

Next, the students should attempt to write laws that are easy to understand. Each student can write what he or she thinks is the single most important law in the world or the single most important rule for home or school. Other students should then criticize the law by pointing out loopholes or ambiguities. If someone wrote: "It is unlawful to commit murder," other students might ask whether killing someone in war or in self-defense would be called "murder." If another student wrote: "Cheating is not allowed in this classroom," the question might be raised: Is helping someone with a homework assignment cheating?

Hopefully, the above experiences will demonstrate that it is almost impossible to write a law that everyone interprets in the same way and that it is the accumulated interpretations of citizens, lawyers, police, judges and others — and the actions based on those interpretations — that give life and meaning to the laws on the books.

Law Day

No. 257

LAWS EVERYWHERE

Ordinarily we encounter laws one at a time — often when we've broken one. Yet one of the most notable things about law is its pervasiveness — the way it seems to touch almost everything we do.

To help your students get this point, try a "mind walk," in which you describe a typical journey to the supermarket. You begin: "I leave the house and get into my car." Ask the children to break into the story wherever a law comes into play. For instance, the law says that the car must be licensed.

The first time through the story, the children may not have spotted many laws. You can jog their imaginations by asking a few questions: Is there a law about wearing clothes? Are there laws about the content of the gasoline in the car tank? about how you drive the car? Is there a law about how the food is prepared before it goes on the shelves? Is there a law about the money used to pay for the food?

The children might create a mural that depicts a shopping trip or the daily journey to school and is annotated with the appropriate laws.

If possible, borrow a set of your city's ordinances, or at least make Xerox copies of the index or table of contents. The children may be astounded by the sheer number of laws as well as the range of items dealt with. In one small western city, for instance, there are laws governing such things as aircraft, barber shops, fortune telling, skateboards and pony rides.

Nonlegal rules are also pervasive. Ask the children to identify the rules that govern life in the school. Areas covered might include talking, dress regulations, classwork, homework, assemblies, emergencies, health and justice (how rules are enforced and punishments given).

A similar survey — again, perhaps culminated by an annotated drawing — can be done for rules at home: TV watching, eating, study habits, allowances, work and family decision making.

Law Day

No. 258

BLEACH PAINTING

Bleach has some decidedly unpleasant qualities. It has a strong smell and eye-watering fumes that should not be breathed. Working with it in a large group in a confined space could be a problem, so you may want to take the kids outside for bleach painting.

Materials: Bleach, paint cups or glass jars, cotton swabs, dark-colored construction paper.

Procedure: Put a small amount of bleach into a paint cup or glass jar. (You might want to make a hole in the cap of a glass jar — such as a peanut-butter jar — large enough to insert the cotton swab easily. In this way you'll cut down on fumes.)

Have the child draw a simple outline picture in crayon on a sheet of dark colored construction paper. The picture needs to be free of detail, since the cotton swab isn't the most delicate of painting instruments.

When the drawing is complete, the child dips a cotton swab in the bleach and "paints" with bold strokes along the lines of the figure. Then the bleach paintings are laid on papers to dry. Slowly the bleach takes the color from the paper, leaving the drawing lines highlighted in gray or off-white against the dark background. The results can be quite striking.

Leave the paintings outside until they dry. At that time, the artists may want to do some touching up with crayons or markers. Some paintings might be treated to construction-paper frames for Mother's Day gifts.
Idea by: Michael and Libby Robold, Columbia School District, Brooklyn, Mich.

No. 259

HOW MANY BRICKS DO YOU WEIGH?

The concept of pounds and ounces (or for that matter, kilograms and grams) may be fairly fuzzy for children, especially in relation to their own weights. To give students a clearer picture of what their own pounds and ounces represent, try using bricks and a teeterboard (or seesaw) in a balancing activity.

First check (or estimate) the weights of children in your class. Then locate a supply of bricks and weigh one to get an idea of how many you'll need to balance the heaviest children.

Invite students to pick up bricks and feel how heavy they are. Then have each child try estimating the number of bricks that might equal his or her own weight.

Next, using a teeterboard, have one child sit on one end of the board and begin placing bricks, one at a time, on the other end, until the board balances. Explain that this is a rather rough and inaccurate way to measure weight, not as accurate as using scales. For this rea-

son, children may have to slide forward or backward slightly to bring the board into balance. A child may actually weigh something *between* nine and ten bricks.

Keep a record of the number of bricks that are needed to balance each child. Later, separate the children into groups according to their weights in bricks. Have children observe a particular "brick group" and compare the general sizes of children in the group. Are most of the children in the ten-brick group about the same size?

Children may set up weight problems, such as: an 11-brick child = an 8-brick child + _____ bricks, and then try proving their answers on the teeterboard.

Idea by: Barbara Michel, Racine, Wis.

May 20

No. 260

JUMP RIGHT IN

Here's a measuring activity (from *Sports*, Activity Resources Co.) that kids will jump right into.

Supply students with a variety of measuring devices (yardstick, meterstick, trundle wheel, ruler, tape measure and so on) and give these directions:

"Mark a line on the playing field with chalk or string.

"Try a standing jump by standing at the edge of the marked line and jumping as far as you can. Measure the distance using different measuring devices.

"Try a running jump where you run toward the line from a comfortable distance, jumping when you reach the line. Measure the distance with various measuring devices.

"Compare your running and standing jumps."

May 20

No. 261

RUBBING

Rubbing is a way to make a picture of something that requires no drawing talent at all. It's also a way to collect a thing without taking it home with you. It's almost as good as a photo except that you don't need a camera and you don't have to wait for the film to get developed.

All you need for a trial run is a pencil, paper, and a coin. Here's what you do:

1. Put the coin under the paper.

2. Rub the spot where you think the coin is lurking with the side of your pencil. Hold the paper still. Keep rubbing until the design shows up.

Now you're ready to move on to bigger things. The following directions are good for tree bark, headstones, or anything else with a raised or depressed surface design. Smooth surfaces like slate or metal plates make the clearest rubbings, but stone and wood make interesting, rough designs. Be careful with old wood and worn stone. You can rub them out.

You will need: (1) Large sheets of paper (how big depends on what you want to rub). Butcher paper, rolls of heavy shelf paper or even sliced-up brown bags will do. (2) A fat crayon or a square stick of artist's charcoal (conti crayon), not too soft. (3) Masking tape. (4) A big, fat paintbrush.

1. Clean the spot you want to rub with your brush. Take your time. Every lump of sand has a way of showing up.

2. Cut a sheet of paper and tape it over the spot.

3. Rub, using the side of the chalk or crayon.

4. Did you forget to ask permission? Some places have grounds keepers or guards. Just smile and tell them what you're doing. Usually it's okay.

Rubbings can be the basis for several different kinds of study projects.

● One way is to look at them as art. Collect samples of curious or decorative items that mark the city. Old buildings have antique lettering, iron curlicues and stone carvings. These artistic and fanciful bits are fun to collect just to look at. Often you wouldn't notice them unless you were on the lookout for them. Think about how styles have changed in architectural decoration.

● Rubbings are often clues to the times and places of things in the city. For instance, sidewalks are often branded with the makers' names and the dates they were laid down. Designs around the doorways of buildings sometimes provide dates and other hints of a building's past. Plaques, plates and cornerstones offer little histories. There are commemorative markers, like "so and so slept here." And don't forget manhole covers and hydrants that reveal the whereabouts of the city's underground circulation system. They mark watermains, sewers, and powerlines with some pretty nice designs.

● A rubber's paradise is the local cemetery. Tombstones offer all sorts of fanciful art and verse, plus a lot of history. Your class might investigate things like the average age of death in 1900 versus now; periods marked by an unusual number of deaths; peoples' origins from surnames; ethnic groups. Be on the lookout for catchy epitaphs!

Idea by: Linda Allison, author of *The Wild Inside*, Sierra Club.

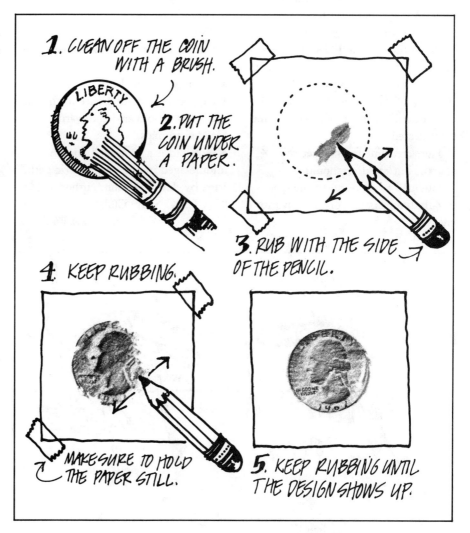

1. CLEAN OFF THE COIN WITH A BRUSH.

2. PUT THE COIN UNDER A PAPER.

3. RUB WITH THE SIDE OF THE PENCIL.

4. KEEP RUBBING. MAKE SURE TO HOLD THE PAPER STILL.

5. KEEP RUBBING UNTIL THE DESIGN SHOWS UP.

No. 262

DOG YEARS DIVISION

"My dog is thirteen years old."

And almost any kid will tell you that in dog years, thirteen is really old. Just *how* old is a good lead-in to a math activity that measures the ages of various animals on a comparative basis.

Start with the idea that our year is measured in how many days it takes the earth to circle the sun—a journey that hasn't much to do with life spans. A better measure is to compare our life span to other animal life spans. How many of our human years equal a dog year? A little long division will provide the answer. You might have your class use a calculator if the arithmetic is too complicated.

Here are some facts to get you started, but children should be encouraged to set out on a life-span fact-finding mission for their favorite creatures.

Life-Span Equivalents

Humans	70 Years	
Dogs	16	
Quail	4 Years	1 quail year = 17 human years
Deer	17	
Crayfish	7	
Rabbits	5	
Elephant	47	
Cat	15	
Turtle	25	

Can you draw any conclusions from your statistics?

● Do bigger animals live longer?

● Do you see any difference in the life-spans of cold-blooded and warm-blooded animals?

● How old is a teen-aged dog? A middle-aged mouse? A geriatric gerbil?

Idea by: Linda Allison, author of *The Wild Inside,* Sierra Club.

National Pet Week

No. 263

SIDEWALK FOSSILS

It's rare to find a real fossil right outside the school door. But sidewalk fossils—leaf, twig or nut imprints that have become preserved in cement and asphalt—are easier to find and can tell students much about fossilization.

Before you take your class on a tour of the surrounding neighborhood, check out the area to be sure "fossil" imprints are to be found. Then give your students a simple working definition of a fossil: A fossil is preserved evidence of past life, or the remains of an organism that lived during ancient geological times, perhaps. You may wish to reinforce the definition by sketching the fossilization process on the board. (For example: a dead animal becomes buried in mud; in time the mud hardens and preserves an imprint of the animal; the organism becomes a fossil.)

Now for the tour. Give each student a guide sheet with the following directions and questions:

Make a simple sketch of two or three leaf, twig or other imprints you find.

Can you identify the tree, plant or bush the "fossil" came from?

Briefly tell how you think the imprints formed in the sidewalk. Why aren't sidewalk fossils real fossils?

Discuss students' answers when you return to class.

A 30-minute fossil hunt will be an eye-opener for most students, making them aware that the fossilization process is going on right underneath their feet.

Idea by: Robert G. Hoehn, Roseville High School, Roseville, Calif.

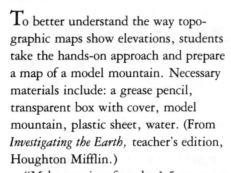

No. 264

MODEL MOUNTAIN MAPPING

To better understand the way topographic maps show elevations, students take the hands-on approach and prepare a map of a model mountain. Necessary materials include: a grease pencil, transparent box with cover, model mountain, plastic sheet, water. (From *Investigating the Earth,* teacher's edition, Houghton Mifflin.)

"Make a series of marks 1.5 cm apart up one side of the [transparent] box. Place the model mountain in the box and pour in water up to the first mark. Draw a line around the mountain at the water line. Add more water up to the second mark and repeat the procedure. Continue doing this until the mountain is covered with water. The peak should be just submerged, but this might occur between marks. If so, stop pouring when the peak is at water level, dot the peak with the grease pencil, calibrate the in-between level, then pour in a little more water so that the peak is covered over.

"When you have finished drawing the lines, put a clear plastic cover on the box. Trace the contour lines on a plastic sheet as you see them from above. If you close one eye, it may be easier.

"How does your map of the model mountain compare with the hills on a topographic map? Do you think the statement 'A map is a paper model of the real world' is a true one?"

May 29

No. 265

FOOTNOTE FOR MOM

Mother's Day. That's when first graders across the land color, paint, cut and paste pictures to be hung with affection on refrigerator doors. How about a greeting with a practical note as well?

Have each child fold an eight-inch-square sheet of construction paper in half. Each child then places the paper on the floor with the fold on the left-hand side. The right foot goes on the paper, with the inside immediately against the fold. Have each child trace the shape of his foot and cut around it on all but the folded edge, so that the paper will open up to make a card in the shape of a pair of feet.

On the outside of the card the message can read: "A Footnote for Mother." Inside goes an important personal message—something each individual intends to do for Mom. "I will help you in the garden."

The card is one Mom is sure to appreciate. It should go nicely on most refrigerator doors, too!

Idea by: Sister Mary Therese Fenton, Sacred Heart Convent, Fargo, N.Dak.

Mother's Day

No. 266

MAGAZINE HOLDER

Magazines of every kind —
Stacks and stacks —you got 'em.
Guaranteed the one you need
Is way down at the bottom.

Sound familiar? This problem can be corrected at the same time the students are enjoying an art project, recycling some waste paper products and maybe creating a gift for Mother's Day.

Begin by collecting empty laundry-detergent boxes. The most practical sizes are the larger ones: the 5-pound-4-ounce size and the 10-pound-11-ounce size. Students will be able to provide some from home. And a foray into a local Laundromat trash bin should yield a bonanza of empties. (The manager may even be willing to save some for you.)

With a sharp knife, slice off the top of the box. (Use your judgment as to who performs the operation.) Draw a line across one end panel about six inches from the top. From the end

points of this line draw lines that curve across the front and back of the box and up to the top on the opposite side. Cut along these lines.

Wipe all detergent residue from the inside of the box with a damp cloth, and the box is ready for decorating.

1. Cut or tear brightly colored magazine pages into irregular shapes.

2. Dip each piece into white glue that's been thinned — two tablespoons of water to each quarter cup of glue.

3. Position glue-covered pieces all over the outside of the box, making sure pieces overlap and leaving no places uncovered.

4. Cover the cut edges of the box by bending glue-covered pieces over them.

Students may enjoy doing collages that follow a theme — all cutouts (pictures and words) relating to a specific topic. This single-theme technique could be useful in personalizing a gift magazine holder. The theme might represent the kind of magazine the receiver would be storing, or the receiver's special interests might be reflected.

Idea by: Louise D. Safron, Canton, Ohio.

Mother's Day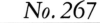

No. 267

HANGING PLANTER

"An attractive hanging planter can be made from a discarded bleach or ammonia bottle and inexpensive items from a variety store. Though several steps require close teacher supervision (one and two), dexterous fifth and sixth graders should be able to complete the entire project independently." (From *An Ecology Craftsbook for the Open Classroom,* Center for Applied Research in Education.)

Gather the following materials: empty plastic bottle, serrated knife, paper hole puncher, acrylic or enamel paint, paintbrush, four 12-inch gold chains, eight double hooks, large gold ring, potting soil and ivy.

"1. Using a serrated knife, cut out an oval section in the side of an empty plastic bottle.

"2. Paint the outside of the bottle with a colorful acrylic or enamel paint.

"3. Punch a hole into the plastic bottle at each of the four sides of the oval with a paper hole puncher.

"4. Place a hook into each of the four holes and then attach a section of chain to each of the hooks.

"5. Now attach all four pieces of chain to the ring using the remaining four hooks."

6. Put some potting soil into the bottom of the container, plant the ivy, and the planter is ready to hang indoors or outdoors.

Variations: Use braid in place of chain. Tie one end of the braid to each hook and attach the other end to the ring.

PRESSED FLOWERS

To make pressed flower panes, use flowers from your press or pick a tiny bouquet of leaves and flowers early in the morning after the dew has evaporated. Choose thin delicate plants so they will dry quickly. Small colorful flowers of the weedy sort work fine, so have your kids scout the gutters, curbs, and wild and weedy back lots.

Pressed flower panes can be displayed in a classroom window. Or, kids can fancy them up with some blanket stitches as springtime gifts for Mother's Day. They can also be made into a set of flower flash cards.

1. When the plants are dry, cut two pieces of clear plastic with sticky backing to mount them on. Con-Tact paper works very well.

2. Peel the paper away from one piece and arrange plants on it, leaving space enough around the edges.

3. Peel the second piece's backing away and stick it on top to form a sort of window.

4. Burnish the window with the back of a spoon. Oops, bubbles? No problem—slit them with a razor blade or mat knife and burnish them flat.

5. Trim the window to an oval or square. Leave a bit of space (about ½ inch) around the specimen. The panes are ready for display now, or you can continue to steps 6 and 7 for the gift and flash card variations.

6. Using a needle and embroidery thread, sew around the edges using a blanket stitch. Make a hanging string at the top and loop it through. Measure it to neck length for Mom to wear.

7. If you want a set of flower flash cards, trim all the panes to a uniform size and skip the embroidery step.

Idea by: Linda Allison, author of *The Wild Inside*, Sierra Club.

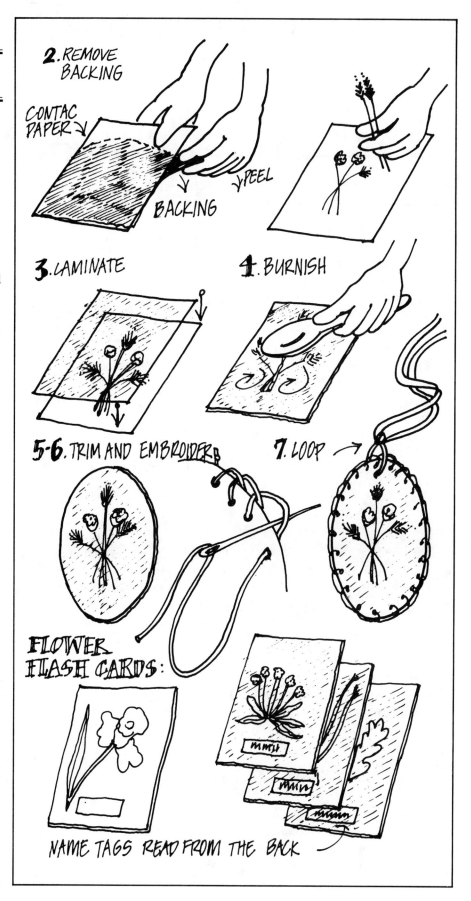

2. REMOVE BACKING

CONTAC PAPER

BACKING   PEEL

3. LAMINATE

4. BURNISH

5-6. TRIM AND EMBROIDER

7. LOOP

FLOWER FLASH CARDS:

NAME TAGS READ FROM THE BACK

No. 269

BIKE SIGNALS

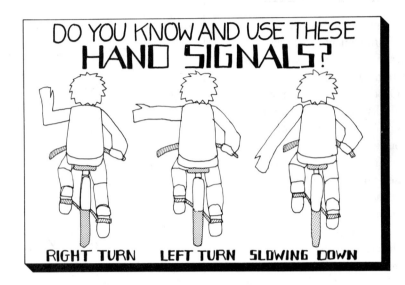

Kids who walk to school have pretty well mastered safety reminders, such as "Look both ways before you cross." But more and more kids — especially those who come a distance and don't like the bus — come to school on their bikes.

As a service to your bicycle commuters and to those adult drivers who have difficulty coping with kids in the bike lane, allocate some bulletin board space for a display or diagram of basic signals. The signals shown in the illustration from *The Big Fearon Bulletin Board Book* (Fearon Pitman) are ones that are universally understood among safe bikers and drivers: right turn, left turn, and slowing down.

From time to time, drill your students on their biking signals, and admonish them to use them regularly when they are on the road. You might also want to review bike safety rules that are enforced in your community and at your school.

American Bike Month

No. 270

TOPICAL T-SHIRTS

A medium for self-expression that seems here to stay is the good old T-shirt. To usher in those warm months when T-shirts seem to be the prevailing fashion, you can construct a colorful bulletin board that's guaranteed to be popular with kids.

First, trace a T-shirt pattern for each youngster on a piece of 18 x 24 inch white construction paper. Distribute the sheets and have the kids crayon in a design or letter in a message or slogan in multiple crayon colors. Be prepared for rock and roll group logos, popular slogans, topical retorts, and some lively jive talk running full breast across the paper. After the design has been colored in with crayons, each kid must paint a watercolor wash over the entire shirt. (The crayon areas will not absorb the paint.) When the paint has dried, have the kids cut out the T-shirt along your tracing.

Staple heavy yarn across a wide bulletin board. This is the clothesline. Help the kids to hang their shirts on the line with clothespins. Laundry never looked so good!

Idea by: Lucille V. Harker, Vineland, N.J.

No. 271

THE TRADING POST

Bulletin boards provide space for showcasing classroom projects and presenting information. They can also be used as central locations for students' advertisements. Ads for rabbits, baseball trading cards, toys and play equipment may appear. If you encourage kids to use their imaginations in creating their ads, to say a lot in a few words and to include zany illustrations, the Trading Post will be an educational as well as a useful classroom feature.
Idea by: Ann Edmonds, Morrison Junior High School, Morrison, Ill.

RESOURCES

BICYCLING ON THE SAFE SIDE — Now that bicycling has become so popular both as a form of recreation/exercise and as a means of transportation, the need for safety education has increased. In an interesting and fast-moving 16 minutes, this color film presents instructions and suggestions for making bicycling safer.

There is technical information on how to determine the proper size of a bicycle, instructions for preventing theft, and general traffic safety rules and precautions. Each rule is demonstrated by a bicyclist facing the potentially hazardous situation. There is even a touch of humor when the narrator suggests being alert for unsuspected problems, at which time a ball comes rolling out on the street followed by a person in a gorilla costume.

Though the bicycles used in the film are the popular 10-speeds, almost all of the information applies to any type of bicycle. The musical accompaniment works well and varies with the scene (a blues tune, for example, plays when a bicyclist is pulled over by a policeman).
Order from: Ramsgate Films, 704 Santa Monica Blvd., Santa Monica, CA 90401. **Grade level:** 4–high school.

SOLAR ENERGY CUBE — For the futurists in your class who recognize the need for a plentiful source of clean energy, here is a device that offers a peek into tomorrow.

The Solar Energy Cube is a simple mechanism made of five clear plexiglass panels, approximately 3½-by-3½ inches, and open at the bottom. Attached to the underside of the top panel are three solar cells made of a silicon material. Wires connect the cells to a small motor with an attached propeller. When exposed to enough direct sunlight or to an artificial light beam (such as from a lamp), the cells generate enough energy to move the propeller.

The speed of the propeller depends upon the amount of available light. Kids can experiment with propeller speed by exposing the cube to different light sources and holding their hands or other objects over the cells to see how the speed is affected.

Though the experience won't tell students how the energy transfer takes place, the results of the transfer will be very visible. The cube should raise many questions and much discussion about the potential uses of solar energy.

The Solar Energy Cube is lightweight and perfectly safe. The propeller is made of plastic and, though it moves rapidly, is harmless even to primaries who feel compelled to stick their fingers into the rotating blades.

A brief descriptive sheet that comes with the cube gives useful information about the composition of the cells.
Order from: Edmund Scientific Co., 380 Edscorp Bldg., Barrington, NJ 08007. **Grade level:** Kindergarten–high school.

BOOKS FOR KIDS —
● *Seven Ways to Collect Plants*. Joan Elma Rahn. Illustrations by the author. Atheneum. Recommended reading for the intermediate and middle grades.
● *Catch A Sunbeam: A Book of Solar Study and Experiments*. Florence Adams. Illustrations by Kiyo Komoda. Harcourt. Recommended reading for the intermediate and middle grades.

1

Brigham Young, leader of the Mormon church, born 1801.

2

First baseball game played under electric lights, 1883.

3

Last great auk captured in 1844.

7

8

Patent granted for sweeping machine, or vacuum cleaner, 1869.

9

The Philadelphia Spelling Book is the first copyrighted book in U.S., 1790.

13

14

Flag Day. U.S. flag adopted in 1777.

15

First ice-cream factory opened, 1854.

19

Ethel and Julius Rosenberg executed for espionage in 1953.

20

Congress adopts the Great Seal of the U.S.

21

25

The Battle of Little Big Horn, or "Custer's Last Stand," 1876.

26

One hundred thirty kids followed the Pied Piper of Hamlin, never to return home, in 1284.

27

Helen Keller, deaf and blind educator and political activist, born 1880.

4

Gemini IV Astronaut White "spacewalks" for twenty minutes in 1965.

5

World Environment Day.

6

D-Day, 1944. Allies begin final campaign against Germany in World War II.

10

First log cabin built, 1800.

11

Oceanographer and ecologist Jacques Cousteau's birthday. Born 1910.

12

First human-powered flight across the English Channel, 1979.

16

The U.S.S.R.'s Valentina Tereshkova becomes the first woman in space, 1963.

17

Anniversary of the Watergate break-in, 1972.

18

Amelia Earhart became the first woman passenger to fly across the Atlantic, 1928. Later she piloted a plane across the same ocean.

22

In 1870, the U.S. Department of Justice created.

23

24

First reported sighting of UFOs, 1947.

28

World War I ends with the signing of the Treaty of Versailles in 1918.

29

30

French tightrope walker Jean Gravelet crosses Niagara Falls, 1859.

No. 272

SUMMER ACTIVITY CALENDAR

You are x-ing out the final days on the school year calendar; summer is about to begin. For some children summer is scheduled tighter than commercials during a TV movie. For others summer vacation is exciting for only a week or so. A calendar of events, such as the one that guided the class through the school year, could be a welcome tool—and very possibly a sanity saver—for the folks at home.

Suggest to students a brainstorming session to collect summer activity ideas. Although initially the ideas may run to "go to the movies," "play miniature

golf," "go for pizza" and other such pay-when-you-go recreations, with a little more time the children may begin to compile some less costly and more creative projects.

If you teach younger children, you may want to provide calendar pages with a substantial core of activities already in place:
● Read a story or a comic strip to someone.
● Pull 15 weeds in the garden. Count the leaves on each stem.
● Find five pebbles and put them in order from smallest to biggest.

● Make a sandwich. Cut it in fourths.
● Guess how many windows your house or apartment has. Count the windows. How good was your guess?

Older students might try somewhat more open-ended projects:
● Keep a list of things you see today that George Washington would have been surprised to encounter.
● Look for metric labeling. Give yourself ten points for every metric marking you find today.
● Estimate what percentage of cars passing a certain spot will have only one person inside. Check your estimate.

Allow several days for collecting ideas. Provide a box for depositing students' inspired thoughts.

Before making up the calendar, plan with your students the number of weeks they want to "cover" and whether they'd prefer a week-by-week datebook or a month-at-a-glance format. The size of the space provided for each day will, of course, depend upon the amount of writing and illustrating your calendar makers intend to do. (Including recipes or craft directions takes additional space.)

Since family plans for the summer will vary widely, it is likely that the children will not be able to carry out all of the suggestions. The calendar will nevertheless be a good place to start the search for answers to "What shall I do today?"

Idea by: Loretta See, Belleville, Ill.

End of School

No. 273

BRIDGING THE GAP

No matter what happens in summer, schools still must contend with the discontinuity of formal learning. The following activities are designed to make the stopping and starting less abrupt.

● *Words From on High.* Have a group of students from the next highest grade level visit your classroom to talk about their experiences of the year. They may bring with them textbooks and examples of work they've done. Hopefully, their juicy tales about being a _____ grader will whet your kids' appetites. Their teacher may join them to outline the upcoming year's work and maybe even suggest some summer reading that will tie in.

● *Sneak Preview.* Arrange to have groups of your students visit a classroom from next year's grade level for a few hours to get a sense of its style and content.

● *Guess Who's Coming to Your Class?* Previewing should be a two-way street. Have each of your children prepare a "Me" book with such topics as: my favorite book, a poem by me, my favorite school subject, my favorite TV shows, my heroes and villains, hobbies, shortcomings and dreams. It can also include sample work done in math, science, writing and art. This information can be of great value to next year's teacher. It will help you prepare individual assignments and recognize the special needs of individual students.

End of School

No. 274

SUMMER RESOURCE

With long summer days not too far away, it's a good time to enlist the talents of students — who've been learning research skills and discovering the usefulness of resource books — in the creation of a reference of summer ideas. Emulating reference book orderliness, set up categories to channel students' thinking. Category one, page one, of the book might be: "Things To Do on a Rainy Day." Encourage each student to contribute one idea and then initiate class brainstorming for others — until there are 40 or 50 ideas for that category.

Follow this process with other categories — asking each student to provide an idea and then encouraging opening class collaboration for a larger collection. Page two might be "Things To Do Within Walking Distance of Home." Page three might expand on this category somewhat — say, within a 10-mile circle. Page four could list activities that help other people. Page five might be ways to make money. More pages and more categories can easily be added. Or a completely different classification system could be devised. For instance, students might want to classify activities into categories such as science projects, word puzzles and games, original entertainment ideas, collections to start and the like.

Students who are really intrigued with reference book formats may want to devise a coding system to facilitate the finding of activities that can be done alone, those that require several participants, activities for the family, short-term activities and those that take an extended period of time.

Students may also want to research and include dates and data on local fairs and festivals as well as hours and fees for nearby sightseeing spots.

Whether the summer source book turns out to be a comprehensive compendium or a slim, concise booklet, it should help make vacation time more productive and enjoyable for everyone.
Idea by: Karen McGillivray, Bush School, Salem, Ore.

End of School

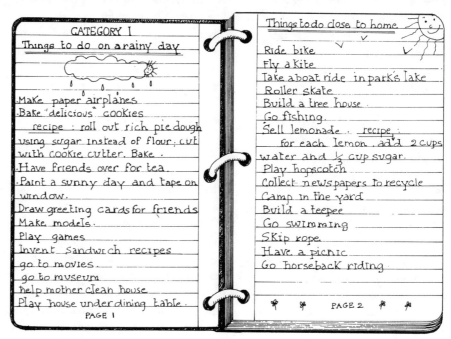

CATEGORY 1
Things to do on a rainy day

-Make paper airplanes
-Bake "delicious" cookies
    recipe: roll out rich pie dough
using sugar instead of flour; cut
with cookie cutter. Bake.
-Have friends over for tea.
-Paint a sunny day and tape on
window.
-Draw greeting cards for friends
-Make models.
-Play games
-Invent sandwich recipes
-go to movies.
-go to museum
-help mother clean house
-Play house under dining table.
PAGE 1

Things to do close to home

-Ride bike
-Fly a kite
-Take a boat ride in park's lake
-Roller skate
-Build a tree house
-Go fishing.
-Sell lemonade. recipe:
    for each lemon, add 2 cups
water and ½ cup sugar.
-Play hopscotch
-Collect newspapers to recycle
-Camp in the yard
-Build a teepee
-Go swimming
-Skip rope.
-Have a picnic
-Go horseback riding
PAGE 2

No. 275

END-OF-THE-YEAR REVIEW

End-of-the-year exams and tests mean review time, but review doesn't have to mean drill. Using games for reviewing can make all the difference.

You might try a game based on the TV show "Jeopardy." The chalkboard serves as the gameboard — a grid with four columns and five rows. Each column represents a category. For instance, if you're reviewing a social studies unit about a country, your categories might be people, products, cities, geography. In math you might have addition, subtraction, shapes and money problems. Each row of the grid has a point value — 10, 20, 30, 40 or 50.

Each box, or cell, on the grid requires a question that you'll need to prepare. Collect the material you wish to review, keeping in mind the categories you've established. For each category prepare five questions that range from easy to difficult, one question for each point-value category.

Divide the class into two teams. A volunteer from Team A selects a category and a point value — for instance, multiplication for 50 points. Drawing from your prepared list, write the appropriate challenge in the bottom box of the multiplication column: $459 \times 27 = \square$.

Both teams work out the problem. The team that called for the problem is checked first. If a predetermined number of the group have the right answer, that team gets the 50 points. If not, Team B is checked. If the members of Team B meet the standard, they get the points. Team B now gets its chance to choose a problem.

The game continues until all the boxes on the gameboard have been filled or until a time limit runs out. The team with the higher score wins.

This is a game that can be used to review any subject and that gives everyone a chance to play and to reinforce learning at the same time.

Idea by: Nancy B. Ludwig, Sporting Hill Elementary School, Manheim, Pa.

End of School

No. 276

SUMMER FAIR

An ambitious summer-gap strategy would be for you (along with other teachers or administrators) to hold an end-of-the-year summer-projects fair. Here you can marshall the ideas and resources of your school and community to help foster home learning experiences.

Your fair might have a variety of booths. Older students can demonstrate science projects doable at home, art activities and so on; local hobby and sports shops can demonstrate camping and hiking techniques; the garden club can explore the learning side of gardening; the local library or bookstore can feature a variety of how-to books for parent-child learning; a representative from the city recreation department can publicize organized events planned for the summer.

Invite a reporter from the local newspaper to write up the fair. This way, those who can't attend will still benefit from the ideas and resources you are able to assemble.

End of School

No. 277

MATH BY MAIL

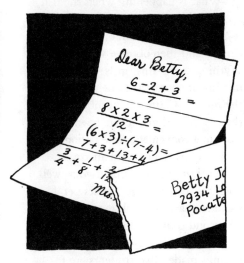

Dear Betty,
$$\frac{6-2+3}{7} =$$
$$\frac{8 \times 2 \times 3}{12} =$$
$$(6 \times 3) \div (7-4) =$$
$$7 + 3 + 13 + 4$$
$$\frac{3}{4} + \frac{1}{8} + \frac{3}{12}$$
mu...

Betty J...
2934 L...
Pocate...

Here's a way to keep all those hard-won math skills from deteriorating or slipping away during the summer. Ask each interested child to bring you 12 (or however many weeks there are of summer vacation) self-addressed stamped envelopes before the end of the school year. Once a week during the summer, send out one envelope to each child, enclosing math sheets worked on in class plus a few new ones for practice. Children may work the problems whenever they wish, and parents may get involved in the checking process. Just receiving mail each week will be an enjoyable experience for the kids, and basic skills and concepts will be reinforced as well.

Idea by: Donna Stevenson, Limestone School, Kankakee, Ill.

End of School

SUMMING ALL THINGS UP

Endings traditionally are a time for review (literally, "to look back"), taking stock, trying to make sense of an event or era and then, perhaps, planning for the future. Students can use the following wrap-up suggestions as a way of bringing the present school year into perspective.

● *Memory Mural.* Have the class sit in a circle. Let each student recall some event of the past year. Try to keep it as free and spontaneous as you can. The events recalled could be of major significance, funny, known to the whole class, a trivial detail — anything that helps bring a piece of the past into the present.

Put up a long sheet of butcher paper and let each student translate his or her recollection into visual terms. Aesthetics and design, not chronology, should dictate the arrangement of the pictured events.

● *Re-creations.* As a class or group activity, students should create poems, cartoons, drawings or collages that capture a single memory of the year or that make a statement about the year as a whole.

● *Yearbook.* Encourage each student to produce a personal yearbook. Items to include may be: my best moment, my worst day, the most important thing I learned, the funniest joke I heard, the most interesting place I visited. Students should add drawings and, of course, invite write-in comments.

● *Making History.* By trying to produce a more formal picture of the school year, students can gain insights into the discipline of historical research and narration.

Divide the class into small research teams. The first task will be for each group to select what it perceives to be the most significant school events of the year.

Next, each team should arrange the events in chronological order. Trying to determine with logic, objectivity and inductive reasoning whether a certain trip to the zoo came before or after the fire in the gym will make clear, as no other activity can, a major problem facing the historian.

Students should utilize as diverse a collection of sources as possible in researching their history. This may include interviewing eyewitnesses (fellow students, the crossing guard, the principal, the janitor, parents). The actual narrative of each team's class history can be written or delivered orally.

Later, by comparing the histories of the different research teams, students will discover firsthand that the validity of works of history are dependent on the skills, objectivity, wisdom, thoroughness and fluency of the historian as well as the availability and untarnished nature of relevant data. Not only might accounts of the same event vary in detail or interpretation, but different histories may deal with totally different happenings. One group may focus on academic happenings (the development of the science lab), while another concerns itself with social events (conflicts or friendships within the class).

● *A Funny Thing Happened . . .* Stretch your kids' imaginations by challenging them to produce comic sketches based on some of the less happy events of the year: the impact of the energy crisis on your school, cafeteria food, lack of supplies. The results may make a happy end-of-the-year assembly for the whole school.

End of Year

No. 279

FISHY BEHAVIOR

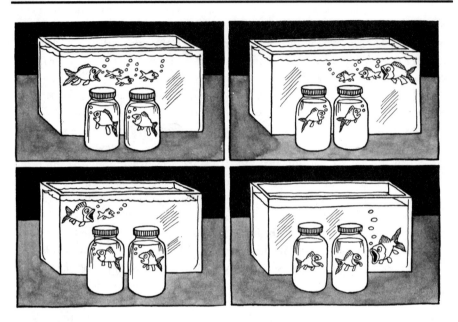

Can you predict how fish will react to changes in their environment? *Fish and Water Temperature: An Environmental Investigation* (National Wildlife Federation) gives questions and procedures to help find out. For the observations, you'll need an aquarium, two large containers with watertight lids, and several goldfish. To begin with, place all the fish in the aquarium.

"Do the fish always stay together in a group?

"Try placing a single fish in each of two small containers set next to each other. Observe whether or not the fish orient themselves toward one another. Do they seem to notice other fish? How do they behave? Separate the containers with a book or piece of paper. Does the behavior change? (Do not suggest what they probably will do. Encourage the

students to describe the actions of their fish.)

"Do the fish prefer light or dark places?

"Cover one half of a container with black paper or some other material so that part of it is darker. Put the lid on for a few moments and turn the jar on its side. Support the jar with books to prevent it from rolling off a desk. . . . Observe the position the fish takes in the container.

"Do the fish always swim near the bottom of the aquarium?

"Observe a fish to see if it moves up and down more freely in a jar than it does in the aquarium.

"What might happen if several fish are placed in the small aquarium?

"Place several fish in one container and compare their behavior with that of

a single fish. Is the group of fish more or less active than the single fish? (This investigation can be done by one group of students. They can then share their observations with the class.)

"What is happening when the fish opens and closes its mouth?

"Observe the mouth opening and closing and then observe whether or not anything else—fins, gills—may also be moving at about the same rate as does the mouth. Count the number of times the mouth and gill covers open and close in a convenient time period. (Fifteen seconds is a convenient time period, but others can be used as well. To get a good average 'counts per 15 seconds,' have the children take several 15-second counts, add all the counts together and divide by the number of timings made. Two students are required to do this—one to time and one to count. If eight 15-second timings were made and found to be the following counts—11, 9, 8, 12, 11, 10, 9, 10—that would be 80 counts in two minutes or an average of ten counts per 15 seconds. Note that in some of the experiments you may also want to adapt the counting procedures and determine, for example, the counts per minute. Again, it would be best to average several timings.) Does there seem to be any relationship between the opening of the mouth and the opening of the gill covers?"

June 11

No. 280

SIMPLE REACTION MOTOR

"The enormous speed of modern jets is achieved without the use of either propellers or piston engines. The principle of a jet engine was based on Sir Isaac Newton's third law of motion: for every action there is an equal and opposite reaction. Try picking up a heavy boulder and throwing it as far as you can. The weight of the boulder may even force you off balance." (*A Sourcebook for Elementary Science*, Harcourt Brace Jovanovich.)

Another example of an action-reaction occurrence is the rotary lawn sprinkler. How it works is easily illustrated.

"With a nail, punch two holes opposite each other near the bottom of a can about the size of a soup can. Also punch two holes near the top of the can so that the can may be suspended by a string. In each of the bottom holes, twist the nail sideways (in the same direction for both holes) while holding it parallel to the bottom. When water is poured into the can, jets of water emerging from the bottom holes in one direction make the can spin in the opposite direction. Repeat the experiment, doubling or tripling the number of angled holes. Note how much faster the can turns."

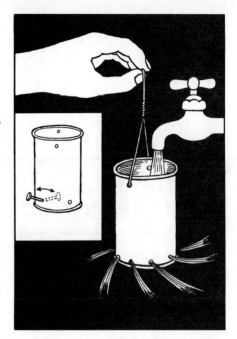

No. 281

WATER DRAWINGS

Water drawings are a fun way to use the sidewalk on a warm day. All you need is some fairly smooth concrete and a supply of ice cubes.

Encourage kids to try tools like a straw dipped in water, or a brush, or to make their own pens by freezing water in cans or plastic (not glass) containers in the freezer.

If it's a very hot day your students will have to draw quickly in order to finish what they start. It's a good project to get kids to draw big, loose and fast. Also, a mistake vanishes quickly. Choose a shaded place if you expect to see the drawings finished.

After a short time, the sketches will disappear into the sidewalk and the air.

This is not unlike what happens to rain when it hits the ground. The type of soil, the wind pressure, temperature and humidity determine the rate of evaporation. Ask your students a couple of challenging questions: On what sort of days do your water drawings last the longest? Is there any relation between how long your drawing "sticks" on the ground and how sweaty you feel?
Idea by: Linda Allison, author of *The Wild Inside*, Sierra Club.

TOOLS: PAINT BRUSHES

WATER

SPONGE BRUSH (FROM A PAINT STORE)

DRINKING STRAW OR PAPER JUICE CAN WITH FROZEN WATER.

STICKS

No. 282

FRESH WATER FROM SALT WATER

Lack of fresh water is a problem in many parts of the world—most recently the western United States. One way of handling the shortage is to remove salt from seawater. This desalinization process can be done by evaporating salty seawater, collecting the vapor and condensing the vapor into fresh water. Salt will not evaporate with the water. Students can demonstrate this process by making a still, described in the *Ginn Science Program* (intermediate level C, Ginn).

Provide students with the following materials: table salt, water, pot, hot plate, jar, ice cubes, heat-resistant glass bowl.

Mix up some salt water and pour it into a pot. Carefully place the pot of salt water on a hot plate. Now fill a jar with cold water. Add one or two ice cubes to the cold water. Then place a heat-resistant glass bowl in the pot of salt water. Put the jar of ice water in the bowl.

"Turn on the burner and bring the salt water to a very slow boil. What do you see forming on the outside of the jar of ice water? Can you describe what is happening?

"Allow the salt water to boil slowly until a good amount of water has collected in the bowl. Let the whole apparatus cool for 15 minutes or more. Using a hot pad or heavy cloth, take out the jar and bowl. Taste some of the water in the bowl. Is it salty or fresh? Do you think the water vapor contained any salt? How do you know? Should the salt water in the pot now taste more salty or less salty? Does it? Why?

"Try boiling other liquids in your still after rinsing all the utensils well. What happens to water colored with food coloring? Does the still separate the coloring from the water? Does distilling make vinegar lose its taste?"

No. 283

SOLAR PORTRAITS

Here is a great outdoor idea featured in *The Sierra Club Summer Book* (Sierra Club Books/Charles Scribner's Sons).

Whenever there is strong sunlight, the conditions are right for solar portraits. Students will need partners, felt markers and large pieces of paper.

The best time to do this is when the sun is either low or high in the sky. In the early morning or late afternoon, tape the paper onto a smooth wall. At noon, put your paper flat on the ground.

Place the paper so that a student's head profile falls onto it. Then the partner traces around the shadow with a felt marker. After one profile is completed, the students replace the piece of paper and reverse roles.

The completed pictures, hung around the classroom, will make an interesting and unusual portrait gallery. And once you've tried portraits, you can go on to silhouettes of still-life objects. It will enable your gallery to feature a changing exhibit.

No. 284

SOLID-STATE TRANSPORT

At the close of school on a muggy day, when the mercury seems stuck in the torrid zone, send your youngsters off with the following: "By the way, please bring in an ice cube tomorrow."

It may take a moment or two for the implications of this unusual request to register. Then a few students may express scorn or puzzlement while others begin to plot strategies for completing this strange assignment.

Don't let discussion run on too long; a greater variety of cube carriers will result if comments are held to a minimum. Just be sure that the students are aware of the challenge: to devise a method to keep ice from rapidly melting, to keep cold cold.

The next morning, as the icepersons come in, check and compare the effectiveness of their insulation methods and devices. The ice cubes and their containers can serve as starters for a discussion of melting, insulation and packaging:
- What materials are good insulators? Which are only fair?
- How do various kinds of commercial "cold keepers" work?
- Once the cube starts melting, can you stop the process?
- How long does it take for an ice cube to melt in an open Styrofoam cup? in a glass jar? in your hand?

Some students may be challenged to devise "the ultimate" in homemade cube carriers. And if they are successful, you may be able to store up a hot afternoon's supply of equipment for an ice-cube relay.

Idea by: Deborah Ferris, Elm School, Vacaville, Calif.

No. 285

IDENTIFIABLE FLOATING OBJECTS

What makes some objects float on water and others head for the bottom? Children will enjoy finding out as they experiment with the conditions that determine flotation. (From *Strategies for Teaching Young Children*, Prentice-Hall.)

You'll need a large variety of objects to conduct the flotation test: Ping-Pong balls, washers, golf tees, poker chips, paper clips, pins, colored wooden cubes, buttons, spools, corks, rubber jar rings, pieces of Styrofoam, pebbles and similar items; a large container for water, such as a plastic dishpan or a water-play table; two smaller containers — one labeled *sink* and the other *float*, and each decorated with a picture of something floating or something sinking; newspaper or towels; ice, food coloring, sugar, soap and salt; small bowls.

"Place water tub on terry towel or newspaper laid on a table or the floor. Make objects available in appropriate container near water tub. Encourage children to place objects in water to see if they sink or float and then to place them into the properly labeled containers. Do not provide too many objects at any one time. New objects can be added and old objects removed every three or four days. Encourage children to try to find ways to make sinking objects float.

"[Some children may] be content to sort objects into sink or float containers rather than to seek reasons for floating or sinking. [Other] children will become interested in solving the problem of what determines flotation. At this point teachers should help children generate possible hypotheses through questioning — 'How are these objects different from these?' 'Do you suppose all of these are heavier than these?' A pan balance can be provided to find out. 'Do you think size has anything to do with it?' 'Are these alike in any way and different from the others in any way?' [The] children might also be interested in altering the condition of the water to see if this affects the flotation of objects in any way. Ice, food coloring, sugar, soap and salt should be provided so that children can experiment. Smaller bowls are helpful at this point so that a great deal of the materials is not consumed. [The] children might notice that there are many gradations of sinking and floating. Some objects float, though almost totally submerged. Others float midway, and others are on top of the water. They may want to test objects for these fine distinctions."

ACTIVITIES

No. 286

INSECT OBSERVATION ZOOS

In the wild, be it an African veld or a nearby vacant lot, it's not easy to keep close tabs on the behavior of individual animals. Thus, zoologists supplement field observations with those made of captive animals. Your students can do likewise.

Because insects fly, crawl, dig and swim, students must learn a variety of methods for collecting specimens. (Since some insects sting, and others carry germs, students should be cautioned to use gloves.) Here are some methods that are used by experienced collectors:

1. *Netting.* Students can fashion their own flying-insect nets using a stick; a coat hanger; wire (to attach the coat hanger to the stick); cotton, muslin or nylon netting for the bag; and thread. Note: Butterflies and moths are easily damaged when netted or when placed into jars. So, for living zoo collections, your entomologists should concentrate on sturdier and smaller flyers like houseflies and mosquitos.

2. *Sieving.* Many water insects can be caught using ordinary household strainers or minnow nets.

3. *Trapping.* Many flying insects can be collected around streetlights. Aggressive collectors can hang up a white sheet with a light shining on it. Place open cartons under the sheet. Some flyers, bumping into the sheet, will be momentarily stunned and tumble to the carton below.

Many insects are attracted to sweet substances (sugar, molasses, overripe fruit) or decaying meat used as bait in a jar. By setting several such jars in various places — near bushes, on ledges, buried in the ground — kids will not only capture specimens but gain further knowledge about which insects live where.

4. *Rearing.* Nurturing insects lets students observe the life history of the species. It's easy to rear flies by scooping up maggots and decaying material from a garbage can. Mosquito larvae can often be obtained from water standing in an open can, wading pool or bird bath. Insect eggs also can be found on the undersides of leaves. Clip the entire leaf and place it in a jar with a screened top.

Naturally, you'll want to identify captured specimens. Direct students to insect identification handbooks found in many libraries. Knowing the identity of an insect is especially useful in planning for its diet in captivity and in guiding observation and experimentation.

There are two basic types of captive environments. The first in no sense resembles normal surroundings. This kind of zoo is convenient for studying the physical characteristics of an animal close up. All that is needed for most insects is a bottle with a screened or hole-punched cover. Students should be able to see the bug from all sides and, with a magnifying glass, get a detailed view of the animal's external structure.

The other kind of zoo simulates the animal's natural habitat. This calls for considering such points as vegetation, soil, climate and space (a fly needs more room than an ant). Use a screen-topped aquarium for water species. Typically, vegetarians are easier to keep going than meat eaters. Ants and cockroaches, being omnivorous, are probably the easiest to keep. (Always remove old food to keep the zoo clean.)

In any and all cases, the key to successful naturalistic zoo-making is field observations. Students should study in detail the insect's real-world environment and try to bring together all its elements in the zoo space.

No. 287

FOLLOW THAT BUG!

If creepy crawlies are your students' passion or if you're about to launch a unit about mapmaking, this activity from *The Learning Center Ideabook: Activities for the Elementary and Middle Grades* (Allyn and Bacon) will be a worthwhile learning experience.

Students will need pencils, paper, casual clothes and something hard to write on before venturing outside on a bug hunt. Each student or pairs of students should choose an insect and observe it for five minutes without disturbing its activity. As the bug travels, students can trace its path on paper. If students watch carefully, they will be able to record a long list of activities on their bug maps. The children will obtain such information as where the bugs stopped, what they met or communicated with (friend or foe), what they stopped to smell or climb over, and what they ate.

No. 288

SATISFY AN INSECT APPETITE

The following experiment examines the eating preferences of insects. (From *Ventures in Science: An Action Thought Laboratory,* level red, Sadlier.)

Partition off seven equal sections of a shoe box by taping pieces of cardboard to the sides. The partitions should not reach the top of the box.

Put equal amounts of different foods—such as salt, gum, cookies, lettuce, candy, bread crumbs and sugar—in six sections, one food per section. In one section place a jar cap filled with water. Cover the box with a thin piece of cheesecloth that students can see through.

Use a butterfly net to collect insects—houseflies are fine. Slip the insects into the covered box.

Over the next several days, examine which foods disappear most quickly.

What conclusions can the students draw from the results? What could have been done to better control the experiment? What kinds of follow-up experiments can students devise on their own?

No. 289

INDOOR ENTOMOLOGY

If you're looking for a good classroom entomology project, have your class watch the life history of lacewings.

First, you need to find a supply of lacewing eggs. They can usually be found on the undersides of leaves in gardens during the spring and early summer. You can get all the facts on how to feed and house lacewings from a free sheet called "Culturing Green Lacewings in the Home and School" by writing the University of California Agriculture Extension Service, Berkeley, California 94720.

Your students might want to raise a colony of lacewings and sell them to gardeners in their neighborhoods in the summer. Lacewings are famous for their appetites for sucking bugs.

Idea by: Linda Allison, author of *The Wild Inside*, Sierra Club.

No. 290

A NEW LOOK AT OLD STORIES

Those stories the class wrote awhile back—the ones you collected and copied and collated and stapled into booklets called "Animals in Autumn" or "My Favorite Folks"—can become a useful and unique resource for language arts task cards. The tasks might touch on a variety of skill areas or focus on reading comprehension, spelling, etc. Each card directs students to look at specific stories in a class story collection; the authors' names are given as reference guides.

For instance:

● Write the plural form of each word listed below. If you have trouble, look at the story of the person named.

bike	(Kristen)
fox	(Jerry S.)
puppy	(Jack)
key	(Betsy)

● Write a synonym for each of the following words. For help check the stories of the persons named:

quiet	(Kim)
fast	(Brian)
fat	(Joey)
spooky	(Linda)

● Give three examples of words that start with the letters "str." For ideas, read the stories of Lauren and Peter.

Be sure to include each student's name at least once in this personalized task card activity. Everyone likes to be "in print."

Idea by: Annette Weinstein, Old Bridge Public Schools, Old Bridge, N.J.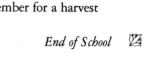

No. 291

SUMMER CROP

Since freshness is a prime factor in produce, have kids look into what kinds of fruits and vegetables are grown locally—or will be as summer comes along. Are there truck gardens in your area? Would a field trip bring a better understanding of the soil-to-salad process? During which months are the various locally grown fruits and vegetables available? During the rest of the year, many of the same items will be available in supermarkets. Kids might select an item, such as a tomato, and, working through a supermarket, research its origin during each month of the year. Have kids taste-test and compare a locally grown food with one that has been shipped in.

You and your students may be interested enough to plant your own vegetable garden. If your school can spare a small area of its grounds, and you have kids who can volunteer time after school and during the summer, you're half way to harvest. All you need now are a few donations—hoes, trowels, watering hoses—and a few purchases—seeds, fertilizer, stakes, plant markers (Popsicle sticks do admirably). Everybody can participate in the initial digging, preparing the soil, and planting. Then the self-appointed farmers can follow through. Who gets the pickings? Whoever's around to pick! But you might like to reunite the class again in September for a harvest celebration.

End of School

No. 292

ALIEN OBSERVER

LONG, SCALED, SLIPPERY, AND CAN SWALLOW A WHOLE PIG?

How would a martian react to some of our earthly (and not so earthly) contrivances? Ask kids to think and write about that question following these guidelines from *Many Americans—One Nation* (teacher's edition, Man and His World series, Noble & Noble).

Divide the class into small groups. Tell each group to write a description of something on earth that might interest someone from another planet, but not to include the name of the object being described. When each group has finished preparing its description, have the groups trade papers. Ask each group to decide what thing is being described and what the description tells about the person or persons who wrote it.

June 24

No. 293

CLASS CREAMERY

Nothing is more tantalizing to kids in the warm weather months than ice-cold ice cream. So, give them an early summer treat. Show them how to make their own ice cream. Here's an easy recipe for the classroom provided the school refrigerator has a little freezer space you can use. The only other equipment you'll want to have on hand is an electric beater, a large bowl, two smaller bowls, and an ice cube tray without grid dividers.

For every six servings you will need 1 cup of milk, 2 eggs, 2/3 cup of honey, 2 teaspoons of vanilla, 1 cup of whipping cream, and a ripe banana.

1. Beat the eggs lightly in the large bowl.

2. Add the milk to the eggs, beating as you pour.

3. Beat in the honey.

4. Stir in the vanilla.

5. Beat the cream in a small bowl until soft peaks form when you lift the beaters. Then, fold the whipped cream into the egg mixture.

6. Mash the banana in another bowl. Then, fold the banana into the egg mixture.

7. Pour the whole mixture into an ice cube tray and freeze it until it is solid about one inch from the edges (about 2 hours).

8. Turn the partially frozen mixture back into the bowl and beat it until it is smooth.

9. Return the mixture to the tray and freeze it again.

10. Serve the ice cream once it is firm, not hard (about 2 hours).

June 15

No. 294

SCOOP CATCH

Toss, grasp, roll, run, scoop, catch. Muscles and eye-hand coordination are given a workout in this fun and challenging game from *Teachables from Trashables* (Toys 'N Things).

The game is played with "scoopers" and a foam or tennis ball. The scoopers are plastic jugs (bleach, milk or juice containers) whose ends have been cut off to form a kind of bucket.

Stand the children several feet apart and have them toss the ball back and forth using their scoops. Younger children may roll their ball on the floor.

Variation: Attach a foam ball to the handle of the container with yarn or string and have individual children try to swing the ball into the scoop.

No. 295

TIE-DYE TIES FOR FATHERS

Here's a way to jazz up that traditional gift for Father's Day — the tie. The project can get a little expensive, depending on how much it will cost students to purchase solid white or pastel ties. If the cost seems prohibitive, you can tie-dye T-shirts instead.

The tie-dye process itself is quite simple. A local crafts store or department store will carry inexpensive color-fast dyes. Read the instructions that come with the dyes to prepare the dye solutions and to correctly time the dye procedure. Provide four or five colors and at least three bowls of each to avoid crowding and spilling. Give each kid several rubber bands. Instruct the kids to gather small areas of the cloth (tie or shirt) into a bunch and secure the gathering with a rubber band. The bunch gets dipped into a dye solution until it turns the preferred intensity of color, then it is removed. When the material is dry, release the rubber band. The process is repeated many times with different colors of dye until a desired effect is achieved. Encourage kids to overlap colors, and to gather bunches of varying diameters.

You might want to provide additional narrow strips of cloth for kids to tie-dye and use as ribbons when they wrap their Father's Day gifts. If you have kids in your classes who don't have dads around, you might suggest that a grandfather or uncle would probably appreciate the gift.

Father's Day

No. 296

SAND CASTING

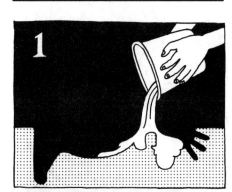

"Turning something to stone is indeed an awesome talent, but doing it without magical powers is nearly as exciting." To produce a stone statue, your artists will need wet sand about 12 inches deep (in a sandbox or at the beach); water; plaster of paris for small statues or a plaster and sand mixture for large statues; a pail or wagon for mixing; sticks or chicken wire; cord or wire; acrylic spray or shellac. (From *Outdoor Art for Kids*, Follett.)

To create a stone statue, students need to imagine a creature lying facedown in wet sand, making an impression where it lies. The impression becomes the mold for the statue. While digging out their molds using fingers, spoons and sticks, the children will need to remember that what is to stick out on the statue (nose, tusks, toes) must be a hole in the mold and what is to be a hole in the statue (mouth, eyes) must be a bump in the mold.

Encourage the children to make simple molds at first, perhaps toothsome monster faces. Shells, cones, seeds and other small objects can be placed in the mold for added effects, and if big, flat feet are made, the statue will stand by itself when finished. Be sure high, thick walls surround the finished molds to contain the plaster.

When the molds are ready to be filled, have the children make only as much plaster of paris or plaster and sand mixture as they think they'll use. The mixtures, stirred by hand in pails or wagons, should be the consistency of cake batter. For best results, plaster should be spattered by hand into details first, then poured to fill each mold halfway. To make the finished statue stronger, sticks or chicken wire can be added at this point, before the pour is completed. If a statue is to be hung, cord or wire should be placed in the back while the mixture is still wet.

Once the statues are dry and hard to the touch, sand should be dug away from the edges of the molds, and the statues should be raised to a standing position. Have the children prop up their statues so that the surfaces can dry undisturbed for a few more hours. Loose sand can be brushed off or sprayed off with water, and a quick misting of acrylic spray or shellac will make the statues waterproof.

No. 297

DESIGN YOUR OWN CLASS FLAG

Celebrate America's legal adoption of the stars and stripes in 1777 with an unusual class craft project. Have your students design and actually stitch together their own class flag.

Encourage your kids to first submit rough sketches of their design conceptions with written explanations of why they chose to use particular colors or symbols. The class as a whole must discuss the various submissions and decide which colors and symbols will finally be incorporated into the flag. A design committee can be appointed to come up with an attractive layout.

Have a sewing committee (comprised of girls *and* boys) transfer the layout onto a large, solid-colored piece of cloth (about two yards wide). The different parts of the design should be carefully cut out of other appropriately colored pieces of cloth and appliqued onto the flag with a running stitch.

Recycle an old broom handle or a long garden stake for a flag pole. Attach one side of the flag to the pole by hammering in small tacks through the cloth. Stand the flag in a corner of the classroom, bracing it with a few wide strips of masking tape. Or, you can forego the flag pole and tack the flag across a wall or bulletin board.

If your kids are very enthusiastic, or if a number have been left out of committees, you might have them compose a classroom "Pledge" to recite as you raise the class flag. You can suggest that the pledge include some mention of arriving to class on time or completing homework, but undoubtedly your students will have more philosophical things in mind.

June 14

No. 298

LITTER BOARD

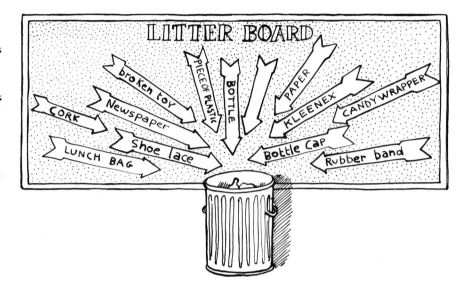

World Environment Day is June 5, a day in which we devote our thoughts to preserving and enhancing the environment. Your students can begin in their own backyard — the playground. And you can commission their efforts with an activity bulletin board entitled, "Operation Clean Up."

Constructing the bulletin board is easy. Display the title prominently at the top of the board. Then, cut out long construction paper arrows. Tack up the arrows so that they all extend from various points on the top half parameters of the board and point downward. Directly below the board, right smack in the center, goes the object of focus — the garbage pail.

Send your kids out to the playground on their environmental mission — a lit-

ter pick-up. Each kid is responsible for picking up and posting one piece of trash. Undoubtedly, the kids will find a lot more than a single specimen of garbage, and they should be encouraged to pick up those others and contribute them to the garbage pail placed strategically under the bulletin board.

When the garbage pail is full, the mission is accomplished. But don't be surprised if your kids are inspired to continue their efforts to clean up their environment, given a little extra recess time and encouragement.

World Environment Day

No. 299

FIRST ENCOUNTERS

Invoke your kids' imagination and science fiction fantasies with a mysterious spaceship that has landed on your bulletin board. All that's missing are the aliens which have deboarded for their first look around Earth. That's where your kids come in.

Have each kid draw, color in, and cut out his or her conception of an in-

tergalactic alien creature. Post these creations all around the base of the spaceship (unless they fly), and save a few to explore some other walls in the classroom. If your kids are particularly turned on, you might want to incorpo-

rate a fun creative writing assignment, "My First Encounter," written from the viewpoint of an alien encountering an earthling, or vice-versa.

June 24

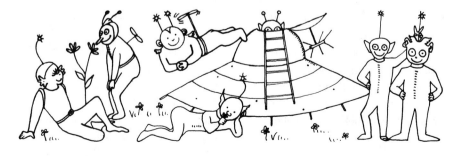

No. 300

WHAT A YEAR!

What better way to remember an activity-packed school year than to let children choose and illustrate those events that were of most importance to them? Ask each child to think of an activity or occasion from the last nine months — humorous or serious, special or of a more everyday nature — that had significance for her or him. Then have each student write a headline that describes the chosen event — "The Day We Made a Tepee" or "Engine Company No. 9 Visits Our Classroom" — and below it draw a picture that brings the event to life. A bulletin board display of each child's special memory can vividly show everyone what a wonderful year it was.

Idea by: Sandra J. Frey, J.E. Fritz Elementary School, Lancaster, Pa.

End of School

RESOURCES

BOOKS FOR KIDS —
● *Animal and Plant Life Spans*. Alice L. Hopf. Illustrated with photographs. Holiday. Recommended reading for the intermediate grades and up.
● *Bug Hunters*. Ada and Frank Graham. Illustrations by D.D. Tyler. Delacorte. Recommended reading for the intermediate grades.
● *A Prairie Boy's Summer*. William Kurelek. Illustrations by the author. Houghton Mifflin. Recommended reading for the intermediate grades.

SCIENCE FICTION — As science fiction quickly becomes science fact, the topics of the genre become increasingly familiar to children. This series of eight intermediate through junior high books, written by well-known children's author Eve Bunting, covers some typical and not-so-typical areas of science fiction, including UFOs, ESP and communicating with beings in the future.

All the books are easy to read, though one or two require the students' special attention at the beginning to keep track of names and details. There is a good balance of male and female characters throughout the stories, and the books present an appropriate amount of scientific information.

The books range in length from 25 to 35 pages and are available individually or as a set. The eight titles are: *The Followers*, *Day of the Earthlings*, *The Island of One*, *The Mask*, *The Mirror Planet*, *The Robot People*, *The Space People* and *The Undersea People*.
Order from: Childrens Press, 1224 W. Van Buren St., Chicago, IL 60607.
Grade level: Intermediate–junior high.

THE WAX MOTH — Any teacher who has had to handle and take care of laboratory animals knows the bother that can go along with the benefits. Enter the wax moth, the lazy scientist's dream. The moth requires absolutely no care and observers can easily follow each of the four stages of metamorphosis. Moreover, because they have a very limited diet, they will not become a permanent feature in the school if accidentally released.

The moths arrive as tiny wormlike larva packed in a plastic tube. They should immediately be dropped into a gallon glass jar along with the food that comes in a separate package. The jar must then be covered tightly with a *wire* screen — cheesecloth has proven itself inadequate for the job.

In several weeks the larva will begin to pupate by spinning silken cocoons on the sides of the jar. In another few weeks the adults hatch, mate, lay eggs and die. The adult stage lasts for about a week and a half, during which the moths never eat. The adult moths are fairly inactive, which makes them easy to handle and examine.

You will also receive a teacher's guide full of useful information. It describes the life history of the moths, techniques for raising the culture, short activities, a recipe for making additional food and large (8½-by-11-inch) reproducible line drawings of male and female wax moths.

Students, either in small groups or as an entire class, will find the wax moth valuable in the study of insects and introductory biology.
Order from: Nasco West, P.O. Box 3837, 1524 Princeton Ave., Modesto, CA 95352. **Grade level:** Kindergarten–12.

INDEX

APPENDIX

STUDENT MAKEMASTERS

The following 22 pages are Makemaster duplicatable worksheets for your students. The pages are perforated so that you can detach them easily. There are two worksheets for each month of the school year—one each for the primary and intermediate levels—and a color-in cover and calendar. Together, the Makemaster pages comprise a year-long scrapbook of creative, calendar-related learning activities.

The worksheets are designed to be completed by students with a minimum of teacher direction or supervision. However, you will want to collect and file the papers as they are completed so that you can keep them out of harm's way until June. You may also want to supplement the *Day By Day* Makemasters with your own worksheet pages. In June, redistribute all the material and have your kids assemble the pages into souvenir scrapbooks to take home with them at the end of the school year.

Here is a list of the Makemaster activities which follow:

Primary	*Intermediate*
Color-In Cover	Color-In Cover
School Month Calendar	School Month Calendar
My Classroom	Classroom Map
Animal Mask	Blend in With the Crowd
Thanksgiving Dinner	Foreign Feast
Make A List	Everybody's Gift List
New Year Plans	Be It Resolved
Heart-to-Heart Talk	Heartfelt Words
Weather Chart	Weather Calendar
Flowers of Spring	First Flowers
Draw Your Own Stamp	Design Your Own Stamp
Friends	Autographs

TEACHERS' PLANNERS

This section is all for you! The Teachers' Planners work like a desk calendar. There is an open calendar grid for each of the ten school months. The calendar pages, like the Makemaster pages, are perforated so they can be easily detached. Use them to jot down *Day By Day* activity ideas and calendar information you want to keep in mind. And of course, include your own learning ideas and personal dates—there's plenty of room.

Write the letters of your own name here. Color in all the letters on the cover.

SCHOOL MONTH CALENDAR

There are ten school months. Count down the months until June. Draw a picture that shows something special about each month — a holiday or the weather or a sport.

SEPTEMBER	FEBRUARY
OCTOBER	MARCH
NOVEMBER	APRIL
DECEMBER	MAY
JANUARY	JUNE

MY CLASSROOM

Draw your classroom. Show all of these things:

1. desks
2. chairs
3. blackboard

4. flag
5. door
6. clock

NAME

CLASSROOM MAP

It's always hard finding your way around a new place. Now, you might say that all classrooms are the same, but they're not. Sometimes the desks are in different places and the waste paper basket seems to move around.

Make a map of your new classroom. Find out what are in the closets, and don't forget to include little things like the pencil sharpener. Use the key or make up one of your own.

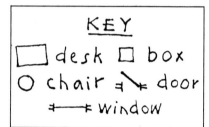

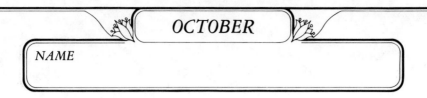
ANIMAL MASK

Draw an animal mask for Halloween.

The mask makes me look like a _____ .

NAME

BLEND IN WITH THE CROWD

The very first masks were probably real animal heads or horns worn by hunters so that men could sneak up on animals.

   Now it's your turn. Make a costume you could use to blend in with one of the following:

a swamp	a row of sunflowers
a museum	a pack of Dalmatians
a living room	a supermarket window
a parking lot	a Christmas tree lot

THANKSGIVING DINNER

What do you eat on Thanksgiving? Here is the dinner table. Put the food on the table for Thanksgiving. Draw the food or cut out pictures. Paste in the pictures.

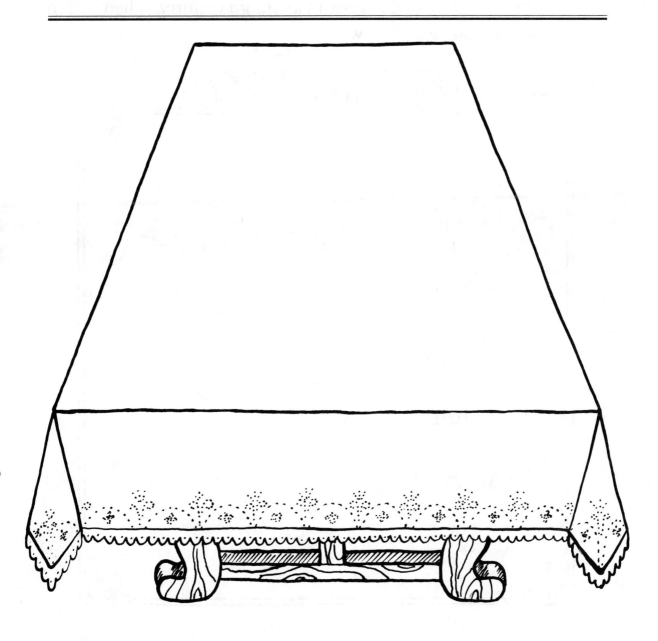

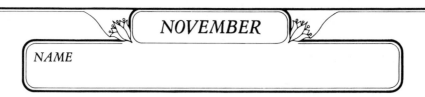

FOREIGN FEAST

Does your Thanksgiving menu include the usual — turkey, stuffing, cranberry sauce, sweet potatoes, pumpkin pie? All over the world, people have special meals for special days. For instance, do you know what people in Sweden have as their main course on Christmas? Not ham or goose or turkey, but fish!

Find out about a holiday feast in a foreign country. Then, fill in the menu for that feast below.

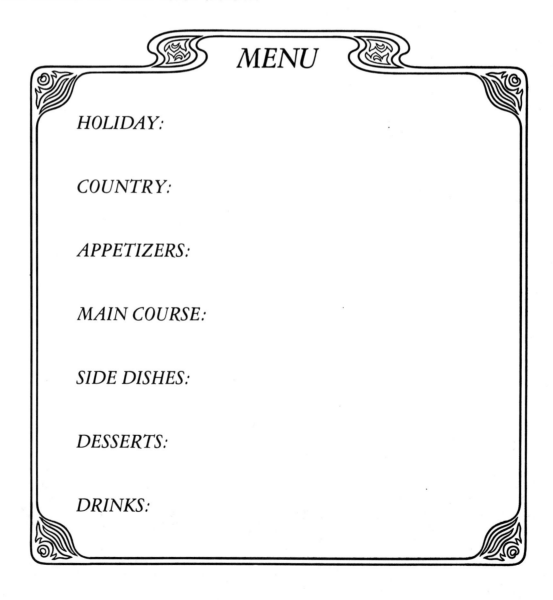

MENU

HOLIDAY:

COUNTRY:

APPETIZERS:

MAIN COURSE:

SIDE DISHES:

DESSERTS:

DRINKS:

MAKE A LIST

What do you want for Christmas or Hanukkah?
Make a list. Draw one present in the box.

1.

2.

3.

4.

5.

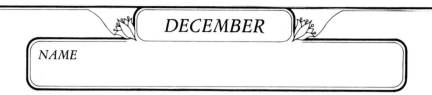
EVERYBODY'S GIFT LIST

Chances are Santa Claus and your parents already have a list of the things you would like for Christmas or Hanukkah. But what about all the shopping and present-making you have to do? Here is a list you can fill in with the gifts you plan to give everybody else.

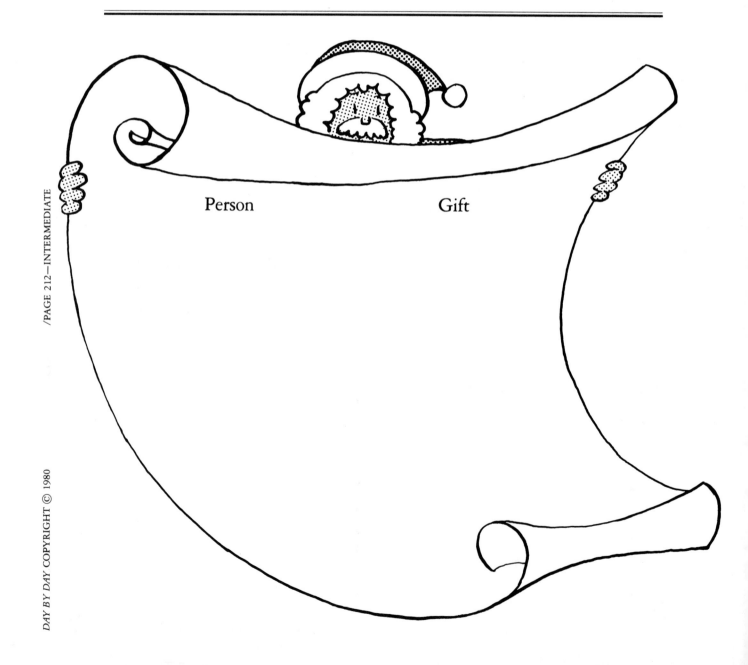

Person   Gift

NAME

NEW YEAR PLANS

It is a new year. Make plans for the new year. Write five things you will do. Then try to do them!

1.

2.

3.

4.

5.

NAME

BE IT RESOLVED

It's that time of the year again — the very beginning! Now that you have a chance to wipe your slate clean and start anew, how about listing some New Year's Resolutions? Fill in the official document below, then stick to it!

New Year's Resolutions

Be it resolved that I, _____, do solemnly resolve to do

the following during the year _____:

1.

2.

3.

4.

5.

6.

7.

8.

9.

10.

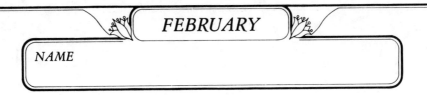

HEART-TO-HEART TALK

What did one heart say to the other heart? You write what they said in the balloons.

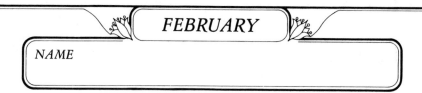
HEARTFELT WORDS

The word *heart* is used to describe many feelings. Here are some expressions with the word *heart* in them. Underneath each one, write what it means.

heartbroken	stout-hearted	heartburn
heavy-hearted	heartless	hearty
chicken-hearted	heart of the matter	hard-hearted
heart-to-heart talk	soft spot in my heart	have a heart

Pick one expression and draw a picture to illustrate it.

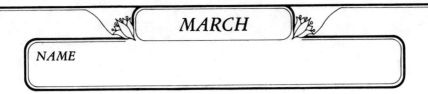

WEATHER CHART

Here is a weather chart for the days in March. There is a box for each day. Look out the window each day. Draw a picture of the weather.

MONDAY	TUESDAY	WEDNESDAY	THURSDAY	FRIDAY

NAME

WEATHER CALENDAR

Just like people, the months are different and special. A month is often described by its weather. For example, March is known as the windy month.

Make a calendar and keep a record of the weather for March. Mark the weather of the day on your calendar just before you leave school each afternoon. Before you begin, make some weather predictions.

Which day in March will have the sunniest weather?

Which day will be cloudiest?

On which day will it rain the most?

Which day will be the coldest?

NAME

FLOWERS OF SPRING

Spring is here. Take a walk. Look all around you.
Draw all the flowers you see.

NAME

FIRST FLOWERS

April showers bring May flowers, so the first flowers will blossom soon. Use the chart below to keep track of the flowers you see at the beginning of the new spring season. Use a flower guide book to find the names of flowers you don't know.

Name of Flower	Picture	Date First Seen	Describe It

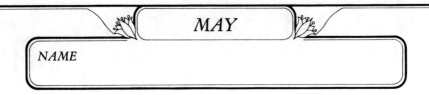

MAY

NAME

DRAW YOUR OWN STAMP

Here is a big stamp. Draw the picture on the stamp.

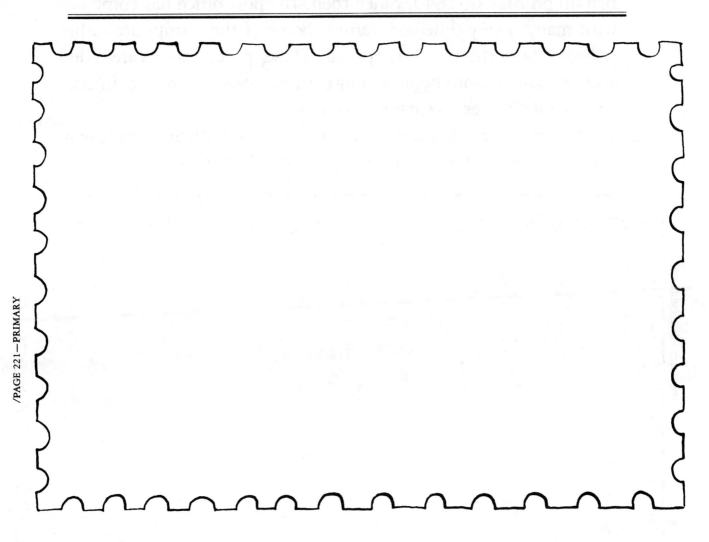

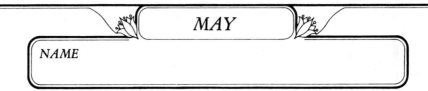
DESIGN YOUR OWN STAMP

The very first lick 'em, stick 'em postage stamps were issued in Great Britain on May 6, 1840. Since then, the post office has come out with many, many different stamps. Some of the stamps are rather ordinary, but others are very special. These special stamps are called *commemorative* stamps because they commemorate, or honor, important people, places, events, and things.

As a way of celebrating the birthday of the postage stamp, why don't you design a commemorative stamp of your own?

NAME

Friends

NAME

Autographs

SEPTEMBER

MON.	TUES.	WED.	THURS.	FRI.

PLANNER

OCTOBER

| MON. | TUES. | WED. | THURS. | FRI. |

PLANNER

NOVEMBER

MON.	TUES.	WED.	THURS.	FRI.

PLANNER

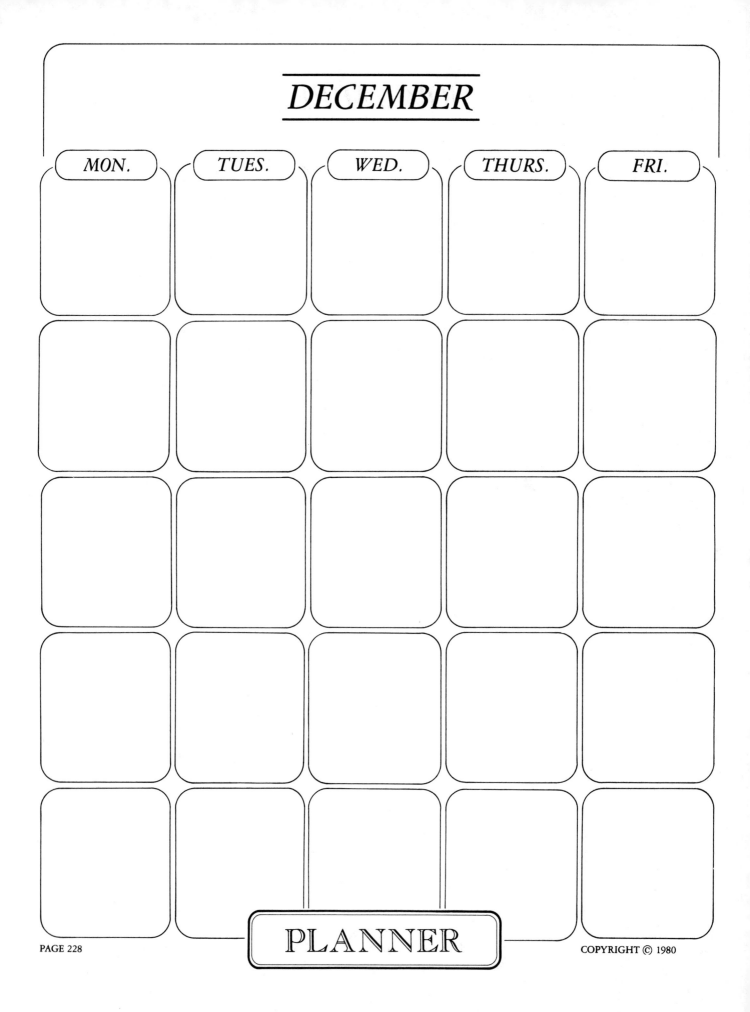

DECEMBER

MON.	TUES.	WED.	THURS.	FRI.

PLANNER

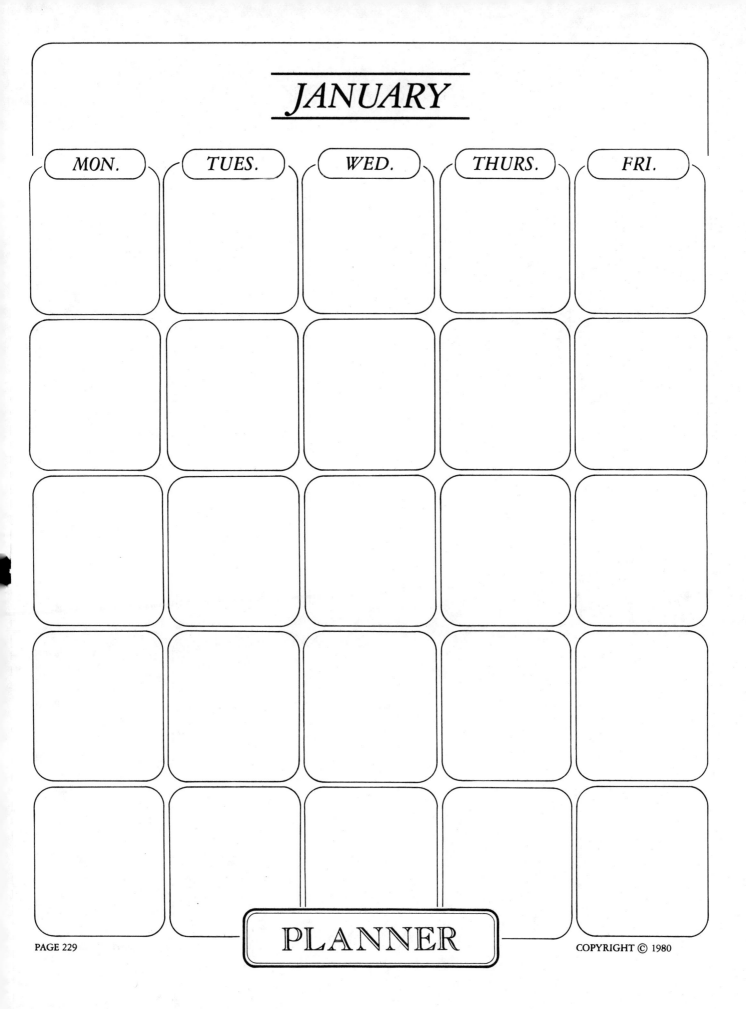

JANUARY

MON.	TUES.	WED.	THURS.	FRI.

PLANNER

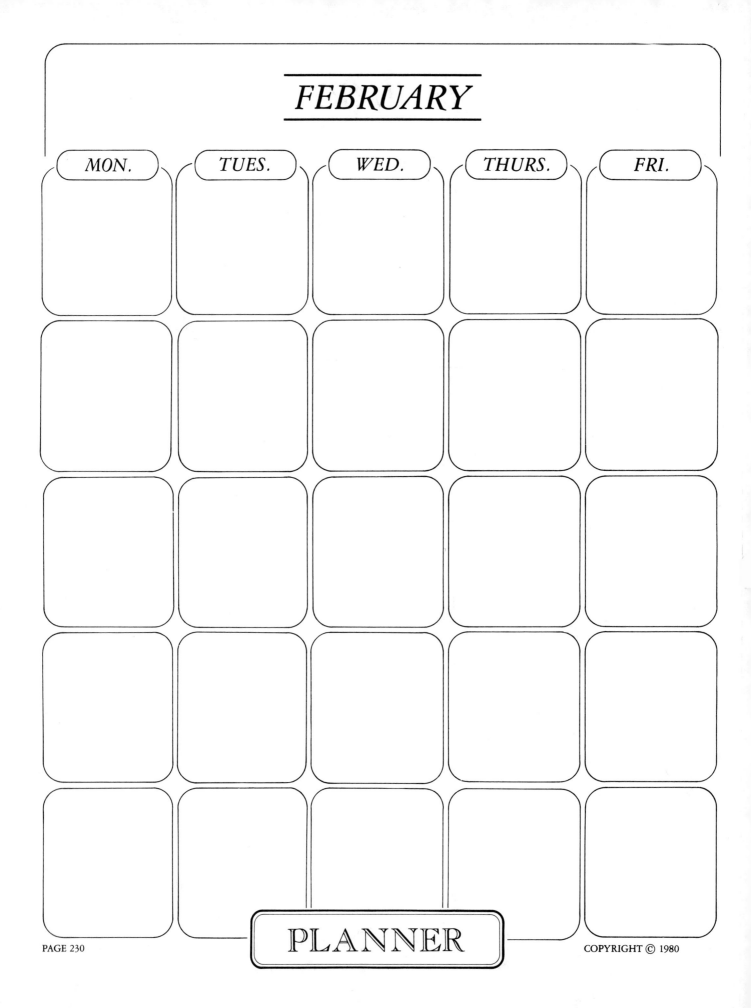

FEBRUARY

MON.	TUES.	WED.	THURS.	FRI.

PLANNER

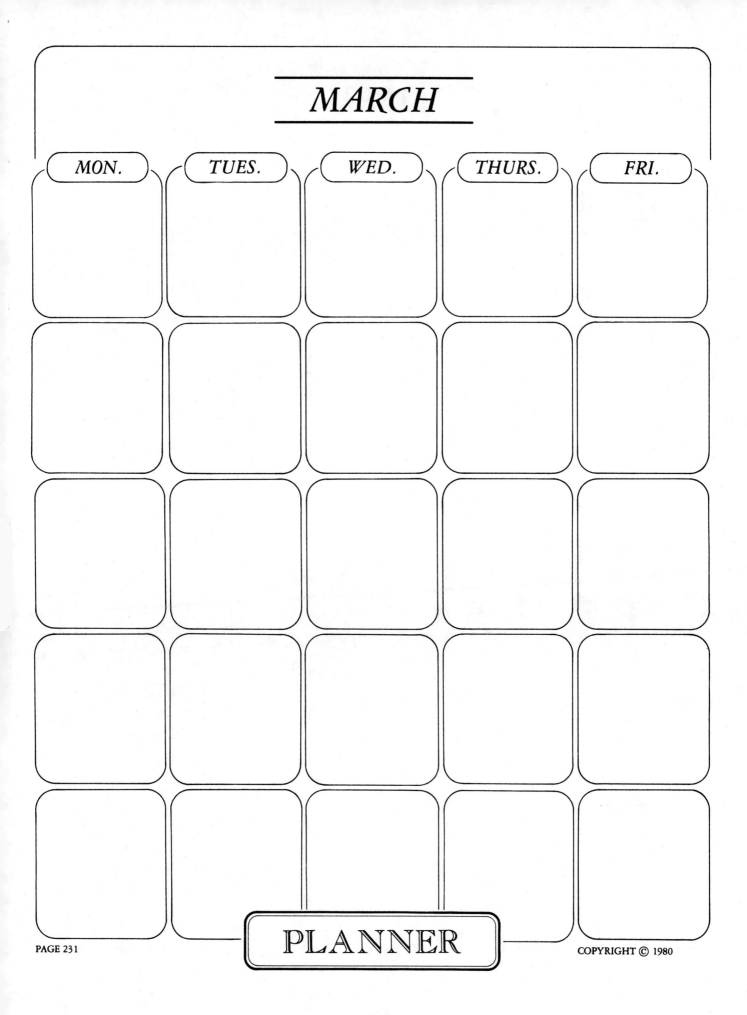

MARCH

MON.	TUES.	WED.	THURS.	FRI.

PLANNER

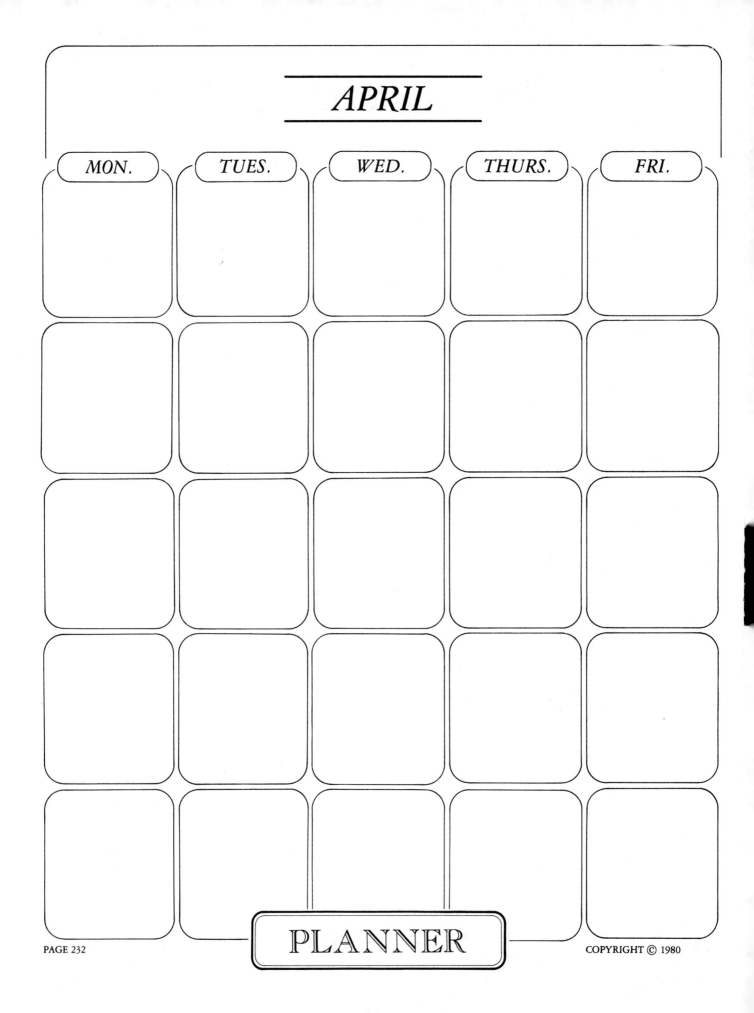

APRIL

| MON. | TUES. | WED. | THURS. | FRI. |

PLANNER

MAY

MON.	TUES.	WED.	THURS.	FRI.

PLANNER

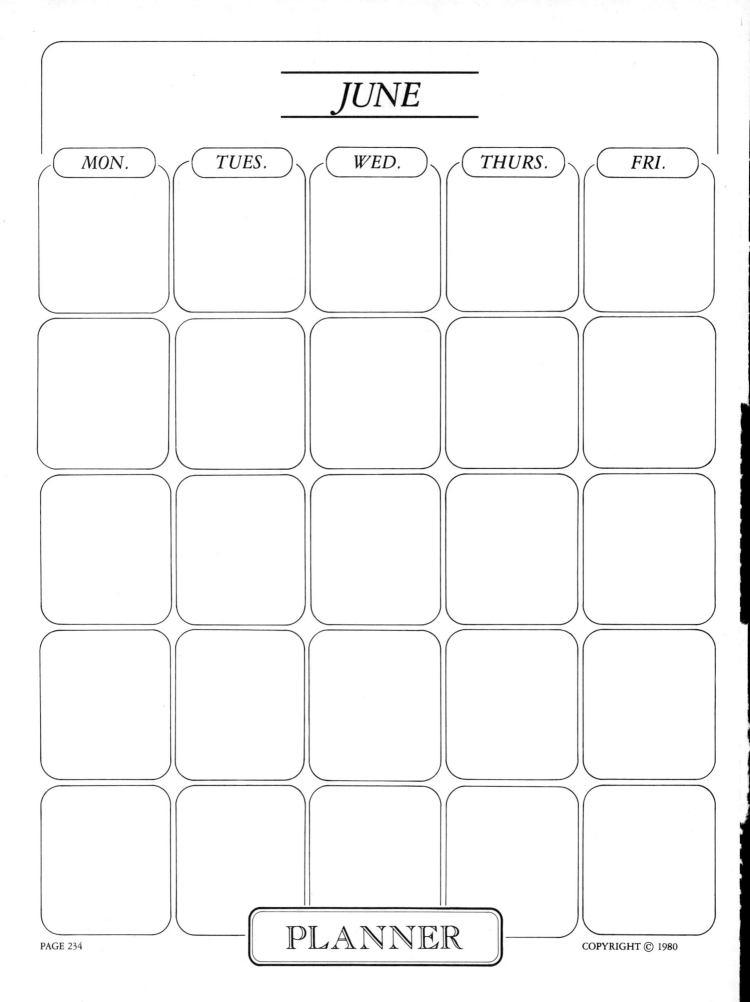

JUNE

MON.	TUES.	WED.	THURS.	FRI.

PLANNER